Floyd's Story: A Letter to Dalilah

Floyd T. Rounds Jr.

Self-published

floydsstory.com

floydsstory@gmail.com

ISBN: 9781099632358

Printed and bound by Kindle Direct Publishing

DEDICATION

This book is dedicated to

EVERYONE that believed in me.

CONTENTS

ACKNOWLEDGMENTS

I would first like to thank my wife for her support throughout the time that she has been in my life, as well as her encouragement and assistance as I wrote this book.

I would also like to thank the child that I write about in this book for her unconditional love and strength. I know she will read these words one day, and I hope that she can be proud of the way that I tell our story.

I must thank my wonderful parents, Janice and Floyd Rounds Sr., for their love and support throughout my entire life.

I want to send a special thanks to Andy Metayer of DNA Videos for his amazing videography and photography in marketing this book.

I would like to thank Edwin Lynn of Edwin Lynn Photography for the amazing front and back cover pictures.

PREFACE

I have been a solid writer for as long as I can remember. People have asked me over the course of my adult life, "When are you going to write a book?" My reply was usually the same: "That is a nice idea, but I do not feel that I have enough to write about. And I do not think I have anything to write about that people would want to read." Of course, as life goes on, things tend to change. After my brother passed away, which I will discuss in this book, I thought that I could possibly have a message that the world may want to hear, and maybe that message could change a few lives. However, as always, I still told myself that I would never write a book because I do not really have much to say. Then guess what - life continued to change. More importantly, life changed ME. And here we are. I have a damn good story to tell. You need to hear it.

This book has come to fruition due to a few reasons. First, I wrote this as a vehicle of release and as a form of therapy to allow me to reflect on things that I have been through. Sometimes reflection can be relieving, but seeing your thoughts and feelings in writing is even better because, while you may still mentally hold them inside, they take a different form when released onto a piece of paper or an electronic screen. I also wrote this book to convey messages that I think can help people that have gone through situations similar to my experiences that you will soon read about. No one person's experience will ever be identical to that of another person, but someone may have dealt with a person or people who may have similar traits to someone that you may read about in this book.

Another reason that I wrote this book is to convey important messages to a few people that are referenced in this book. Some names will be changed for legal reasons but the people that know me will know whom I am talking to, and those people that I discuss in the book will also know who they are. For those that do not know me personally, I make a good effort to explain what I learned from each situation that I discuss, and how this knowledge or advice can be applied to something that you or someone you know is going through or has been through. This book is personal in a sense, but it is also a vessel to help those who are seeking to understand why some things happen in their lives, as well as explore ways to deal with different situations, both mentally and physically.

I will cover different areas of my life and situations that are representative of those that many people go through, while one specific situation that a good part of this book covers is unique to me. That situation involves a child that I raised as a co-parent for eight solid years of her life. It may not be totally unique as other fathers have been in and are going through similar situations. However, the child and definitely her mother are unique, and you will see this as you come to that part of the book. I will speak on losing a sibling, and how this affected me, as well as how I dealt with it and how it has helped shaped me into the man that I am today. I will also discuss how this loss has affected my family.

I will talk about myself - where I came from, my background, and where I am today. Some other topics will be mixed in throughout this book, but they will all be worthwhile. I will mention that, while this is my story, and I still have not created the title for this book as I write this Preface, every event and situation that I write about in the pages to follow has actually occurred. This is a true story. I have documented and saved many messages and records over the last ten years or so that this book covers that can provide validation for what you can read. However, most of it consists of things that simply cannot be denied because people were there to witness it with me. Honestly, much of what you will read could not be made up in my wildest dreams, and that is what makes my story so intriguing.

For the readers that are not related to me or do not know me, I hope that you can read my story and take something from it that will have a positive impact on your life. I want you to be able to look at situations or people in your own life and try to understand that you may not always know what they are dealing with. I want you to see that people go through some of the same things that you do, and some go through situations that you cannot ever imagine until you see it or read it for yourself.

To the family and friends that know me, you know my personality and those that have interacted with me at some point in my life know my heart. You know some of my story. I cannot really think of a friend or family member that does not support me living a great, productive life. I love you all for that, and I am looking forward to reliving with you the memories in my life that you were present for, sharing with you the little details of my life that you may not have known about, and revealing the part of my story that most of you have not been fully aware of until the releasing of this book.

Last, but not least, to those of you who have roles in this story that will be written about, I hope you not only hear but also LISTEN to my messages. From the person that has caused a good deal of resentment towards themselves from my entire family and many others due to their decisions and actions, to the beautiful, young soul who is helpless at the time this book is being written but will one day blossom into an incredible, powerful force - there are messages in the following pages for you. For those of you mentioned in this book who have always been positive influences in my life, enjoy what I have to say because you are so worthy, and your impact on my life has been meaningful. No matter how big or small you may feel your impact has been on my life, it still matters.

Some of you know that when I put the pen to paper, I can make magic happen and it is powerful. However, I will keep it entertaining and fun as much as possible while it will be impossible to smile at some parts of the story because they are truly unexplainable. This is my book, so I will write it the way that I want to. This means that if I want to laugh aloud or I want you to laugh aloud, I will use the "lol" acronym. Actually, I am going to "lol" the hell out of you. Lol. If I want to cuss, then damnit I will cuss! You just need to soak it up, get the message and move on, ok? I will also put certain words in ALL CAPS to emphasize them, such as saying "I did this for YOU." Can you see how that changes the sound of that word in YOUR mind? I will try not to do this too much, but it is prevalent throughout the book where I feel it is appropriate.

Now, I do live in reality, and I debated on putting this in the Preface, but I know that some people may not want to hear about who I am and where I come from, although I put some good, funny stuff in the first few chapters, especially good things about relationships and marriage that you can definitely learn from. Those chapters also shed some light on the person that I am, which may better help you understand my logic and the choices that I made regarding my life in the later chapters. Therefore, in an effort not to lose any impatient readers, if you have heard about this book from another person and you just want to jump to some of the "juicy" stuff, I will give you permission to jump to Chapter Three, the Adulthood chapter, because there is where I start to talk about relationships, and offer my perspectives on many issues that pertain to couples as well as single people. Chapter Four is about my dog, literally, but Chapters Five and Six contain the situations that you may have heard about if you were directed to this book by someone else, and those are the situations that will put this book on the map so if you want to jump to those, feel free to do that as well. I say this with confidence because I truly believe that after you read those chapters, you will go back and read the rest of the book. Prove me wrong...

Thank you for allowing me to introduce to my story. I hope it affects you as a reader as much as it has affected me as the writer and the person that lived through this. Thank you for reading the Preface and enjoy the book.

Floyd T. Rounds Jr.

I. F.L.O.Y.D.

1

WHO AM I?

(Disclaimer: Please go read the ***Preface*** *if you have not read it yet as it provides some good details to help you better understand the book and my writing style.)*

Who am I, you ask? Well, my name is Floyd. I am a Black male (or African American, whatever you want to call it). I am thirty-seven years old as I write this book. However, I will be thirty-eight years old when I finish. I am representing for the Capricorns, bitch! I told you my mouth may get foul at times throughout this book and I meant that so put your seatbelt on and get used to the ride.

Anyway, I am 6'4 and right at 200 lbs. at the moment. I have pretty good, paper bag brown skin, and a nice grade of shiny hair of which nearly half, if not a full half, is gray. My beard is just about all gray.

I get that from my wonderful father. I am married to a wonderful woman who you will know fairly well by the end of this book. Our marriage has just passed the 5-year mark a few months ago and we are cruising. No marriage is perfect, and I will not pretend like mine is, but we are doing well, especially after cutting some negative things and negative people out of our lives. We have raised a wonderful, sweet child that is eight at the time this book is being written. Her name for the purposes of this book is Dalilah, and you will also know her well by the time you finish this book because she has an entire chapter devoted to her life and the events that my family and I have encountered as a result of her existence. This is at no fault of her own, of course - I want to make sure that is clear as a contact lens because I know one day she will be reading these words, and I do not want her to be confused about how I feel about her. I love you, little girl!

I resided in a suburb west of Atlanta known as Lithia Springs. I lived in that area ever since my parents moved us to Atlanta back in 1988. However, in March 2019, my wife and I moved to Smyrna, which borders the Atlanta city limits. I have worked in the field of commercial real estate lease administration since I graduated from college, which now puts me at nearly fifteen years into my field. I like it, and I am damn good at it, too. My bachelor's degree from Georgia State University is actually in Real Estate so that foundation helped me to fall into my line of work. I also have other ventures that I am a part of. My mom and I run a 501(c)3 not-for-profit organization that we created in memory of my late, great little brother Brian. You will meet him through the later chapter that is devoted to him and his large impact on my life.

Writing has also been a passion of mine for as long as I can remember, as you can see, so I have a small, part-time business called Acacia Writing Solutions through which I offer writing services such as composing content for websites and other types of business materials. Writing content for small business websites generates most of the small income that I make from this business, but who knows - after this book is released and read, some people may want me to write things for them. Then I can quit my day job and go back to working from home as I had done for the past four years lol. Hey - that has always been a vision of mine waiting for me to make it happen. Your mind controls your destiny - remember that because I definitely try to make sure I never forget that myself. I also had a part-time gig operating a photo booth that I worked about once a week or so during the warmer months. It paid well for the little time that it involved but I recently ceased this gig and I explain why in a little more detail later in the book.

I keep myself busy through various hobbies and organizations. I started bowling in 2007 and I do that occasionally - mostly in the summers now but I plan to start putting more time into that. I play flag football in what I consider to be the most competitive 8-man league in the City of Atlanta. I am a member of the OUTSIDERS team and we have won multiple championships in our league, as well as performed well at the annual Flag Football Nationals and numerous tournaments throughout the Southeastern U.S. However, due to personal endeavors and the demand for my time and presence in other organizations that I am involved in, along with the composing of this masterpiece that I call my book, I have not seen the field as often as I have over the past few years. I cannot retire officially because I love the exercise, competition, and camaraderie among the guys that I play with. But yes, my days on the field will not be as plentiful as they have been over the past four years. You will hear a little more about flag football later in the book. I am also a Prince Hall Master Mason. I love the organization and what I have learned from it, and I will talk more about how it has positively affected me later in the book but, of course, I am not talking TOO much about it lol. If you want to dive into that subject more deeply, do as we Masons say: "To be one, ask one." I will leave that right there for now.

What else should you know about me? Well, I am ambitious but also a great procrastinator, if that makes sense. That is almost an oxymoron, huh? In other words, I have big dreams, but I am sometimes slow to take the steps to make them a reality. Sure, I live what most would be considered to be a good middle-class life. I may even be what they call "lower middle-class" - I should research that one day to see where I unofficially fall. I have a wonderful, supportive family. This stretches from my immediate family all the way to my extended family, and even distant family. I can honestly say that I have never really had a falling out with a family member, aside from the disagreements that come with having parents and a wife, but that is damn near every person with either of those. I can say that all of my family supports me, and I love that. I have had a relatively good life when it comes to my family and I know many people cannot say that. I love them for that and I know they love me, and I believe they will love me even more and be drawn closer to me in spirit after reading this entire book. That keeps me going. I also have wonderful friends. My close childhood friends are still in my life and have always been great. They have affected me in so many ways, and I love those guys and gals. They have been there to laugh at me when

I have done stupid shit, as well as save me at times when I was about to do stupid shit. They did not save me every time I did stupid shit, but I would not be the Floyd that I am today without seeing the consequences of some of that stupid shit. Are you tired of me saying "stupid shit" yet?

Anyway, I have other friends, both male and female, that have shaped me into the person that I am today through many different interactions. Even if it was for a season or for a second, I have been touched by many, and all of those moments have played a part in developing the F.L.O.Y.D. that is behind these words.

This is my short introduction. Now let us dive into the book.

2

CHILDHOOD

My story starts in St. Louis, Missouri. However, it would not be right if I did not start before that with the people that birthed the amazing Floyd that is behind these wonderful words :-)

My maternal grandmother, named Ruby, is from West Point, Mississippi. She met my grandfather, C.L. Vasser, in West Point and later moved to Amite, Louisiana where my mother and her six siblings were born. My grandfather passed away when my mother was thirteen years old. Shortly after that, my grandmother moved the family to St. Louis, Missouri. My father, Floyd Sr., was born and raised in St. Louis and comes from a family of eight siblings, including two stepsisters. My paternal grandfather was not around much so my father did not have the closest relationship with him. My paternal grandmother put in most of the work in raising her kids, along with my Uncle June and Aunt Pat that also resided at her home. Both of my parents resided in North St. Louis, and yes - it was in the hood. My mom and her people lived on a street named Genevieve, and my dad's family stayed within a mile on Garesche. This area is commonly known as Walnut Park and is characterized by a large, one-building elementary school that was also called Walnut Park Elementary but is now defunct. I attended that school for my kindergarten year, and I started when I was only 4 years old. Just some interesting tidbits to feed your mind. At least I think they are interesting.

My parents each had a childhood that would be somewhat normal for people that were raised in this part of town. Just like any real hood, they saw their share of fights as well as deaths, which were mostly drug-related. It was the typical hood, so nothing happened here that would not happen in most ghettos. When my father was in his twenties, his youngest brother was murdered. His brother's name was Brian. I say this separately because this name has much significance in our lives, and you will see why as you get further into the book. After high school, my dad served in the army for four years and was honorably discharged.

When my mom was eighteen years old, she applied for and got a job at a neighborhood Arby's, where she worked for a while. My dad was hungry one day, and that is how he met my mom - at Arby's lol. He was twenty-three years old at the time and living his life, as was she. With my mom being the beautiful woman that she was and still is, my dad could not stay away after setting his eyes on her, so he would go visit her at work when he was not working. Sometimes he would come with one of his best friends named Keith and they would just hang out at Arby's. My mom and dad begin to date and had a good relationship. My dad was a car and motorcycle enthusiast, so he enjoyed his toys. He had a motorcycle, so he and his friends would ride around St. Louis and do what young men did - basically party and drink lol. My mom rode with my dad sometimes and they would both enjoy that. Yes, my mom knows more about riding a motorcycle than I do, but that is neither here nor there - I will learn one day.

Now, back to me.

I was born at 3:15 a.m. at Barnes Hospital, which is one of the largest, if not the largest, hospital in Missouri. I was a healthy but bald baby, with an island sprout of hair on top of my head. I was seven pounds and one-half of an ounce. I was born Floyd Tilford Rounds Jr., but my family has always called me "Mann." My mother said I got that name at birth. She said that when I came out of her womb, I was not crying - I was just looking around the room like a little man, and that the doctor that delivered me had to pop me on my ass so that I could cry to make sure I was all right. I am not sure how true it is but that is what I was told. My mom was twenty-one years old when she had me so that was five years after her and my dad had been dating, and they got married four months before I was born so that is how I remember their anniversary. Money was tight for my parents around this time, but they still made things happen. My father was a bus driver for the metropolitan transportation system while my mother worked as an administrative assistant at Washington University. These are not exactly the most glamorous jobs, but they put food on the table.

Now is probably a decent time to mention that I have an older sister named Sharee. She was seven years old when I was born so yes, you guessed it - we are seven years apart! We do not share the same mother so I think you may call that a "half-sister" but I have never called her that. To me, my sister is my "sister" if we share some of the same blood. She lived with my parents and me off and on growing up, and when she was not with us, she resided in California with her mother. I do not have many details on the relationship between my sister's mother and my parents, so I will not discuss that any further, but I can say it has not been the best over the years. Mentioning this now does not really have any direct relevance to my life as a baby but I want you to know that she exists, and she was a wonderful part of my childhood. She is great, by the way, and she is one of my biggest supporters in everything that I do and have done. One of my "Day Ones," as people like to say nowadays. She is my real Day One because she was literally there on my "Day One" on this Earth lol. I have never had any real issues with my sister and she will be mentioned again as you learn more about me.

Anyway, back to my parents. My dad drove buses for the city but, as a real man that knows that his family is his priority, he had hopes of providing more for us and he knew that he could only achieve that through exploring other opportunities and career paths. He took an interest in the heating, ventilation and air conditioning field so he decided to attend school to become a licensed HVAC technician. My mom believed in his abilities and determination, so she made the sacrifice to support our home on her income while he pursued his license. My dad earned his license and that opened so many more doors for him, and it ended up changing our lives for the better. My dad has told me how he had to deal with subtle, and sometimes blatant, racism as he took his HVAC classes and completed his apprenticeships. St. Louis used to be a very segregated city in many areas, and some areas still have some progress to achieve as was brought to light by the more recent incidents in Ferguson, Missouri. My dad's elaboration on these experiences during my pre-teen years was essentially my first introduction to the concept of racism as I had never really experienced it directly. I knew the word but never felt the action.

My life as a young child was good. We went from an apartment to a small house, and then to a bigger ranch style home in the Jennings area of St. Louis. While this was your normal suburban area, we were just a hop, skip and a jump from the hood where my parents grew up, and where most of my family lived for much of lives before dispersing to other areas of town. My parents were good with their money, so I pretty much had all the necessities that I needed, and I was able to enjoy the things that most kids from similar economic environments did. I loved my Atari, getting candy and honey buns when we went to the store, toys, and all the other goodness of childhood.

When we lived in Jennings, our cul-de-sac was literally across the street from a small mall called River Roads, so we would walk over and frequent the stores, and I started bowling at the alley that was connected to the mall when I was around the age of five. My parents bowled in a league there; they put me into a youth league and this was my introduction to the sport that eventually became a staple in my life. The elementary, middle and high schools for our area were all on the same street that ran behind the mall, so my sister and I walked to school every day. Rain or snow, we were walking! Sometimes I would walk over to the middle school with my sister and get candy from their school store before walking back to my school, which was called Northview Elementary School. If I had my entrepreneurial mind back then, I could have made a killing selling candy. However, I was a five-year-old kid, and I loved candy like every other five-year-old kid on the face of the Earth so I was not selling shit. That candy never had a chance once it hit my hands.

I attended Northview from first to third grade. I have some memories from that school. However, just about all of them are too faint to remember since that was about thirty-two years before the time that this book is being written. One thing that I do remember is my best friend at the school, who was named Alonzo. He was what us black folks normally call a "bad ass kid" while I was probably one of the best-behaved kids you would find so I guess opposite personalities do tend to attract sometimes when it comes to friendships at every age. I think I also hung with Alonzo because I knew that if any kid at that school ever tried me, they would have to deal with him. I learned at an early age to keep some thugs on my squad so I would never have to get my hands dirty if someone threatened me, and that kept me pretty much fight-free during all of my school years. But let us get back to Alonzo. We hung out hard at school and on the playground. The playground was like a small city - do you remember those days? Every component was like a different building and each had different groups of kids that gravitated towards it. I was a merry-go-round and monkey bars kind of guy myself.

I remember my kindergarten teacher at Walnut Park (Mrs. Twelveman) but I cannot remember my first, second or third-grade teachers from Northview at all - isn't that weird? I also cannot vividly remember any other kids that I went to school with during that time except Alonzo. It is crazy how good friends can cement memories in your brain that never go away. Anyway, if you are from the St. Louis area and know of an Alonzo that may have gone to Northview Elementary in Jennings between 1986 and 1989, tell him to holler at me if he remembers a guy named Floyd.

In 1988, shortly after my little brother was born, we took a family trip to Atlanta to visit my parents' friends Henry and Maxine. They were an older couple that my parents enjoyed being around. They had a nice house in a neighborhood called Cameron's Crossing, which is situated in Austell, a suburb that is fifteen minutes west of Downtown Atlanta. I remember it being so refreshing and free in the South, and a change of pace from the monotonous Midwest vibe that I was used to. We stayed with Henry and Maxine for a few days, and apparently my parents felt the same way that I did about Atlanta because after returning home for a few weeks, my parents told me that we were moving to Atlanta. I was so excited! I get to move to a cool new place with a cool new little brother! Of course, I loved my St. Louis family but, at that age, I was primarily fascinated with the idea of moving to a new place and meeting new friends. We loaded up in our family's 1984 Toyota Corolla and hit the road. Georgia, here we come! Yes, we actually moved to Atlanta in a Corolla. My parents now own a BMW SUV, a nice Toyota Tacoma, a BMW motorcycle and my brother's old Maxima. Man, how things do change over the years…

Our first residence in Metro Atlanta was on the infamous Six Flags Drive, in the Whisperwood Apartments that still exist in the same spot today. So, to my fellow folks from what we call "The Drive": yes, I was a member of The Drive! We lived in our apartment on the ground floor of our building for a year, and I have good memories from that place. I watched my brother take his first steps in that living room. I also had a good friend that lived in my complex named Randy. He was a year or two older than I was, and we would play and ride our bikes down the steep driveway that ran through the apartment complex. The main thing that I remember about Randy is that he would ride his bike behind mine and would always stay really close to my bike when we rode down the steep hill. He would always end up slightly touching his front wheel to my back wheel, and then he would fall off his bike. This happened just about every day that we rode down the hill. Many years later, I was driving by Whisperwood and it totally hit me out of the blue: Randy was actually trying to clip my bike so that I would fall while riding down the hill. However, he never succeeded in making me fall. I guess God was keeping an eye on my naive ass and punishing Randy at the same time. Based on his actions to try to hurt me at that young age, I am assuming he is probably locked up at this stage in his life. But hey, I do not know everything so prove me wrong. Randy - if you are out there and are reading this, holler at your boy!

Since we moved from St. Louis right in the middle of my third grade year, I had to finish the academic year in a new school, in a class that was already established. I was placed in Mrs. Polke's class at Riverside Elementary in Austell. I have two vivid memories from that school year - the first was watching Reading Rainbow on the large Laserdiscs in the classroom. Do you remember those? The teacher or paraprofessional would push the TV cart into the classroom with the television on top and the Laserdisc player on the middle shelf. I thought that thing was an amazing piece of technology because we did not have the Internet nor cable television in classrooms back in those days. Now I can watch an entire movie on a flash drive the size of my pinky finger. Man, how things do change.

My other memory from this school year was bittersweet because while it hurt me at first, it turned out better in the end and it taught me something important. One day Mrs. Polke asked the class to write an assignment on paper. I cannot remember what it was that we were asked to write but I remember putting my little seven-year-old heart and soul into that assignment. When we were done, Mrs. Polke collected the papers and started to read some of them aloud to the class. When she got to my paper, I was excited to hear my words about to be read aloud to the class. Then she did something very unexpected. She turned my paper around to the class so they could see it, and said some words I would never forget: "Look at Floyd's handwriting. It looks like chicken scratch!" The class burst into laughter. Umm…who does that! I do not think I showed any expression because I did not want the class to know that my feelings were hurt. I felt bad, but I did not realize exactly how bad Mrs. Polke's poor choice of action was until I was at home that evening and my mom asked me how my day at school was. I told her what Mrs. Polke did, and my mom said, "Really? She really said that?" I said, "Yes, that is what happened." She said, "Baby, your writing is beautiful, and do not ever let anyone ever tell you any different, ok?" I said, "Ok, Mom." You know a mother can make you feel good no matter what the outside world tries to do to you.

My mom took me to school the next morning and walked me to my class. We went in, and my mom went over to Mrs. Polke's desk and asked her to step aside with her for a moment. When the teacher saw my mom's face, she had a look that was partly startled but also exuded some "I think I fucked up" vibes because I felt that at that moment it hit her that what she did the day before probably should have stayed in her head instead of bringing it to the class's attention. My mom started talking to her quietly, and I could tell that she was going off on her in a low voice because I saw that same stern face that she would display when she would tell me to put candy and toys down at the store that I wanted her to buy for me. To this day, I do not know what my mom said to Mrs. Polke for five minutes in that corner of the classroom and I do not think I want to ever know, but I know that for the rest of the school year I did not have any further issues with Mrs. Polke embarrassing me in class. I was young back then and focused on other things such as having fun, but I think that I had no further issues with Mrs. Polke because I do not recall her talking to me as much after that visit from my mom. I also cannot recall if she treated me differently from the other kids after that, but I did pass on to the fourth grade so it is what it is. And she did not want to see Mrs. Rounds again

I switched to Clay Elementary for the fourth and fifth grades because this school was in the district that I actually lived in. These were good years because it was during this time that I met some of the childhood friends that are still in my life today. I also started playing little league sports around this time. I played football for the South Cobb Vipers, and also played little league baseball at Wallace Park, which was the home of both the Vipers program and the baseball league. It was through these leagues that I was able to travel to different parks in the Cobb County area to play different teams, and it was interesting to see how different kids lived and the areas they were from.

From the middle-upper class kids of Lost Mountain and Acworth to the lower-middle class kids from the South Marietta/Fair Oaks area, I learned during these years that no matter where you are from, talent is talent. Your sports program can have money and no talent, talent and no money, or a mixture of both. I think our Wallace Park program had what I would call an average amount of money and a shitload of talent. I say that because we won the little league Super Bowl in three of the four years that I played little league football there. I was a tall, lanky running back paired with a shorter, fast bruising running back named Vincent that would always take it to the house if he was able to turn the corner on your defense, which he did just about every game. Vincent was also one of my best friends back then and is still a good friend to this day that I still see often. We also had an awesome quarterback and a good leader that we called Sly (short for Sylvanus). He was from the hood so he had that mentality, and he was not that big but was fast and would run your ass over. He was the hardest hitter on our team aside from Vincent, and that was because he was tough "mentally." I have not seen Sly since one day during my college years when I was playing pickup basketball at the legendary Run N' Shoot in Atlanta, but I learned the importance of confidence from him, and the concept of telling people that they cannot beat you, and then showing them why.

I spent my middle school years at Lindley Middle School in Mableton. Middle school was an interesting time because kids are emotional as hell during this period of their lives. As a middle schooler, you are caught between being a kid and being a teenager so things are confusing. You are growing hair in places you never had it before, but you are still not quite a man or woman yet. I saw some of the best fights that I have ever seen during middle school. I first joined the band in sixth grade and decided to play the tuba. I was good at it but I was a skinny kid so lifting a big ass tuba every day was not the move. In seventh grade, I switched to the trumpet. I was good on this instrument and made it all the way up to third chair by eighth grade. We had an awesome band director named Mr. White, who was a very cool guy. One day, at the beginning of the eighth grade school year, he asked if any trumpet or trombone players wanted to try playing the baritone. Not knowing what that was, we all sat quietly looking at each other. Once he brought out the instrument and showed us what it looked like, I fell in love with it. You mean to tell me that I can play an instrument that looks like a tuba but is smaller and sounds good like a trombone? Hell yes, I will play baritone! So, my friend Clarence and I volunteered to play the baritone. That instrument took me through high school and beyond as you will hear later. I had some good years while in middle school. They were not too eventful as far as memories go but they were good, innocent years.

During my late elementary and middle school years, I would go home to St. Louis for a couple weeks each summer to visit family. I spent most of my time at four places while I was there: at my Uncle Bud's house where I hung with my cousins Dana and Putt (Bud's son, whose real name is C.L. like his dad), my Aunt Ann's apartment complex near downtown, and at both of my grandmothers' houses on Garesche and Genevieve in the Walnut Park area in North St. Louis. All of these areas were ghetto, but they were in two different parts of the St. Louis city limits. Uncle Bud and my grandmothers all stayed within a mile of each other in Walnut Park while Ann's apartment complex was located about five to seven miles into the city.

From crabapple fights to nigga-knocking (knocking on people's doors in the apartment complex and then running away before they could answer), from fire hydrant water dancing to box Chevy's riding up the one-way streets ten times a day with two fifteen-inch speakers or three twelve-inch speakers bumping Spice 1's 'Trigga Gots No Heart', I experienced some of the most fun, carefree times of my life during these years. Sure, you would hear gunshots sometimes and see grown men fighting from time to time but that was part of being in the hood. I will have to say that St. Louis is probably the firework capital of the United States on July 4th because people there would spend $1,000 or more on fireworks to pop in front of their houses. You had dope boys and other hood-rich people with money to blow so the streets would sound like Baghdad in the early 2000's with cherry bombs and M-80 fireworks shaking the ground, while Roman Candles and bottle rockets would light up the night sky. I liked the simple Black Cat fireworks that looked like mini sticks of dynamite. I would light them one by one and throw them on the sidewalk as soon as I lit them or light a small portion of the brick form that they come in and watch them pop. Sometimes I would light the whole damn brick pack, which would go off like a machine gun for about sixty to ninety seconds straight. I will never forget the fun we had with all the sounds and vibrations, firecracker smells in the air, guns shooting into the sky…

…and the box Chevy Impalas and Caprices still riding up the one-way street with the two fifteen's or three twelve's bumping 'Trigga Gots No Heart.'

As I transitioned into high school, I did not go back home to visit St. Louis quite as much because I was busy with…well, being a high schooler. I attended Pebblebrook High School in Mableton. High school was a unique experience because it was interesting to see friends grow up and choose their own paths. Most of my fellow students got jobs and spent most of their after-school time at work, while others just hung out and did the other things that high school teenagers did. Many of us boys started to dabble with that thing called the "opposite sex" so most of us went out with girls during those years and started to learn about women. We thought we were some G's back then but realized later in life that we did not know shit lol. And there were a few students that decided to dabble with the same sex. Back in those days, the ones that decided to do this kept that on the low because society was not as accepting of alternative lifestyles as they are today, especially at the high school age. Therefore, some students that decided to go that way were subject to getting hands put on them. Nowadays, they call them "hate crimes." Back then, it was just called "a good ole' ass whooping because you were gay." Anyway, that is not exactly my area of expertise since I am as straight as Katt William's perm, and I do not have a problem with whatever sexual orientation a person chooses, but I am just speaking on how it was back then. We live in very different times now.

Most of my close friends were working nearly full-time during our junior and senior years, and they just wanted to get through high school for the most part. I am glad that they all learned from their life experiences because the ones that now have teenage kids are pushing them to get educated and be better than they were. It takes real parents to push their kids to reach new heights that they could not imagine when they were their children's ages. I was a little different back in high school because while I liked the same things that most other teenage boys liked - video games, girls and food - I always wanted to go to college, and everything that I did in high school was focused on that ultimate goal. I made good grades in each year, never bringing home anything less than a B in any class. I played on the freshman football team and would dress out for varsity games with a few other freshmen during my ninth grade year. I was skinny compared to everyone else, but I played linebacker because I loved to hit people. I felt that as long as I had pads on, I would not hurt myself, and this led me to knocking the shit out of people that came into my zone behind the defensive line. However, after hitting the varsity fullback in a spring training practice as that first year was ending and feeling that impact in every bone of my 5'10", 137-pound body, I decided that my pad football career would end then and there. Even after some urging from the head coach, I never put on shoulder pads again after that day. However, I probably should have kept playing because I sprouted from 5'11" to 6'2" during my junior and senior years. If I would have stayed in the weight room and on the field, I could have possibly developed a body that may have led me to catching touchdowns on Saturday afternoons at someone's Division I school.

That clearly did not happen, but what did happen was my joining the high school band class, and eventually jumping into the marching band after my freshman football season. I stuck with this and eventually earned the position of sole drum major for the marching band at summer camp in 1997, as I went into my senior year. This was a great lesson in leadership because, while it was a challenge leading over fifty band members every day throughout an entire football season, I did it successfully. I cannot say that the football team had their best season, but "my" band was solid. I played junior varsity baseball during my sophomore year and played varsity in my senior year. I was also a member of the Student Leadership Team. To this day, I am still not sure what we did as members of this leadership team besides tell people that they could be like us lol.

It was during my high school days that I first realized that I had a gift. I was able to make very good use of the written word. I realized that I was a writer. Writing just seemed to come easy to me, and it was something that I never struggled with. It was something that I could literally do without thinking. Almost like the way that I am writing this book that you are reading. Back then, I was on another level with it. I knew that because of the letters that I used to write to the girls back in high school when I thought I knew a little something about "macking" lol. I would write a letter to a girl that I was going out with and give it to her at lunch. At the end of the day, I would see her, and she would be on the verge of crying, asking me why I do not like her. I would then ask her to pull out the letter that I wrote, and I would actually have to explain line by line what I was trying to say. Then she would be happy again lol. This happened on more than one occasion, with different girls. Once I decided to try to "dumb" my letters down a little, I did not have any further misunderstandings. Maybe it was just me not being clear, but I still think it was them not being able to comprehend what I was saying. This is when I first learned that when you are communicating with people, be concise because sometimes less is more. I have always loved to read and write, and I have never made less than an A in any English class that I have taken. I am not saying that I am perfect with my craft because I know that I am not, but I am damn good at it. I guess I will know for sure after my editor gets ahold of this book. I also wrote some poetry back in my high school and early college days. I have some of it saved, and maybe one day I will publish it. We will see.

As you can see from some of the grades that I mentioned in the above paragraphs, I had a nice high school resume that was very fitting for some college admission applications. I remember speaking to my guidance counselor early in my senior year about my college options. I was going to mention her last name here, but due to what I am about to say about my "guidance" experience with her, I will digress. I remember being excited that I was a senior and telling her about my desire to apply to a few big schools. Not Ivy League schools, but big schools - I feel it is important to note that. As I sat in her office and discussed some of these options with great enthusiasm, she totally shut me down, and I will never forget what she said to me: "Floyd, those options sound nice and all, but do you think you should try some smaller local schools such as Kennesaw State, or maybe Chattahoochee Tech?" In my head, I was like, "Bitch, I am pushing a 3.5 grade point average, got extracurricular and leadership accolades out the ass and a 1200 SAT score? And you are gonna play me like that? Really? Have you seen my damn grades?" Of course, I did not say any of this out loud because my major college hopes would have been ruined then and there by being expelled, but you know I was sure as hell thinking that. It is funny because, in later years, I have chatted with some of my close friends that also dealt with the guidance counselors at our school back then, and they have told me that they were also steered towards local schools, and not just by this particular counselor. I wonder if they just did that to the black kids. I am not trying to speculate or anything, but why not encourage students to shoot for the stars, especially ones with credentials that can get them there. My school was the premier performing arts school in the county so maybe this counselor's mind was focused on pushing those (mostly white) kids. But still…

Anyway, my response to her question was, "No."

Let me tell you how things worked out. I applied to and was accepted into the University of Georgia, Morehouse College, and Florida State University. I also applied to the Georgia Institute of Technology - this was the last school to accept me but was my first choice so that is where I decided to go. I was also awarded the HOPE Scholarship as well as a scholarship from one of the premier black Greek fraternities. All this was announced on Senior Day a few weeks before my class graduated in June 1998. It was nice to hear my name read along with my chosen college and the scholarships that I had earned. I saw that same guidance counselor sitting on the front row of the bleachers, smiling as if she had something to do with my accomplishments. I have to give her some credit - she was always nice to me no matter how bad the advice she gave me may have been. As I walked down the stairs of the stage and locked eyes with her sitting to the side, I silently worded a "Thank you" in her direction and formed a smile with my lips, but my mind was saying…

"Kick rocks, trick."

My lesson to any parents reading this who have teenage kids in school, or to any teenagers reading about my foul-mouthed experience, is to remember that if you have a goal to do something when you graduate, do not let anyone steer you away from it. Visualize it, and if you truly believe it, you will have no choice but to achieve it.

I figure that my college days that I am about to entertain you with should fall under the Childhood chapter because, while I thought I was a grown man at this time in my life, I later realized that I clearly was not anywhere near that lol. No, I was not a wild, crazy college kid by any means, but I still was not what I consider the true definition of a "man." Most college males are legally considered men simply because they are eighteen years or older, not because they are mentally grown. I enrolled at Georgia Tech in the summer quarter of 1998, only a few weeks after I graduated from high school. Why so soon? Well, the school had a program in which they were taking a handful of the students that were not accepted into the general fall admission and allowing us to start in the summer quarter, and work our way into the fall class (the school was on a quarter system back then). So, we were basically a group of freshman rejects that they were giving a shot to.

Georgia Tech is a tough school, and I did not realize just how difficult it was until I got into it, especially since I never really had to study before I got there. I stayed on campus for most of my freshman year, and it was intimidating being around other students who were so smart. I remember eating lunch one day in one of the campus cafeterias with a few white guys from my dorm and a couple of females that also stayed on campus. We were talking about taking the SATs during high school, and one of the guys said that he fell asleep while taking the SAT the first time. I said, "Wow. What kinda score did you come away with?" He said, "1200." Really, dude? I stayed up the whole time I was taking the test and got a 1200, and that was on my second try! It was these kinds of conversations with other students that had me intimidated while I was at the school. I really stressed myself out because in my mind I felt that my knowledge was inferior to the other people that went to the institution. They did not really act as if they were superior, and many of the people that I met on campus were actually really cool, but that was just how I felt. I could not fathom back then that I was just as smart as they were, but I did not know how to apply myself.

This intimidation led me to eventually stop attending class, and on most days when I should have been on campus, I was instead back in Austell hanging with my best friend Ben, playing video games or just riding around the city and hanging out. There was a major black fraternity at the institution that wanted me to go online with four other guys and pledge, but my grades were so bad at that time that I told them I would not make it through school if I pledged. They were still trying to get me in because the frat's membership at Georgia Tech was so low at the time that they had to do a lot of stuff with their fellow chapters from the Atlanta University Center schools, so they needed to get their numbers up. I was even given my materials to learn like the other guys. However, I did the right thing for me at that time and continued to decline. Only one guy crossed that quarter, but the other three guys eventually crossed in later quarters. I often talk about going back and pledging the grad chapter for this fraternity, and I may still do it one day. If you are an Alpha and you are reading this, holler at your boy.

I made it through my freshman year, which is an accomplishment at Georgia Tech because in the new student orientation they told us that many freshmen did not make it through their first year there. The school also switched to a semester system, so going into the fall 1999 semester my GPA was down to a 2.00, and with three math classes on my schedule that I completely did not understand, I knew that would be my last semester at Georgia Tech. I was introduced to calculus while at the institution, and this is when I learned that there are two types of mathematics: scientific math and what I call "money" math. I had a great degree of difficulty understanding scientific math such as discrete math and differential equations. However, I was great at counting money and I could do that kind of math all day, which most people often call accounting. It was around this time that Georgia Tech introduced a major called Science, Technology, and Culture - which became commonly known by the acronym "STAC." They came up with a fancy 10-second spill explaining what the major was, and I memorized the hell out of it so I could explain it to people when they asked me what individuals with my major do. It was basically an English major that took some technical classes. That is all that it was, or at least that is what I perceived it to be.

I remember going to a career fair that was being held in the basketball coliseum that semester. I had on my sweater, tie, and slacks, thinking I was hot shit! I walked around to the different company recruiting tables and they had signs on the tables listing the majors that they were interested in talking to. I read the signs on each table as I passed them. Electrical Engineering and Mechanical Engineering majors…...Civil Engineering majors……Computer Science majors…...Industrial Engineering majors…...Textiles Engineering majors……Electrical Engineering and Computer Science again……..Mathematics majors. I remember thinking to myself, "Damn, I do not think that I can get a job with this STAC shit." Then, on a table tucked away in the back corner of the lobby, I saw a sign that said ALL MAJORS. That sign shined like a light from above! I was like, "This is your big break - pop a Cert in your mouth and hit it hard, Young Floyd!"

I walked over to the table and introduced myself to the nice-looking, young Caucasian female and young Caucasian male recruiters. They asked me how I liked Georgia Tech, and then the golden question came: "So, what is your major?" I said, proudly, "I am a STAC major. It stands for Science, Technology, and Culture." The lady replied, with a slightly puzzled look, "Ok, umm...interesting. What is that?" I immediately smiled and went into the spill that I had memorized so well, "Well, the STAC major blends the sciences and technology with a study of literature…blah…blah…blah…blah...blah...blah…" When I was done, the two recruiters looked at me for about two seconds, and then looked at each other for another two seconds. Then they both just burst out in laughter. And I mean loud laughter, as if I had just told them a joke. They were laughing too hard to even say that they were not interested in me. I turned smoothly and eased away from the table, kind of like I was just passing by and picking up a brochure as if I never had the prior conversation with them. They pretty much kicked me in the kidney with that one, but I kept it moving like a G. As I walked away, I heard the female recruiter say, "You think we hurt his feelings?" The male recruiter responded, "I don't give a shit. What the fuck is STAC?" And the laughter continued. And with that, my Georgia Tech days soon came to a close. I wonder if the STAC major still exists or if they just call it English now? Lol.

The lesson that I learned from this experience is that the world does not give a shit about how you label yourself. It only cares about what you do AFTER you label yourself. So, why label yourself in the first place? *Figure out who you are and just do "you."*

Oh, and if you are going to be a STAC major, please minor in something else. You will thank me later.

I withdrew from Georgia Tech right after that embarrassment at the coliseum. Not necessarily because of that experience, but because of the fact that I was well on my way to flunking all of my classes that semester. At that time, the institution would only let a student withdraw that far into the semester if he or she had some dire hardship such as a death in the family or something drastic. I did not have that at the time, but what I did have was an old obituary of a distant female family member that I snuck and found in one of the old photo albums that my mom kept downstairs in their den. I took it to campus, scanned it into a photo editing software, changed the date to a week prior to that moment, printed it out and submitted it along with my request to withdraw due to the stress of losing my great-aunt. It was accepted, and just like that - my Tech days were over. Until now, no one ever knew about that. Well, you do now. This book is about telling the world about things that I haven't told many people. And trust me - I am just getting started......

My parents were the type that made it seem like they would kill me if I dropped out of college. This is mainly why I gave them no clue of my withdrawal from Tech for a little while. Imagine the pressure dropping out of college and not telling your parents when you know that their ultimate dream for you is to graduate from college! After I withdrew, I spent a few days literally riding around Atlanta during school hours and drinking Bud Ice trying to figure out how to tell my parents that their son, who they had put their hopes, blood, sweat, and tears into, had dropped out of college. Ben, my best friend, just constantly reminded me of how far my dad was going to put his foot up my ass once he found out what I did. But that was Ben - being my best friend while also not being my best friend at that time in my life lol. Eventually, I decided to tell my parents, and luckily I did not have to pick my head up off of the floor after I told them. They knew that I was struggling at Tech, but they were about as shocked about me withdrawing as I was. They were partly angry, but more along the lines of, "Well, you need to go somewhere and finish because you are not giving up on school." I was with that. I did not like my experience at Tech, but I still loved college because I felt that any other school that I could go to would not be as difficult as Tech was to me. That turned out to be very true for the next college experiences that I had. Moreover, I am still glad my parents never teed off in my ass over that withdrawal.

So, one day shortly after I talked to my parents, I was chatting with my friend Sol on the phone. He was a year under me at Pebblebrook High School and was a cool dude, and probably one of the cleanest and best-dressed cats that I have ever met. He also served as drum major of the marching band the year after I graduated. Sol loved music, and he ended up going to Grambling State University in Louisiana. We were just chopping it up on this particular day, catching up as friends do when they have not talked for a while. He was telling me about his band experience at Grambling, and how he was enjoying it so much. I told him about what happened to me at Georgia Tech, and that I had left the school. He asked, "Well, why don't you come down here? I auditioned and got a P1 scholarship. I am sure you can get a scholarship too." The P1 scholarship is usually known at historically black colleges and universities (HBCUs) as the highest band scholarship that the program offers. I was always slightly above average on my baritone, so I thought, "Why not? That is actually not a bad idea, Sol!" My mom did suggest that I now consider going somewhere outside of Atlanta, so I applied to Grambling and requested to audition for the band. I auditioned and was awarded a P2 scholarship. I truly believed that I should have received a P1. However, the P2 still covered my tuition so I was cool with it, but I later learned that members of the band somewhat gauged other members by the type of scholarship that they received.

I remember my mom and cousin Geneva driving me down to Grambling for band camp in the summer of 2000. We rode through the country towns such as Meridian, Mississippi, and the town of Tallulah that you encounter as soon as you hit the Eastern Louisiana border on Interstate 20. I remember thinking to myself at this time, "Do I really want to do this?" Sure, I had been down that way before, but it was different since I was not going back home lol. We arrived on the Grambling campus and it was as dead as roadkill. It was an extremely hot day when I moved into my room in the Pinchback men's dormitory. Anyone familiar with Grambling's campus back in the early 2000's knows about Pinchback. It was sort of like the projects compared to the other dorms on campus, with the exception of the Martha Adams dorm, which was just about as dilapidated as Pinchback but was located on the other side of campus.

I was on campus for about a week and a half before band camp started so I just chilled out during most days, which involved writing the last poems that I would write for years, eating food from Sonic or the Tasty's Restaurant because that was about all they had near the campus at the time, and getting someone at the gas station that was over twenty-one years old to buy me Budweiser that I would take back and drink in my room. As other students started to arrive for band camp and for the fall semester, things livened up around campus and it started to look like a real HBCU.

I had good, interesting years at Grambling. I met some good friends on my floor in my dorm that I still keep in touch with to this day. I would hang out on the yard with those fellas and watch the cars ride by on the twenty-inch rims, especially around refund check time. Of course, the females would be out and about, and as college males we were always looking at them. We even fried fish and pork chops in the hallway in our dorm from time to time. You would not see something like this done in dorms on most campuses but this was Grambling, and you had students here from every part of Louisiana. Therefore, these guys could cook like I have never seen before, and those were good days.

Being in the Grambling Tiger Marching Band was a good experience that made me stronger as a person, and I also saw a culture up close that I really did not know existed - the HBCU band culture. During band camp, we practiced every day, twice a day. It was grueling but I was relatively healthy, thin and in decent shape so I did not have any issues handling the heat and the work. I learned how to play my instrument while dancing and I really enjoyed that. I also had to learn how to play as loud as I could because I was transitioning from a glide step background, also known as "white folks' marching" to the Grambling folks, to a show band style where I had to high step. Glide step bands raise and lower the volume throughout the show, while show bands basically play their asses off for the entire show. If you are not tired after performing a halftime show in a show band, then you are not doing something right. And if you are not a little fatigued after just watching an HBCU halftime show, either the band is not doing something right or you are not doing something right!

Movies and TV shows have been made about band members competing for spots on the field in HBCU-style marching bands, and these movies are somewhat accurate for the most part. I was always on the field throughout my only season in the band, and I performed in every halftime show that year, including the Battle of the Bands in New Orleans and the Bayou Classic that takes place the next day where Grambling's football team plays Southern University. All of the work that the band members put in during the season makes them go extra hard in the Bayou Classic because you have not "officially" completed your first year in the band until you have performed in that event, and I will never forget that performance as long as I live.

While in the marching band, I noticed that some of those people took the band culture just a little too seriously. I used to laugh internally at the way some of those guys would talk big shit about anything and everything at band practice, and then when you see them on campus away from the band room they would be as quiet as a mouse. It always tickled me when I saw that. Sure, you would have some members who would try to put you on the spot around campus, but eventually they would be reminded that it is a little lame to try to pull "band rank" in the cafeteria, and my fellas from the dorm and myself would just stare at them blankly when they said something off the wall to me. For the most part, I did not have any real issues with anyone in particular in the band.

It was also during this time that I learned the interesting concept of a "crab." If you have been around any HBCU band for any length of time or saw movies on the subject, you have likely heard of a crab. Crabs are the label given to students who are in their first year in the band. Freshmen are called crabs because of the crabs-in-a-bucket mentality. If you were to observe a bucket of actual live crabs, you will often see that when one tries to escape, the others pull it back into the bucket. This is referred to in other walks of life as one person's efforts being undermined by others, ensuring the group's collective demise. However, in the marching band, it refers to the concept of togetherness - when one member tries to quit and bail out, the other crabs work hard to keep him or her in the band. This does not always work as some people decide to leave the band and do what they think is best for them, but often fellow crabs do keep each other going throughout band camp and the football season.

I had an issue with being a crab for two reasons. The first reason was that the crabs were treated like a bag of pit bull shit by older members of the band, and this came largely from the sophomores who had just graduated from crabhood themselves and were eager to inflict the treatment that they had received as crabs. My issue with this was that I was technically a sophomore, so I was the same age as the assholes that were treating me like a crab. I really did not like that at all. The second reason was that when you play in a show band, one person's sound is often overshadowed by the much louder whole. Therefore, it was difficult to find out exactly how good or bad someone was because they rarely had to play their instrument alone. Over time, I learned that many of those people that treated the crabs like shit were often shitty on their own instrument because no matter how much shit they talked, you would never hear them play their instrument alone. I also learned that the people that were actually good on their instruments did not bother you much because they were more focused on doing just that - being great at what they do. There were some annoying people that were also good on their instrument, so they sort of had a right to mess with crabs because they also worked hard at their craft. This concept taught me that sometimes people will ridicule others to hide their own insecurities and weaknesses. Therefore, there is a good chance that the loudest person in a room is often the most insecure and most sensitive person in the room. I will put money on those odds.

Many of the people in the band were from either New Orleans or Shreveport. Combine that with their seriousness for the band culture and it became tough for me to relate to many of them. This caused me not to have any real close friends in the band other than Sol, my fellow crab sister Crystal and crab brother Maceo that also played the baritone, and my friend Derrick from New Orleans who also happened to stay next door to me in Pinchback, and is still one of my closest friends to this day. Crystal, Maceo and I were all good on our baritones so we could hold our own if anyone challenged us, and that was very cool. However, no one ever did because they knew we were good, and Maceo has to be the best baritone player that I have ever seen to this day. He was a music major, and he also later composed music that the band played at some games - his rendition of Love Does not Live Here Anymore will give you shivers because it sounds so good. Most of the people I hung out with when I was not around the band were from my dorm floor, and I also met some cool people in Ruston, which was the next town over east of Grambling. It was about 5 minutes away from our campus and is the home of Louisiana Tech University, which was where all of the people that I knew from Ruston were students.

The other reason that I went at Grambling involved getting my grades up. I do not know the difficulty of Grambling's curriculum now, but back in 2000 and 2001, it was a breeze to me. I do not want to say that it was too easy, but it was too easy, and that may have been because of the rigorous curriculum I had encountered at Georgia Tech before I came there. Anyone that went to Grambling back then that was not majoring in a tough major such as Computer Science or Mathematics that ended up dropping out due to low grades (that were not baby, jail or death-related) seriously did not apply themselves. I do not think that any of the people that would fall into that category will ever read this book, so I can safely say that. My GPA was around 2.0 when I started in the fall semester of 2000. When I transferred out of Grambling after the summer of 2001, three semesters later, my GPA was a 3.25. I accomplished this, to my recollection, without cracking open a book outside of class more than 5 times during the entire time I was there.

The school did serve its purpose - it was my first time truly being away from home, it showed me the limits that I could be pushed to physically, and I redeemed myself in academia. I had planned to stay and finish my college career at Grambling, but some unfortunate things started to happen. During the spring 2001 semester, there were some violent acts that took place on or near the campus, and at least one resulted in the loss of a life. There were also dorm robberies where people would kick in someone's door, duct tape them and take their stuff. They would also burglarize dorm rooms when students were not there, and I was a victim of this as my computer and books were stolen. My car was also broken into. Then, while staying in the Martha Adams dorm during the summer 2001 semester, someone was shot a few floors below me, and I actually heard the shots. They survived, but I thought to myself, "I cannot be this far from home and something happens to me." Can you imagine the pain my parents would have to endure if I was seriously injured and they had to ride in a car for eight hours wondering what my condition would be when they arrive down there to see me? I was not serious enough about the marching band to stay there, although I really wanted to experience a year in the band while not being a crab, and I had also pledged my section (Lords of Sound, Fall 2000) so I was looking forward to enjoying my next year while representing our section. However, I knew it was my time to go. I called and discussed it with my parents and, within a week, I was on my way back to Atlanta. My days at Grambling silently ended but I took some great memories from that institution that are still near and dear to my heart today. I also believed that the school has made some large strides since the time that I had attended it.

I transferred to Georgia State University in downtown Atlanta as a junior. I liked Georgia State because of the hustle and bustle of the commuter life. It was not like the traditional campuses that I had experienced at my past two institutions of higher learning. Many of the people that I encountered at GSU either transferred in from somewhere else or were trying to come back and attend college after working in their careers for a while. Therefore, people seemed to be about their business - they commuted to campus, attended their classes, and got the hell on. It was not much of a campus atmosphere as the main yard sat between some classroom buildings, and it was not much bigger than the yard area of some of the larger high schools around the Metro Atlanta area. However, the school has expanded for blocks since I left there in 2003 so the current students have access to an entirely different campus experience.

I came to the school in 2001 as a Computer Information Systems major. While in my first semester, I decided to explore some other majors in the College of Business to see what was available to me. I was shocked to see an actual Real Estate major. I inquired about this and found out that it had its own curriculum, and it was very interesting. It was also closely tied to the Finance major as I could take four additional classes and have a minor in that as well. At this time, my parents had a few rental properties and were involved in real estate on a part-time basis. They seemed to enjoy it and I was interested in it as well, so I changed my major to Real Estate and pursued it. I enjoyed this major and every class that I took, and it thoroughly prepared me for the career in corporate real estate that I currently enjoy as I write this book, although I probably use only about 15% of what I actually studied there with the rest of my field knowledge gained through actual work experience. By this time, there was nothing else in my life to worry about but school, so I finished my college career with no issues and graduated at the end of the summer 2003 semester with a major GPA of 3.33, and an overall GPA of 3.15. Georgia State's Real Estate program was ranked in the top 10 in the entire country at that time, so I was very proud of my accomplishment. I would also say that my first "real" relationship started here as it was at GSU that I met the person who I would consider my first "real" girlfriend.

3

ADULTHOOD

Adulthood started right after I graduated from college because that is when the world became "real" to me. I was fresh out of school, and I still had a little help from the parents here and there, but I was a grown man now. So I thought lol. I had a bachelor's degree in Real Estate, so I was not quite sure of what I was going to do with it at that time. I figured I would go into commercial brokerage as a salesperson, but I really was not a fan of sales. I performed really well in my real estate market analysis and real estate investment analysis classes at GSU, so I thought I could probably get a good gig doing that line of work. However, at that time the job market was not exactly hot, so I went and worked some contract gigs here and there for the rest of 2003.

One of those contract gigs included a stint at the MCI WorldCom building for a few months, shortly after the fall of that company from the executive-level fraud that was going on. My friend Todd had got me on with him there, and our sole job was to sit in a room with no windows and go through every physical document printed onsite at this company before it fell, label the document types and record them in Microsoft Excel, and file them in boxes that would later be sent to an offsite document storage company. I guess this had to be done to comply with document retention laws, along with the litigation that may have still been going on at that time or had ended shortly before we started the job. I was amazed at some of the things I saw in those emails between coworkers and bosses, and it gave me a clear idea of why things worked out the way they did there. I am talking about frivolous lunchtime spending and even more interesting lunchtime "relations" between employees. I guess many of them were unaware of the concept of "your email belongs to the company" because they were clearly talking about everything and everyone under the sun in those correspondences. I saw other documents that blew my mind, but I do not want to get into any trouble so I will not comment on this any further. However, it was an interesting introduction to the internal operations and happenings of a large corporation in the early 2000's.

The manager named Dee that supervised us was too cool. We would all go out to a nearby hibachi restaurant on Fridays, drink sake and then go back to work for an hour or two before leaving. Those were good days for me. This position lasted from the fall of 2003 into the early part of 2004. There were roughly eight of us, and after a few months, Dee started to pull people aside one by one on what seemed like every Friday and privately tell them that the contract was winding down, and that it would be their last day. I knew my time was coming so I was prepared for the conversation, and I had no hostility towards her as I knew it was out of her control. Aside from Todd, I have not seen any of those people since then, but I remember having good times and laughs with them in that cluttered room with no windows.

For a couple of weeks after this job ended, I did not do much but apply for professional jobs, some of which were actually in my field. In March 2004, I received a call from a company called ACS, Incorporated. They were an outsourcing company that held a large information technology contract with General Motors. General Motors also needed a vendor to handle its real estate lease administration, so they decided to ask ACS to do that as well. Now, people outside of my field ask me all of the time what lease administration is so let me take a second to explain it before moving forward. Let's use an imaginary department store such as J.C. Nickel's (JCN) as an example. JCN has hundreds of stores at malls all across America. The malls are run by property management specialists on behalf of larger companies that own the malls themselves. The property managers operate and maintain the properties, which includes keeping the parking lots and landscaping nice, repairing and maintaining the building, keeping the utilities on, as well as paying for the property insurance and real estate taxes. These costs are referred to as common area maintenance (CAM) expenses. The landlords are then reimbursed by the tenants (stores) for the common area expenses by charging each store a monthly CAM rate along with a base rental rate, just like tenants in an apartment building. In most cases, the malls charge each store based on its size compared to the rest of the mall, which is known as the store's proportionate share. When the mall landlords bill JCN, there is a person at JCN's corporate office who makes sure that the rent and operating expenses are paid for each JCN at its respective mall. JCN may also use an independent commercial real estate company or its own in-house real estate managers that negotiate new leases for the stores at each mall, and once the leases are signed and sent to the corporate office, the person that monitors the rents will also input these leases into JCN's lease administration system and set them up so that the rents are paid for the new locations. Well, this person that I am talking about would be the role that I would play. There are also other things that lease analysts do, such as requesting insurance certificates and paying property tax bills, but this should give you a good idea of what lease administration covers.

Now, back to the ACS job that I was discussing. ACS had no prior experience doing this line of work, so they hired a manager with experience in this field along with a team of five lease analysts and two lease abstractors to do the work. The manager and human resources team loved my degree, but since I had no real experience in the field, they wanted me to fill one of the lease abstractor roles, which involved strictly inputting the information from the leases into the lease administration system. I did not have shit else to do so I was happy to take the job! This was a weird situation because all of the employees that were hired for this department were interviewed remotely, so when we arrived for our first day of work in a brand new office area that they had built out just for us in the company's Marietta warehouse, it was the first day that we all actually met each other. Luckily, we all were laid back and we clicked pretty well so we were able to complete our work, and there were no serious personality conflicts to deal with. The office consisted of one long room where each person had their own cubicle along with an open conference area at the other end of the room by the exit. If I had to guess, it was a rectangular shape with about 1,000 to 1,500 square feet of usable space but it provided plenty of space for each person. There was also a separate office for our manager. I enjoyed the abstraction work, and it was a good introduction to the lease administration field. I was able to get an understanding of how commercial real estate leases were structured, and most of the leases were dealership leases in which General Motors leased the dealerships from the landlords that owned the land and buildings, and were then paid a percentage back from the actual dealership that used the properties. After nearly a year on the job, my manager said she wanted to hire an additional lease abstractor, so I had my friend Todd interview for the job. She hired him, and it was even more fun now because I had a friend at work that I could crack up with as well as a lunch buddy.

About six months after Todd had come aboard at ACS, one of the lease analysts mentioned to us that he had a friend at Wachovia Bank that was looking for a lease analyst to join their team at their Sandy Springs office. This would have naturally been the next step for me in my career with my bachelor's degree in real estate, so I applied for it. Todd decided to apply for it too, which I was fine with me because his degree was in telecommunications and networking, so I figured I would be the top choice anyway. I clearly remember the day we interviewed - Todd's interview was right before mine so I arrived right when he was coming out. His armpits were soaked through his shirt, and he was saying it was a tough interview, but they were cool people. I said, "That's what's up," because I was looking forward to my interview and talking about my degree in real estate. I had my interview, and it was my first time doing a panel interview as there were three interviewers. I thought it went pretty smoothly, and after it was over, I was looking forward to the call in the upcoming days with my offer for the job.

After a week had passed, Todd and I arrived at ACS at the same time one morning. As we got out of our cars, Todd came up to me and said, "Floyd, I got the Wachovia job!" It felt like someone had stabbed me in the side with a knife. While I was genuinely happy for Todd, I could not help but wonder how he got the job over me with my qualifications and all. It was a little awkward at work for the next few weeks before and after Todd left as I know my coworkers were probably wondering how I felt since I had brought Todd into the lease administration field, and he just hopped over me and moved on to a better gig. I was still a young man at this time, so it did not bother me as much as it would have if this happened in later years since I knew I still had a bright future. A few days after Todd started working at Wachovia, he told me that the managers that interviewed us told him that I seemed a little too laid back in my interview and a little too confident due to my education, and that they felt that they could better train Todd to do the job the way that they wanted it done. I also knew that it was a little charm that gave Todd the edge as well because he is a good-looking dude ("no homo" as they say but just being real), and he has worked his charm in many situations with the ladies so I could see why they went with him, as two of the interviewers were female and I'm pretty sure that one of them liked him a lot.

I learned a valuable lesson from this that I want you to learn as well: *sometimes it is not about what you know, but how you sell yourself and package your brand, which is YOU.*

You can have the exact qualifications required for a position that you are going for, but if there is a person who may not be as qualified as you who interviews for the position and convinces the company that he can do the job, and that person is more likable than you, more often than not this person will get the job over you. It happens every day. The Wachovia job that Todd got went on to jumpstart his professional career, and even though he later went through hardships as his position was later eliminated, he went on to move into another department at the company that launched a wonderful career for him in a totally unrelated field of work, and I am proud to say that as of the time I am writing this, he has recently started a position as the national director of supplier diversity for a major global healthcare system, and is not too far from C-level status. He did this using his God-given skills and being the person that he is, and he has made strides that I probably could never have due to who I am and my comfort level.

Todd has also returned the favor because while serving in a few good positions since he left ACS, he invited me to a number of professional conferences and got me into all of them free of charge, and put me in positions to network with some dynamic people. It was through these conferences that he taught me to never subordinate myself when I am around other professional people. Sure, some of them may have multi-million dollar businesses and are pretty well off while I just had an entry-level job and a dream, but if we are at a conference of our peers, then I should treat them as just that and I should expect to be treated the same – as peers on the same level. Todd also served as a professional reference for a few of the corporate jobs that I successfully obtained later in my career, and he was the person that made the most important introduction for me thus far in my personal life, which you will hear about later in this book. Over the years, I have learned from

Todd and other personal experiences along the way that everything happens for a reason, and what is ordained for you is just that - it is for YOU.

Now, back to ACS. Todd left the company in the summer of 2005 for the job that he earned. I continued to work at ACS for a few months and then decided that, since I had a year of experience under my belt, I should start looking to advance my career. I posted my resume on the popular job websites and applied for some lease administration positions around Atlanta. I came across a contract position with AT&T as a Senior Lease Analyst, where I would review abstracts for cell tower leases done by junior analysts and either approve them to be entered into AT&T's lease administration system for payment or reject them back to the analysts to be corrected. While it was a contract position, it was paying nearly twice as much as what ACS was giving me, and I had no real responsibilities at the time besides paying rent, so I decided to go for it. I gave my notice at ACS and started the AT&T contract in October 2005. While I was not crazy about driving 45 minutes to work in Norcross each day, the job itself was gravy. I was getting paid twenty-five dollars an hour to grade abstracts like a teacher grades papers, and it was extremely easy. I was amazed at the number of mistakes that those analysts made because the leases were not that complicated but that is why I had a job, so I rolled with it. I was notified in the middle of December 2005 that the contract would cease at the end of the month. I felt that I would find something else after that, so I was not worried.

I had been with my girlfriend from Georgia State for roughly three years before we decided to part ways when I started the AT&T contract, so it was a weird time for me as I had to get back used to being single after being with someone for so long and living with them for a couple of years. After talking with my mom, I decided to broaden my horizons and open my resume up to employers nationwide. In January 2006, I was contacted by a large commercial real estate firm that had an opening for a Portfolio Analyst position in St. Louis, Missouri. With most of my family being in St. Louis, I decided to go interview for it. I traveled to St. Louis for the interview and it went well, and while I was at the Lambert International Airport waiting to board my flight back to Atlanta, I received a voicemail from the hiring manager with a good offer for employment. They wanted me to join their team - that quickly! Unbelievably, I turned them down. Why would I do this, you may ask? Well, I was still in a stage where I was not sure if I was ready to leave Atlanta, and while I was not really into my now ex-girlfriend like that, I still felt like that friendship was keeping me in Atlanta. I always wondered how my life would have turned out if I had taken that job and moved to St. Louis because it certainly would have taken me down a different path in life.

The good Lord would continue to work. In early February of 2006, I received a call from PetSmart's corporate office in Phoenix, Arizona. I talked to the Director of Lease Administration and the HR manager for a little while, and then they asked me if I would be willing to come out to Phoenix for a face-to-face interview if they flew me out there. I said, "Of course, I'd love to come and talk with you," while in my head I was like, "Hell yeah! Let me know when the flight leaves Atlanta!" They said, "Ok. We'll set it up." I was at my mom's house at the time and I had gone downstairs to take the call, so I ran back up the stairs and told her the good news. We were both yelling and jumping up and down lol. PetSmart flew me out to the Phoenix the next week and I interviewed at their beautiful corporate headquarters. They offered me the job as soon as I got back to Atlanta and, after I had accepted it, the company even flew me back out there the next week for a few days to look for a place to live. I was amazed at how well they treated me because the salary was not that great, and they gave me a relocation bonus on top of that! At this point, I was more than ready to finally put my previous relationship behind me and go live my life as God intended it. I left for Phoenix in mid-February of 2006. I was ready to start the next chapter of my life.

Moving to Phoenix marked a big change in my life because it was my first time being truly on my own as an adult, meaning there was no more classes or graduations to look forward to - just bills and living. I was a grown ass man now. In my last phone conversation with my ex-girlfriend, which took place after I first arrived in Arizona, I remember saying to her, "You know, this is the first time I've ever had to make a rent payment or pay a utility bill. And I'm 25 years old." Before that, I had just given the money to her and she paid the bills. The things you take for granted until you have to do them on your own. However, while I had more responsibility for myself, the freedom of being a grown man also came with this. A SINGLE, grown man. I could go wherever I wanted, whenever I wanted. I could do this with whoever I wanted if I so chose to. I am an explorer at heart, and I damn sure explored the city of Phoenix during my time there.

I started my position as a real estate lease analyst with PetSmart and it was great to work at such a cool company. You can bring any animal or animals that you owned to work on Fridays, so on that day each week it looked like a zoo in the office! You could walk by cubicles and see a cat sitting on top of a filing cabinet, or a Great Dane leaning on a desk and slapping his owner in the back of the head while she typed on her computer. There were all types of animals around there, from lizards to snakes. It was amazing to see. As a lease analyst, I had seen but never actually done much of the duties that I was hired to do outside of abstracting. However, my background and experience at ACS allowed me to catch on quick, and soon I was excelling at my job. After a year, I was promoted to a senior lease analyst position where I was responsible for training new analysts on the lease administration and lease audit process. I can say that I trained some people that went on to have good careers at PetSmart, and one of them went on to serve as Lease Audit Manager. The company planned fun outings for us throughout the year, and they would also bring in celebrities to speak to the employees and sign autographs, such as Kurt Warner, who played quarterback for the Arizona Cardinals from 2005 to 2009. I met some great people at PetSmart, and I still keep in touch with some of them to this day.

One fun part of my PetSmart experience included meeting my friend Kris. He was a Construction Manager that worked on my floor, and we met through different interactions in passing. Kris was a few years older than me but we clicked, and he has always been one of the coolest white boys that I know. He is also the only white man that I know who can tell you the artist that sings any Motown record that you may hear, but he cannot dance worth a damn lol. One day, Kris came to my cubicle and said, "Hey Floyd, come join our bowling league. We have our own team and it'll be fun to have you out there with us." I said, "Man, I used to bowl when I was younger, but I haven't really done shit since then besides bowling for fun." He said, "We buy a pitcher of beer each night, dude." All I needed to hear was "pitcher…" and I was like, "I'm there, bro!" So, I started to bowl on Kris's bowling team and it was so much fun. It was then I realized that there was a whole different world in bowling, and that there was so much to the sport. I bought some bowling shoes and a cheap bowling ball to get started. Later, Kris introduced me to a woman that we worked with named Tina. She was a nice woman, and her age was somewhere between Kris's age and mine. It turns out that Tina was actually a pro bowler, and had bowled numerous perfect games, which is a score of 300 and the highest possible score you can achieve in one game, in case you are not familiar with bowling. She agreed to give us some lessons, and while Kris was already an experienced bowler with a very decent bowling average, I was way on the novice end, so she showed us both some things that I know still stick with me today at the lanes.

A bowling ball company had sponsored Tina due to her accomplishments, so she had an assortment of bowling balls at home. She gave Kris and me a couple of balls each, and those balls were very good. I went on to improve as the season progressed, and I told Kris and my other crazy, funny bowling teammate Medley that the night I bowl a game over 200, I was going to get fucked up! Well, one night towards the end of that season I was in my third and last game of the evening in our Thursday night league. I was stroking that game and picking up all spares, and I noticed that Kris and Medley were sitting back chilling but were not really saying much to me. After I bowled my last ball of the night, which was a strike, I walked back towards them and they were standing there with some funny smiles on their faces. I said, "What's the deal with y'all?" They just smiled and looked up over my head. I turned around and looked up at the screen.

It said *"Floyd R...........203."* Damn, I did it!

After shaking the hands of the other team and my teammates as this was a big accomplishment for me at that time, Kris and Medley happily reminded me, "Well Floyd, you said you were getting fucked up when you get your first 200 game. Time to get fucked up!" We went over to the bar and started with some Jägermeister shots. The City of Phoenix turned me on to Jager and I appreciate that lol. Anyway, we all definitely got fucked up, and Kris ended up having to drive me home that night. I achieved both goals that I set for that accomplishment - I bowled over 200 for the first time and I got fucked up. It was a great night and the start of my journey into league bowling that would continue for years after. I still have the score sheet from that night in my bowling bag today.

On the personal front, Phoenix was an interesting place. I encountered many different personalities while living out there. From what I observed, it seemed like many of the people that I came across away from work were not from Arizona, and it was rare to actually meet a person that was born and raised in the Phoenix area. It also seemed as if many people that I met around my age came out there to take on a persona that was not really them, as if they came to Arizona to be someone that they could not be where they were originally from. In other words, they were lame at home so they came to Phoenix to not be lame, if that makes sense. Now, let me reiterate again that this does not apply to the people that I worked with at PetSmart because they were all cool - I am referring to people that I engaged with while experiencing the city socially. I did meet some cool people from Phoenix, as well as other places such as Michigan and Chicago, and even Georgia. I am still friends with some of them on social media today, and it is good to see them doing well. From my friend J.V. from Columbus, Georgia to my boy Patrick that I partied hard with during the Super Bowl festivities in Phoenix in 2008 and my friend Kris that I mentioned earlier, I met some great friends in Phoenix and I am so thankful for my time out there.

Now, the women out there were something else. First, many ethnicities reside in the Phoenix area. However, I first assumed that everyone that looked to be of Latino descent was Mexican because, in Atlanta, most people that looked Mexican were Mexican. I was quickly corrected when I asked one woman, "You're Mexican, right?" She quickly fired back, "No, I'm Guatemalan! Every person out here that isn't white isn't always a damn Mexican!" Well, how the fuck was I supposed to know? All those damn countries in Central America lol. While I met some cool women out there, there were some weird ones as well. While I am definitely an advocate of my black sisters, they were actually the ones that gave me the most shit when attempting to socialize in Phoenix. It almost seemed like they had a chip on their shoulder. I could be sitting and chatting with a black woman that I had just met at a bar, and almost always one of the first questions that would come out of her mouth would be, "Do you like white women?" My response would be, "Don't you see me sitting here talking to your black ass?" Well, I did not quite say it in those words, but I would say something to the point of, "If that was my preference, then I wouldn't be talking to you." They would then say something like, "Well, I asked because all black men out here seem to like white girls." I would be thinking in my mind, "Shit, I see why." With many black women acting in this fashion, I saw early on during my time in Phoenix why black men out there gravitated towards Caucasian women and women of other races. In most cases, they were more down to earth and just flat out cool. They did not want drama or bullshit - they just wanted to hang and have a good time. I also met a few cool black women so I cannot say that they all were like the one I discussed above, but a good many of them did act like that.

One of my best memories from my time in Phoenix actually did not take place in Phoenix. Yes, let me explain this. One of my childhood friends named Devonte called me up one day and told me that he was in Las Vegas, and if I wanted to come out there for the weekend, I could stay with him in a room that he already had reserved. I was like, "Shit, I don't have much going on this weekend. Yeah, I'll be out there, bro!" Now, Devonte is my homie, but he is that one friend you know that always has a good amount of money but you have never seen him go to a nine to five job lol. So, it was not a surprise that he was out in Vegas kicking it.

Devonte had called me on a Wednesday, so when I got off work on Thursday evening, I hopped in my 1997 Toyota Avalon and hit I-10 West. The skies had fallen dark by the time I hit the mountains between Phoenix and Vegas. It also happened to be a full moon that night, so the light from the moon shined on the surrounding mountains and lit them up in a way that was so beautiful. I was amazed as I saw this wonderful sight while I winded through the mountains on the highway, and there were no other cars within at least a few miles of me, so I had this all to myself. The way I felt as I drove through these mountains was a feeling that I have never felt. This was a sight that I had never seen until this moment. I felt like this was "my world." It was a beautiful one. I did not want that drive to ever end. Of course, it did end and I made it to Vegas. I had fun weekend hanging out with Devonte on Friday and Saturday, and my friend Leroy and his wife also happened to be in Vegas celebrating a birthday along with another couple so we all hit the club on the rooftop of the Rio Hotel that Saturday night and partied hard. It was a great weekend to remember, and I have made a promise to myself to one day track the full moon in that stretch between Vegas and Phoenix, and make that nighttime, moonlit drive at least once more in my lifetime.

In early 2008, I started to become a little homesick after talking to my friends back in Atlanta. They were raising their kids and doing what grown people do. I was also enjoying my life, but I felt that I was ready to be back in the presence of the people that I knew and that knew me. While Phoenix was a beautiful place, I felt that I was at a point where I had seen and done enough in the city, and I was ready to go back home. Therefore, in June 2008, I packed up and made the move back home to Atlanta. It was nice to be back home, and it seemed like the city had made some exciting strides when it came to the nightlife options and entertainment so I was hitting it hard. I had a couple of phone interviews lined up when I got back but they did not quite move past that stage, so I was not employed during the Summer of 2008. Therefore, I continued to apply for jobs while just enjoying being back home.

I received a call from Aaron Rents' corporate office in Buckhead in August 2008 regarding a lease administrator position that they had available. I had heard through the grapevine that the Aaron Rents' office was like a sweatshop - no one hardly talked in there during the work day and it was boring. I remember the lease administration manager calling me up and asking me if I was interested in the position. I told her what I heard about the office and asked her if it was something like that. She said, "Well, it's still a little like that." I told her that I do not think the environment would fit me, so I was going to pass on the opportunity. The balls I had to turn down a job opportunity as if I actually had options lol! A month or so passed after that call and the hotline was somewhat dry, as I had not received hardly any calls about lease administration jobs. Sure, I could have gone and done sales somewhere but that is just not my thing.

One day, I was searching the job websites that I usually use, and I saw that the Aaron Rents' lease administrator job was still posted. I started thinking to myself that not much else was out there, so I better go ahead and hop on this position. I applied for the job and the same manager that I talked to the first time brought me in for an interview. She liked me, offered me an acceptable salary and I took the job. I am glad I did because it really was not that bad of a gig, and the office was not that bad either. It gave me a chance to polish my lease administration and lease auditing skills in a low-pressure environment while working with genuinely cool people. I was chatting with my manager a few weeks after she hired me, and she said to me, in her Russian accent because she was originally from that part of the world, "You know, I talked to job candidate a couple of months ago that sounded a lot like you, and they told me that they didn't want to work here because they heard it was awful. That is weird, huh? Hmmm..."

Umm...No, that was not me. Funny story though. What's for lunch today?

While Aaron Rents was a public company, it still had a family-owned atmosphere because it seemed that a few of the leaders across the different departments had a majority of the power when it came to decision-making for the organization. While there may have been opportunities for growth at some spots in the company, the culture in my department at that time did not seem to encourage employee growth, and I felt like I could sit in my cubicle and do the same exact thing for 25 years without anyone asking me if I wanted to apply for something else, or if I wanted to discuss a path for growth. The manager and lease administration team that I worked with were great people, but there just seemed to be nowhere to go outside of my position in the near future. In February 2012, I received a call from a company called Studley, which was a large commercial tenant real estate broker based out of Manhattan, New York. They were looking for a Lease Auditor to join their Atlanta team. I interviewed via phone with the Manager of Lease Audit and Lease Administration who was based out of California, and then I went in and met with a few people from the Atlanta office. I was offered a position with a higher salary and much more flexibility, so I made the decision to leave Aaron Rents. I still keep in touch with some of the people I worked with there to this day, even though only about four of the probably 15 to 20 people that I talked to regularly are still there.

The job at Studley was a cool gig. I was able to focus only on lease auditing, so the number of daily miscellaneous tasks decreased while I was able to learn more about working in a third party capacity. We worked for our clients so the relationship was different from me working as an employee of the company that is receiving the service, and I enjoyed the monthly meetings and keeping the clients updated on the cost savings I was achieving for them. However, it started to thin out in the office as the company merged with an overseas firm, and some of the employees from my group ended up going over to a large commercial real estate competitor that most of them were with before they came to Studley. After leaving Studley in early 2015, I spent a little over a year working as a contractor, and the latter part of that contracting period was spent working back at Aaron Rents. That was fun because I got to work with some of my former coworkers, and I was tasked with doing only the lease auditing function instead of the full lease administration responsibilities that I had when I was an employee there so this was easy for me.

In April 2016, I received a call from a company based in Washington, D.C., called RGR. I interviewed with them and was offered a position where I could do lease auditing from my home for their clients and still come to D.C. a few times a year to interact with the office, so I accepted it. I enjoyed visiting D.C. and seeing the culture there. The city has great food spots, and I usually ate Chinese most of the time while I was there because it was "real" Chinese food that reminded me of the good stuff that you can find in St. Louis, but not necessarily in Georgia. It was not like the bland stuff that you get from most Chinese spots in the Atlanta area where the food is cooked by Koreans and Mexicans. However, if you know of a spot in Atlanta that makes truly authentic Chinese cuisine, please let me know. Anyway, while in D.C., I was also able to interact with a good friend from high school named Nick, who showed me some of the nightspots. In fact, I invited him to the happy hour outings that my job would hold every time me and the other remote employees came into town so eventually my coworkers knew him as well. We would go hard on the town because that would always be my last night in D.C. before returning to Atlanta, so that next half-day at work was always a long one as I often was sitting there red-eyed from the long night before. I could not wait for that airline alert to pop up on my phone around noon reminding me of my upcoming flight home so I could use that as my signal to leave the office, head to the airport and get to my seat on the plane so I could sleep.

Working from home was wonderful but the job with RGR itself proved to be a little stressful for me. It was partly due to me struggling to get used to their work processes, and partly due to the leadership. I will not go into details about that, but it was a challenge for me to gel with their management culture, and it appeared that some of other employees were burned out by the culture as well because a few more ended up leaving the company after I left in August 2018. Shortly before I gave my two-week notice at RGR, I had solid irons in the fire with three other great companies in the Atlanta area and that was a blessing in itself. I had a round of final interviews in one week, and I ended up getting a great offer from the company that I am currently with as I write this book, who offered me a substantially higher salary than what I received at RGR. In fact, I was actually on my way to another interview when I got the call with an offer from my current company! It was an easy choice as my current place of employment is wonderful and they have a lovely building, along with an amazing culture. I am glad I made the choice to join them. I love being able to be involved in so many things, from running the rent process for the business unit that I work in to doing financial analyses for upcoming deals and being involved in document execution, as well as other facets of the company's real estate decisions and operations. Another cool part of this is that I get to do it all from the top floor of the company's brand new building that sits right by the highway with a great view of northwest Atlanta. Oh yeah - I still have a two-monitor setup at the crib and get to work from home in my drawers, occasionally.

Now, when I came back home to Atlanta in 2008, I was as single as a one-dollar bill at the strip club and definitely ready to mingle! I often hung out with my cousin Zaire from Buffalo, New York. He moved to Atlanta to attend Morehouse College, and he was my riding buddy as we were all over the city partying just about every weekend. I guess I should say I was his riding buddy because we rode out in his Jaguar most of the time, and then in his Mercedes S500 once he got that. I actually do not believe that we missed a weekend on the town unless one of us was sick or had a date with a lady lol. Those were good times and we were everywhere. First Friday parties, Professional Relaxation parties, house parties, the hottest lounges and strip clubs - you name it and there is a strong chance that we hit it up. Throughout this time, I dated different women here and there but not seriously as I was just looking to have fun while I acclimated myself back to Atlanta and attempted to figure out exactly what I wanted to do with my life. Not necessarily from a professional aspect, but just in general.

One day, during the fall of 2010, I made my normal commute home from work. Since I worked in Buckhead, I would normally take the backroads, which involved coming down Moores Mill Road, which eventually turns into Bolton Road and crosses I-285. The road then crosses Veterans Memorial Highway (also known as the infamous Bankhead Highway) before turning into Fulton Industrial Boulevard. I made it to my home, which at this time was a small two-bedroom house that I was renting, located near a cemetery on South Sweetwater Road in Lithia Springs. It was my usual custom to iron my clothes, and then hop on the couch and get on social media to see what was going on with everyone else while watching TV.

While on the couch, I saw an alert pop up on my phone from Facebook Messenger and, as a single man, I opened up my inbox as fast as I could because there may have been some soft legs to climb in between at the other end of that message lol. I checked my inbox, and it was a message from a woman named Paula that I had not spoken to since my college days. I knew her from back in my high school days as she attended the rival high school in my area. However, some of her good friends attended the school I went to, and my good friends also knew her so that is how I came across her occasionally back then. Anyway, in her message, she said, "Hey Floyd! How are you? I saw you in traffic today crossing Bankhead. I blew the horn, but I know you didn't see or hear me." I replied, "What's up, Paula! Long time, no see! Yeah, I take that way home from work because I work in Buckhead and I try to avoid the highways as much as possible." She said, "I work in Dunwoody so I feel you - I have to take the highway to Bankhead, and then I try to do back roads from there." We chopped it up for a few minutes and talked about old friends that we still kept in touch with, as well as those that we had not seen in a while. I had seen Paula in a few pics on social media, so I knew that she still looked good. Therefore, of course, I had to go ahead and shoot my shot like Kobe: "So, maybe we should get together sometime and grab a bite to eat from Applebee's or something." She said, "That sounds good to me." And that is exactly how my relationship with Paula started - from us crossing paths in traffic to grabbing dinner at Applebee's.

Paula and I dated for roughly seven months. Towards the end of the relationship, I started to feel as if I was not completely happy. Paula was a beautiful person, both inside and out, and a great mother to her two young sons who I also spent time with during my period with her. However, I felt that she truly did not know how to cater to me, and our relationship became more like a routine. Every day started to become the same, and I had an issue with her paying more attention to her college-aged sister and friends on social media than she paid to me. I used to ask her to put her phone down sometimes and she would, but she would eventually get back on it, and I do not think that she realized how detrimental this lack of attention was to our relationship until I decided to call it quits. Once I got to a point where, when I got off work, I would rather just go home and chill for the evening instead of packing my overnight bag and going over to her house as I usually did, I knew that this was something that I did not want to be in any longer. I also learned an important lesson from this situation - well, it was more of a concept that I had always ignored until this point:

It is good to go with your gut, within reason. If something is keeping you from being truly happy and you know it, get rid of it.

In this case, it was not the person that was keeping me from living my best life - it was the relationship itself. Two people may be great individually, but not so great when they are together. Similar to the two like poles of magnets.

F.A.I.T.H.E.

I started to roll this section of my life into a separate chapter. However, since it was and still is the most significant part of my adulthood, I figured it would fit well in this chapter.

I was talking to my good friend Todd on the phone one day about my relationship with Paula being on the fence. And yes, this is the same Todd from earlier in the book. He never really goes away lol. He was currently engaged to a woman named Asha, who lived in Chattanooga, Tennessee. I do not think he knew her very long at all but he seemed to be somewhat happy with her. Therefore, as his boy, if that is what he was into then I was cool with it. I talked about how things seemed to be going downhill on my end with Paula. He listened with patience and lent a good ear as he had often done over the years. After I finished venting about my unhappiness with the situation, he said something that I will never forget, and we still laugh about it to this day: "Aww man, I hate to hear about that, Tizzle (that is what he calls me since my middle initial is the letter T). Well, maybe you should come with me to Chattanooga this weekend and meet Asha's friend Faithe. She's a really good girl, man. She's pretty, too." I laughed and said, "Damn, Todd - you want a brotha to just go ahead and pull the plug, huh?" He was like, "Well, you might as well. Why not do something that will make you happier than what you're doing right now?" That light bulb went off in my head, and I said, "You know, you're exactly right." Now, I have some great friends, but Todd is that one friend that pulls the trigger in life - if he wants a new car, he goes out and buys it, and deals with the payments later. If he wants a new phone, he goes and gets it because he knows that it will make his life better in some way, and he will get the money back eventually. He told me Faithe's full name, so I went online and found her Facebook page. Once I saw those first pictures of her with that light, pretty skin, beautiful smile and curly hair, I was completely sold. So, I decided to pull the trigger as well. I called Todd back later that evening and said, "Yeah, Todd. I'm going to do that. Can you get Faithe's number for me?" His answer: "I already got it for ya. You got a pen? It's……" *My nigga.*

At this point, I was still technically with Paula. As I mentioned earlier, I was at a point where I was looking for any reason not to go over to her house, especially on a weekend. Therefore, I told Paula that my parents were driving down to Louisiana for the weekend to visit family and that I was rolling with them, so I would be leaving out Friday after work and coming back to Atlanta on Sunday evening. Once I saw that she was on board and that I was definitely free for Chattanooga, I decided to call up Faithe. She did not answer when first I called her. She returned my call the next day and it happened to be while I was at my bowling league. I talked to her for a few minutes before telling her that

I could not talk long because it would be my turn to bowl again in a minute. She was nice, and she understood, so she said I could just call her back later (in a later conversation she admitted that she thought I was out bowling with some other chick lol).

I called Faithe that evening, and we had a good conversation. I learned that she was born and raised in Chattanooga, and that she was a hair stylist. I also learned that, while she did do Asha's hair a few times, they were not necessarily "friends" in the true sense of the word, but more like acquaintances. So, with Asha's wedding coming up, she asked Faithe to do her hair. She worked in a hair salon at Hamilton Place Mall in Chattanooga and she loved her craft. Faithe has a sister named Myra that is one year older than her; Myra has a teenage son and a daughter that is a few years younger than him. Just as Faithe told me a little about herself, I told her about myself and talked a little about my family. She was really nice, and her voice was so soft and sweet - I think I fell in love with that before anything else. We had a good vibe going so I told her that I would be coming to Chattanooga with Todd that coming weekend. She said that was cool and she looked forward to meeting me.

Friday finally came, and Paula and I had texted each other a few times earlier in the day, talking about the usual stuff. When the afternoon came, I told her I was heading to Louisiana and that I would talk to her when I get back, but she could hit me up if she wanted to. Now it was time to go to Chattanooga! Lol. I was coming from my job in Buckhead, and I already had my weekend duffle bag packed in the back seat, so I stopped by the gas station before I hit I-75 North and grabbed a Red Bull and a couple of Slim Jim's, and hit the highway. This would become my bi-weekly ritual for my Chattanooga runs: get off work, ride up I-75 about one-third of the way to Adairsville, stop at QuikTrip and grab a Red Bull and some Slim Jim's, crank the trap music back up and cruise until I reached Chattanooga. I talked to Todd on the way up there during this first trip because he was going for the weekend as well, and we were planning to double date with Asha and Faithe on Saturday.

I arrived at the La Quinta Inn in Chattanooga after an hour and a half of leaving Atlanta. It was around 6:30 p.m., and Faithe said she would meet me at the hotel at 7:30 p.m. so I had good time to get ready before we left for the spoken word event that we were going to in Downtown Chattanooga. She called me when she was pulling up and asked me which room I was in. I said, "Room 108." I will never forget that room number as that was the date that I officially met Faithe. I was looking out of the window because I wanted to see what she looked like as soon as she got out of the car. And there she was! Light-skinned with long black hair, with a black turtleneck shirt and some nice jeans. I backed away from the curtains and did a fist pump as I whispered "Yeaaaahh!" She was beautiful! I gained my composure as if I had not been celebrating, and then I opened the door and said "Hi Faithe. It's nice to finally meet you. You look amazing." She said, "It's nice to meet you as well, Floyd! You look great yourself." I replied, "Well, I'm ready so let's head out!" She originally offered to follow me over to the event in her vehicle and I could tell that it was an attempt to be cautious on her end, which I appreciated. I told her, "You can just ride with me. It'll be fun!" She agreed to ride with me and we headed out.

As we rode to the event, we talked and it was nice. Faithe had a humble, down-to-earth air about her that made her easy to talk with. She was pretty but far from intimidating; she reminded me of a country girl that was not actually a country girl. We made it to the event and we had a good time. We ate and had a few drinks as we watched the spoken word artists and singers. I was shocked to see such quality and talented artists in Chattanooga as I was not aware that they had an entertainment scene that would foster such an event. We got back to the hotel around 2 a.m. and I told Faithe that she could stay if she wanted to avoid the late drive home. Yeah, I know - as the reader you are thinking, "Yeah, yeah - just like a man.....trying to get some ass.....uh huh...." Haha! No, I was actually nice and let her have a side of the bed to herself, and I stayed on my side the entire night. See, I can be a gentleman.

Faithe had to work the next day since it was Saturday, so I spent that day exploring the Hamilton Place area of Chattanooga until she got off work that evening. I went to the mall where she worked and walked around. I also went to the Fresh Market store and got some rotisserie chicken for lunch. Faithe met me at the hotel again that evening, and we then went to meet up with Todd and Asha. Faithe was sexy that day as well with her hair in a bun; the bun brought out her smile and her pretty face. She had on a nice blue top with some brown jeans that matched the accent colors in the top. We all had dinner and drinks, and after that we were ready to party. We left my car near the restaurant in Downtown Chattanooga and rode with Todd and Asha to a club called Midtown, in what I assume was the midtown area of the city. We had a good time, and Faithe danced on me throughout the night. I thought I was a G with my Corona in my hand as I stood behind her for some songs while she danced in front of me lol. We all had a great night, and that was the night I got my first kiss. It was a good one...

I got back home Sunday evening and relaxed in front of the television. As Monday morning rolled around, I knew what I had to do that day. It actually did not take place until the evening. Paula texted me and asked what time I was coming over because that was my usual routine as I mentioned earlier. I told her that I was not coming. Before she could reply and ask why, I just went ahead and said what I had to say, "Paula, I'm not happy. I don't feel that this working for me." She replied and asked why, and I told her that while I think she is a great person, I do not feel that this relationship is where I need to be right now. She then called me, which was what I should have done in the first place for a conversation like this and I do understand that now. It caught her off guard and it hurt her, but she did not seem devastated from my perspective, and if she was then she was doing a good job of holding it together. We talked a little more and I just explained to her that it was not necessarily her - I just felt that we were great as friends, but we were not compatible in a relationship. She seemed to accept it after a couple of days, and it was right after that when I went to her house and picked up the things that I had left over there. I pulled out of the driveway after I loaded my car with my belongings, and that closed the chapter with Paula. This was in March 2011 and we have not spoken to each other since. However, with her knowing many of the people that I know and the omnipresence of social media, I know that about a year or so after we split up she got into a relationship with a person that we both knew previously. They had a daughter together, and I do not know the status of that relationship at this moment (even though I have heard things) but I hope Paula and her family are doing well.

Now, back to the woman of the hour, or day, or my life - however you want to put it! Faithe and I started to date, and I enjoyed my bi-weekly trips to Chattanooga. I would book a hotel for Friday and Saturday, which was usually the La Quinta because the company I worked for at that time had a discount code for the hotel. I would drive up there and we would hang out in the evenings while I kept myself occupied by going to stores during the days while she worked. I met her beautiful mother during my second trip up there and she was so cool. She took Faithe and I to some of her favorite hole-in-the-wall clubs around the city and I enjoyed those so much. They were usually about as big as someone's living room with a small bar, and it was nice to kick back, sip and watch the older folks enjoy the music without having to deal with the hustle and bustle of a club in Atlanta where people were there to basically be seen instead of actually enjoying their surroundings.

Atlanta has a few official hole-in-the-walls but not many like the ones that I went to in the smaller Chattanooga. Faithe came down to visit me in Atlanta for the first time after 3 weeks of dating. I took her by my parents' house (because if you know me, you know damn well that I am a true momma's boy). Faithe had some cute curls in her hair and I was glad that she was looking so good that day because I knew my parents would like her. And they did.

We made our relationship official after about a month when I asked her if she wanted to be exclusive with me, and she said yes. We also made it official in other ways but I do not kiss and tell, ha! Now, I want to drop some game for the single women that are reading this book, and the fellas, too, as you may learn something from this. Faithe has told me over the years that she knew I was the one after I did two things. First, she melted at the fact that I introduced her to my parents early on before we became official, and that I did it with such admiration for her that she could actually feel it. Secondly, and I do not even remember doing this but apparently it was significant to her decision to be with me, she talks about how she came down to Atlanta to visit me at my house one weekend while we were dating. She left and returned home that Sunday, and that evening as we spoke on the phone, she said, "Oh, I just remembered that I left my tennis shoes on the side of your sofa, the end closest to the kitchen." I replied, "Oh, you did? I didn't even notice them there but they'll be in the same spot when you come back so they won't get lost." That was all that I said, and it was the truth - I did not really think anything of it. She later explained that for a man to say that he is not going to move something that a woman leaves at his home until she comes back and gets it, and actually holds true to that, is a major thing to a woman because he is indicating that he is carving a place in his domain for her. Especially for a man that lives in a place like Atlanta, where the women outnumber the men and are looking for good guys like me.

So, remember not to get caught up so much in one's flaws that you never notice the beautiful things that they do for you. Especially if your garden is not exactly Eden. You do not want to miss out on your Adam or Eve.

Faithe and I continued to date into the fall of that year. Everything was going very smoothly and we both were happy with the path that our relationship was taking. We had a lot in common, and we both liked to explore and try new things such as restaurants and lounges. Neither of us were homebodies so we liked venturing out to enjoy the city. Some weekends I would go to Chattanooga, and some weekends she would come to Atlanta. It got to a point where my friends would ask me every Thursday or Friday, "Are you going to Chattanooga to see your girl this weekend?" They knew the routine about as well as Faithe and I did. We were about seven months into our relationship when I decided to take Faithe to the famous Shout Restaurant in Midtown Atlanta on one Saturday night. I had taken her there before since this was one of my favorite restaurants, and I hate that it eventually went out of business. Shout was an excellent restaurant that consisted of a highly rated sushi bar on the ground floor and a sexy, trendy lounge on the top floor that connected to one of the nicest patio areas in the city that overlooked Peachtree Street. The drinks there were priced ridiculously high but I loved the patio, and on any given clear summer night it was a challenge to find a seat on the patio due to the large crowd.

This particular night that we went happened to be on an unseasonably warm night in October with a smaller crowd than usual. We found a seat on the patio that had a clear view of Peachtree Street, and we sat down to enjoy the music from the DJ, along with the warm air and city views. We were talking and Faithe mentioned that she wanted to move out because she did not want to live at home for too long since she had been on her own since college. She told me when we first started dating that she moved back in with her mother after leaving a very toxic relationship in which she lived out of state, so I definitely understood that. I told her that I was planning to move to a larger house around the end of the year when my lease is up, so she could just come down and move in with me. By this point, I knew she was serious about being with me and she knew I was serious about being with her, so it was pretty much an easy decision on both ends. She agreed, and that was that. Time to celebrate the future!

Excuse me, Ms. Waitress! Can we get two long islands over here?

We moved into a home in Mableton towards the end of 2011. It was a nice, older ranch-style home near Veterans Memorial that had been very well kept and had an excellent landlord. We enjoyed the home and our relationship continued to flourish. Our one-year anniversary rolled around that next March, and this was the anniversary of the day we first met, not the day we made it official - just for the record. We went to dinner on that actual day and we were talking. I cannot remember what we were chatting about because that was nearly eight years from the time that I am writing this sentence, but I remember looking at her face and thinking to myself, "I'm actually going to marry this woman. Ol' Fleezy is gonna get married!" The crazy part about it is that I had absolutely no doubts or questions. That was the way God was steering me. As the reader, I want you to remember that last sentence and my next few sentences when you are in the process of considering someone for marriage, or your next relationship or marriage if you have been down that road before. While no relationship is perfect, your decision to be with someone should be "easy" in a sense. You should feel God's wind behind you, and it will push you towards that person that is the object of your eye much like the romantic comedy movies where two people that are experiencing love at first sight are pushed towards each other with the wind blowing their hair and clothes as if they are on a sled! And if it does not feel just like that, look for something similar lol. However, the person that you want to be with should be also drawn to you in much of the same manner, as you should not be working harder to be with them than they are working to be with you, and vice versa. It should be a nice, comfortable balance. If you are not sure if you should marry someone, wait until you are sure. Do not rush this decision because it will affect the course of your life, and definitely do not decide to marry someone just because someone else you know is getting married, or you want to be like other people that are close to you. If that is your reason for choosing to pursue someone for marriage, I suggest that you first figure out who YOU are, because if your friends' decisions for their lives serve as the basis for yours, you truly do not know who YOU are.

Look in the mirror and do not just SEE who you are - KNOW who you are.

Please remember that there is nothing wrong with being single because it is the period in which you are being prepared for the relationship that is destined for you. Many people miss out on living their best life because they mentally cannot step outside of their own minds and BELIEVE that their life should be better than what it is, and this often leads them to settle for less than they deserve. Our minds determine our happiness, and we wake up to this when we are wise enough to realize that we can only control what we can control, so there is no need to stress about the things that we cannot control. So yeah, go ahead and enjoy that apple martini. Sure, go ahead and dance with that man that is showing interest in you, and get that next free drink that he is going to buy for you. In other words, enjoy the life that God put you here to live while you can and stop worrying about what everyone else is doing. Just do not miss that diamond when it rolls and bumps into your big toe.

I designed a very nice proposal for Faithe and I set it for Thanksgiving Day. She was always figuring out surprises but I got her pretty good with this one. I told her that we were going to do a holiday photo shoot at my parents' house, so she needed to wear a nice dress. When that day came, she and I were getting dressed that morning while, unbeknownst to her, all my friends and family were gathering at my parents' home. Her mother, sister, niece, and nephew were also coming. I was not really nervous until that day, and while she was finishing her hair that morning, I was in the kitchen taking shots of Jim Beam Black and trying to make sure that all of my friends were going to arrive at my parents' house before we got there lol. We then drove on over to my parents' home. As we walked in, I can tell that Faithe was a little surprised at all of the family that was there, but it was Thanksgiving so she had not caught on to what was really going on yet. I steered her towards a chair in the living room near the larger sofa that was left clear for her, in a spot that gave everyone that was upstairs clear visibility of her. All of my friends were downstairs in the basement, and I had them park up on the next street up from the house because I knew she would start calculating what was going on if she recognized any of their cars. I also had one of my brother's friends and her boyfriend there to help with the proposal. When I felt ready to pull the trigger, I looked at my mother and said, "It's time."

I went downstairs while my mom silently directed everyone to start inconspicuously looking towards the living room. As I entered the den in the basement, all of my friends were smiling at me as I said, "It's time, folks." And it began. Everyone lined up in a single file line. My brother's friend and her boyfriend that I mentioned earlier were at the front, and they started by walking up the stairs singing "Spend My Life With You" by Eric Benet and Tamia. My friends all followed, and I was at the end of the line. As the singers got to Faithe, they stood behind her while they continued singing the song, and they sounded so damn good! Once all of my friends had stopped in their spots, she saw me with a rose in my hand and that is when it finally hit her. I got down on one knee and started my short dialogue. Her mother and sister were running behind so they arrived while I was in the middle of the proposal. When

I was done with my spill, I asked her to be my wife. She was softly crying by this time and she said "Yes!" Then the applause came.

What I did next was pretty cool, if I must say. I spent the previous month reaching out to good friends of hers that she had not seen in a while, along with some of her family members that could not be at the proposal. I told them that I was proposing to Faithe, and I had them send me videos saying congratulations to her and whatever else they wanted to add. I compiled them into one video in which I did an introduction with me and our dog Lady (who you will hear more about in the next chapter). After the proposal, I pulled a chair to the middle of the living room so she could sit and face the flat screen television on the wall. I played the video for her and everyone else to see. She absolutely loved this, and the video made her cry even harder than the proposal itself. Yeah, I know what you are thinking: "Yeah, that was pretty slick, Floyd. You go, boy!" I had to pat myself on the back for that proposal because it was smooth. We continued to enjoy Thanksgiving Day by eating and then going outside with my fellas and playing football on the empty lot next to the house. We had so much fun that day, and that had to be the most memorable Thanksgiving holiday for me and all of my friends that were there. Later on that day, as Faithe and I talked about the proposal, she said that I had really surprised her this time but she mentioned that my taking shots in the kitchen had her thinking that I had something on my mind. However, she had no clue what it was so I still pulled it off. One win for Floyd.

We had a smooth engagement period, and during that next spring in 2013 we moved to a larger home in Lithia Springs. It was a nice home in the same subdivision that my parents lived in so that was convenient for some things. We were smart with our wedding plans. We accumulated all of the liquor for the wedding over the period between the proposal and wedding by grabbing a couple of big bottles of vodka, bourbon, and tequila every time we went to the liquor store. This proved to be a great move because we were able to get all the liquor that we needed for cheap without breaking the bank, and it was nearly the same as making small payments instead of paying thousands of dollars in lump sums to an event planner for an open bar. My aunts from St. Louis and my mom got together to cook all the food the day before the wedding.

We used two popular tuxedo and dress rental companies for the bridesmaids' dresses and groomsmen's tuxedos. A quick note on that because this is something that we discussed during the process: if you and your fiancé are open to doing non-traditional outfits instead of renting clothes, please go with that option because it is less stress and less money that everyone has to pay, including you. This could mean something as simple as all of the groomsmen wearing the same shirt and slacks, or the bridesmaids wearing dresses that may not be exactly the same in design but are the same color. People often go the route of renting attire for their wedding parties because it is a long tradition. However, just as it is up to you to define your marriage, you also have the freedom to define your own wedding. Therefore, do not be afraid to do just that. Now, as a man, you may be open to non-traditional wedding attire but your woman may not be, and that is fine because the wedding is mostly for her anyway. However, even though you may get shot down, you should still be able to simply have the conversation with her. If you are in a position where you feel like bringing this idea up to your woman or bringing up something else that is important to you will cause a big argument, it may be a good idea to seek premarital counseling because this is an indicator that the lines of communication may not be as open as they should be, and all married people know very well that communication is very important in a marriage. I am just trying to save you some money, heartache and time!

I am a big fan of the Converse Classic Chuck Taylor tennis shoes so this is the style of shoe that I chose for me and all of my groomsmen to wear at my wedding, which is a little non-traditional although many people do get married in tennis shoes. Our wedding colors were gray and plum, so what I did to save money was to buy Faithe and I a pair of plum Chucks while I bought the rest of the groomsmen gray Faded Glory shoes that looked like Chucks for $9.99 a pair from Walmart's website. No one could tell the difference except for the guys wearing them, and even some of them did not know until I told them what they were. So, take that with you and save some money if you are considering Chucks for your wedding.

Our wedding took place on a hot day in August 2013. The venue was in Roswell and it sits on the Chattahoochee River. Our ceremony occurred on the large patio that sits beside the river so the brown water served as our background. I know the color "brown" does not sound too aesthetic, but it was beautiful. I still remember watching most of our guests struggling to keep themselves cool with the customized fans that we placed in each chair while the pastor and I were awaiting the arrival of my bride. It was a funny sight to see - about 100 fans going at different speeds. The wedding was wonderful, and the reception was off the chain. The crazy thing is that it poured down raining the next day, and I mean it really poured, so the good Lord looked out for us and made Mother Nature hold her pee for one more day while we joined in holy matrimony.

I can go on and on about our marriage since the wedding but with this book being the length that it is, I have decided to just quickly touch on life since then and talk about some of the things that I have learned during my union with Faithe. We resided in the Lithia Springs home up until March 2019, when we moved to a townhouse over in the exciting SunTrust Park area (Atlanta Braves Stadium) where we currently reside as I write this book. It is an exciting area and we love enjoying the surrounding attractions such as the Battery and the many restaurants that are within walking distance. I have had several job changes since then and have now landed at the great job that I discussed a little earlier in the book. Faithe was hired on as a stylist at a popular hair cutting chain shortly after she moved in with me back in 2011. She worked there up until the summer of 2018, when she finally arrived at a point where she could no longer comfortably deal with the processes and work culture that was fostered by the owner and his management that ran the multiple franchises. After leaving that job, we leased a salon suite for her at a building in Smyrna. She loves her freedom and independence, and she is steadily building her business so I am very proud of her.

I would now like to discuss some things that I have learned before and during my marriage. One key component to a good marriage that I mentioned just a little while ago is communication. If a couple cannot talk to each other and understand each other, they will not survive a long-term relationship. Why? Well, it is simple. Anyone can get along when things are good, but when a couple hits rough patches, you must be able to navigate through them successfully. How do you do that? You do it by talking to each other. No marriage is perfect, and yes - my wife and I do argue from time to time and we have had some bad "falling outs" as many other couples have. You show me a couple that says they have never argued, and I will show you two liars.

When things get heated, you must be able to calm down and talk about what caused the rift, and how to try to stop it from happening again. I will not sit here and lie - Faithe and I have had disagreements sometimes and we may not have worked it out right away so there have been some periods of silent treatment from one or both of us for a day or so. However, we have had to learn how to eventually talk to each other and understand how each other feels about what is going on, and that is the first step to repairing the problem. Early on in our marriage, and this is something that many couples struggle with, we were talking out our issues after we argued but we were not trying to understand how each other was feeling about each issue. Over time, you learn that if you do not understand your spouse's perspective on a situation, it is very likely to repeat itself. Do you know what happens when it repeats itself? You guessed it - it leads to another argument. I found it interesting that, after talking to some people that have gone through divorces, they admitted that they did not truly understand their spouse until they were divorced. The reason for this phenomenon leads to my next point: those two people were hearing each other, but they were not LISTENING to each other.

Listening is the most important part of communicating because that is the only way you will come to understand your spouse and their perspectives on different situations. I struggled with listening early in my marriage, and I am still working on it, but I have gotten much better at it. I have actually learned how to avoid some disagreements just by refraining from talking and listening to my wife. It is hard at times, especially when I think she is flat out wrong, and I used to be quick with the trigger as soon as she said something that I did not agree with. However, I had to learn that, in life, no one wins a shootout until someone is shot. Some people shoot at each other so much in marital disagreements that they end up killing each other emotionally and spiritually, and the marriage is essentially over at this point because there are some things you just cannot come back from. I will never say that I am the perfect husband because I am not, and I do not believe that any man is. However, as long as I try and my wife knows that I am trying to be the person that she knows me to be inside and out, we will be together. This comes from communicating, which starts with listening.

Another thing that is important in marriage is financial health. If you are considering marrying someone, you must be on the same page financially or your marriage will be much harder than it has to be. Of course, I dated women before I met Faithe, and they were all different from each other because they are all different people. I dated some women that had expensive tastes while I am a cheapskate, at least when it comes to me. After dating some of those women, I realized that I would not ever be compatible with a woman who had such tastes because I would have to spend my time, energy and money keeping her happy with material things, losing myself and my happiness in the process because I would continue to give this person more than I would probably receive in return. Now, do not get me wrong - I want my wife to have the best of everything and I want to give it to her, but she loves me for me and knows that I am ambitious, and she knows she will have it when I can give it to her. So, our love for each other allows her to enjoy what we have now until we achieve the goals that will bring us material wealth.

Now, do not get it twisted - we are not living in poverty by any means, but we always aspire to gain more financially, and we have done that each year we have been together as it relates to our income. Income and assets are two related but different things. Therefore, while we are building our income, we are also working to build our assets as well because that is the measure of your true worth. If your partner wants to spend your money without putting much back in the pot and expects you to always pick up the slack before you get married, that will continue after you get married, and I would put money on that in a heartbeat if someone believes otherwise. If you are ok with that, then you do not have a problem. If you are not ok with that, and you want a spouse that is equally yoked and brings a little more financially to the table, you need to wait until you find that.

Something else that comes with marriage is FAMILY. Let me repeat that: Another thing that comes with marriage is FAMILY. Your girlfriend/boyfriend, fiancé or spouse had their family before they met you, they will have their family while they are with you, and they will have their family after you if things do not work out. You must be able to understand that, if your partner comes from a close-knit family, they will need to interact with their family from time to time to stay mentally healthy. This interaction can be in person, via phone or through video calling. Sometimes a person may not get along with their partner's parents or family members, and this happens because people simply have different personalities. However, if you choose not to interact with their family, you should not attempt to keep your partner from interacting with their family either because this may cause your partner to not be as happy as they could be, and those feelings can have a trickle-down effect that will affect your marriage. This is something that I have not had to deal with personally, but I know people that have dealt with this or are dealing with it as I write this paragraph.

Now, I know there are some mothers with sons who are in relationships that will read this book, and I know that there are some wives with husbands that are close to their mothers that will also read this book. I fall right in the middle of this scenario because I am the husband lol. When it comes to the mothers, understand that, as a mother, you are and will always be your son's first love. However, the Holy Bible tells us that, as a man leaves his father and mother, he is to cleave unto his wife, and they shall be one flesh. A married man and woman become one unit, and his wife becomes his number one priority. Therefore, if you do not see or hear from your son, or sons, as much as you may like, understand that they are being just who you taught them to be: good men. If a man makes a decision based on his woman's input and this goes against your opinion as his mother, he has an obligation to make the decision that is going to keep his home free of injury and negativity, and this is likely his reason for going with her counsel and not yours. If a man is a true "momma's boy" and has always had a good relationship with his mother, he is always going to love you and respect you, regardless of if he chooses to take your advice or not. This means he may drive you crazy to the point where you do not want to talk to him for a few days but understand he is just being the man you raised him to be. Let your son or sons guide their home in the manner that they choose to, and they will always be there to be a part of yours.

Some of you reading this book are wives or girlfriends that are on the other end of this scenario. When you decide to enter a relationship with a man that could lead to marriage, understand that while you may have just met this man, he has known his mother since birth. If he has always had a close relationship with his mother and she has been active in his life, then she has guided his life directly and indirectly for years, and this is something that you must take into consideration as you interact with him. You must know that he will listen to you, but he will also listen to his mother. He will also naturally want to see and hear from his mother. While his time should prioritize you first, you should allow him to have reasonable interaction with his mother because it is good for his emotional health. If you put your man in a position where he feels like he is choosing to make either you or his mother happy, it causes a level of stress that you would never understand. It can also cause him to feel as if you care more about your feelings instead of his, and this can cause other issues to arise in the relationship. His mother has provided for him and given him many things over the course of his life and, as he grows up, he naturally wants to return the favor by being the man his mother raised him to be. Therefore, telling her "No" or that he does not agree with her can be tough for him sometimes and that should be understood. However, a man must be ready to tell his mother "No" or that he will choose his own path once he is in a relationship at this level. If your man cannot do that, it may cause issues further down the road because his mother will ultimately control him, which in turn will mean that she will control your relationship or marriage. Keep this in mind. Now, as a disclaimer so I do not make the women in my life mad (lol), my mother and wife get along well, and over time we all have learned to create a balance in our relationships and communicate better with one another so we do not experience the drama that I know some mother and wives have created in other relationships.

I also must talk to the men and husbands that are reading this book because you do not get off the hook that easily. Your woman or wife is a very important person in your life, and your mother (if you are close to her) is an important part of your life as well. While it may seem hard at times, you must accept that no matter what is going on between your mother and your woman, it is ultimately YOUR responsibility to create harmony. Some of you may be thinking, "My mom and my woman hate each other's guts. That ain't happening, bro." You also may be thinking, "Why is this my responsibility? They're both grown so they need to grow up and act like it." Well, I will tell you why. First, you are the MAN, so you need to act like it. You set the tone. Second, it is your responsibility to convey to your wife that while she may not be on one accord with your mother, she will respect her, and you will do the same for her parents and family members. You also must convey to your mother that, while she may not be on the same wavelength as your woman, she will respect the fact that this woman is your priority and you will govern yourself accordingly, and she must do the same. Some mothers and their son's significant others talk every day, and some may talk once a year. However, if they both can understand and soak in the fact that if the man in between them is at peace with himself and the relationship between the mother and woman, he will be much happier in his own home as well as when he spends time with his mother and parents. I know that in some situations it may be virtually impossible to create the harmony that I speak of due to things that have happened in some families, and I understand that every family is different. However, my goal here is to shed light on things to keep in mind that may help you foster a better relationship when it comes to the mother-son-spouse framework.

You may notice that I did not speak much about fathers. This is because I am writing from my perspective. While my father has always been in my life and we have always been somewhat close but have grown closer over the past 10 years or so, my mother has interacted with my wife much more than he has. We are men - and I know that, as black men, sometimes fathers and sons get along best by saying the least to each other lol. Growing up, I could be in the house with my father all day on a Saturday and we might not say one word to each other but we both were just fine. When it comes to my relationships during my adulthood, my father has been largely hands off and it is pretty simple with us: if I am happy, he is happy. He was more involved in my life when it comes to the child that I will write about later in this book and I am very thankful for that. However, he has always supported my relationships as long as I was happy.

I understand that for some men their fathers played more of a part in their life than their mothers did. My parents were both there as I grew up in a two-parent household so I cannot speak on some things regarding that dynamic, but some of the things I spoke about above can apply to similar situations that involve a father instead of a mother. For example, your father should know that once you jump that broom, your wife is your priority, but you will still always be there for him and support him in every way that you reasonably can. Your woman should also realize that, if you are a man that was raised by your biological father, you will without a doubt possess some of his traits and ways, and she can actually observe your father to get a better understanding of why you act the way you do. I always said that I would not ever turn into my dad, and now every day I watch myself slowly do that - from his mannerisms to his gray hair, down to the way our breath smells (and no, we do not have stank breath so do not go there – it is just an observation) - I am almost a spitting image of him. You can learn from that, women. So, pay attention. You cannot say I never gave you anything!

Another nugget that I want to give to those that are in relationships is that you should not get caught up in the people that were in your partner's life before you appeared, and I am speaking from a romantic standpoint, not family or platonic friends. They had a life before you. Get over it. I know my wife was with other men before me, and that is fine because she did not know I existed until we met. And vice versa. Thinking extremely hard about what someone did before they were with you is wasted energy that I am sure can be better used somewhere else in the universe. My wife can mention that she went to a place with an ex or talk about some things that she experienced in previous relationships, and that is ok because it sheds some light on things that she has been through. To truly know and understand someone involves knowing where they came from and what they have experienced throughout their life. Now, my woman is not about to sit in front of me and talk about sexual experiences that she had with other people or how someone rocked her world before I came along - hell no, we are not doing that shit. However, some couples are comfortable talking about that kind of stuff, and if you are then "do you" because you define your relationship. Talking about things like that may actually help some relationships so that is something to think about. However, I define my relationship, and I know that my wife and I are not comfortable talking about past sexual relationships so we do not do that. This is what works for us. You do what works for you. I will say that when it comes to possible diseases or health risks that one person possesses and could expose their significant other to that resulted from a past experience, these kinds of issues should be discussed openly because they are extremely critical to your future and will likely play an important part in your decisions to further a relationship or marriage.

When you are married to someone or have been in a long-term relationship with a person for a while, sometimes things can get mundane, both mentally and sometimes sexually. This is when you have to remember to keep things fun. It may not be as easy when you have kids, but you have to make time to do some of the things you did as a couple before you got married to keep your marital sanity. Some people asked me during my first year or so of marriage, "So, what has changed in your relationship since you got married?" My response: "Just her name." That was the truth because we continued to live life the exact same way that we did before we got married. People may see Faithe and I on social media out at a restaurant or bar at least once a week, and they tell us that they see us living it up. My mother also sees us and says, "Y'all just be out spending money, huh?" That is a mom for you! However, we actually do not spend much. Well, we spend a little but it is really not that much lol. If you think about it, on a Friday evening you may get a to-go order of 10 wings for you and another order for your partner. Once you add some fries and a 2-liter soda to that, you are already at close to $25. Now, Faithe and I can go to one of our favorite Mexican spots and get a few margaritas that are on special during happy hour or on sale on a particular day during the week, and a couple of enchilada or burrito plates and keep it at around $35. Doing that once a week should not break your bank, and by trying different restaurants around Atlanta, we are able to keep an element of newness in our marriage. Try a different restaurant or bar that you have never been to once a month and see how it impacts your marriage.

It is also during these evenings out that you can talk about things such as your goals and plans for the future. You can discuss these things at home on your couch or at a bar over a cold margarita. Which option sounds more fun to you? One thing that we always do is discuss our budget for dinner on a particular day before we step into the restaurant because we like being on one accord with no surprises. If you are dating someone seriously that you are considering for marriage and you cannot even bring up a conversation about what your budget is for the evening without them looking at you funny or getting irritated, then you should really think about that because it is a financial-related and communication-related red flag, and it should be nipped in the bud before the ring goes on.

My last point on making the decision to marry someone is extremely important, and I have some close friends that are in the stage of their relationships where they are trying to figure out if the person they are with could be the mate that will make the rest of their life a wonderful one. I want you to listen to me carefully because if you are one of those people that are close to me, I know you are reading this book and I care about you and your future:

Things do not change just because you get married.

Please, let me say this again.

Things do not change just because you get married.

So often people make the mistake of thinking they can change a person by marrying them or having a baby. YOU cannot change a person with either of those. The person has to be willing to change themselves, and it can only happen when they are ready to. In addition, if a person promises you that negative habits that they may possess will magically disappear with marriage or a baby, I would strongly advise you not to believe it. I say this for the same reason above. I believe that a person can be changed and enhanced mentally and spiritually in some ways through marriage or by having a child, but the literal act of marriage itself, meaning signing a marriage certificate and having a ceremony where you exchange rings, alone cannot and will not change a person. If your partner has had bad spending habits for as long as you have known them, they will continue to spend badly after you get married. If your partner has been extremely jealous and insecure since you have been together and promises that it will change after you put a ring on their finger, I would bet one hundred dollars each time that those traits will continue to linger after you are married.

The point that I am trying to drive home is that relationship problems do not mysteriously disappear when you jump over a broom. If that were the case, every marriage counselor in America would be without a job. In most cases, *the problems get worse.* I will say this again - in most cases, *problems that exist before marriage often get worse after marriage.* If a person is working on changing unfavorable habits or traits before marriage and they are showing progress, then after marriage, things can get better and that is great. I do not want you to go away from this section thinking that people just do not change after marriage, but there is a process to it, and change does not just happen simply because a person says it will. However, I still truly believe that you should not make the mistake of thinking that by marrying a person you will magically change them because you will not.

When someone shows you who they are, BELIEVE THEM.

4

L.A.D.Y.

Before I dive into this chapter, I understand that, as you read it, you are going to realize that it is based on an animal. You may wonder why I have devoted an entire chapter to a dog. Well, there is a good reason for it, and I want you to read the entire chapter before going to the next one because I teach an important lesson about a great concept. I told you that this is a book unlike any that you have ever read, and I meant that. However, this is a fun chapter so sit back, laugh and enjoy!

I mentioned earlier in the previous chapter that I spent nearly three years working at PetSmart's corporate campus in Phoenix, Arizona. I also talked about how employees could bring their pets to work. One day, one of my coworkers asked me why I did not have a pet, outside of Frank. Before I move forward, I must tell you about Frank the Fish. Frank was a beautiful betta fish that I got from one of our company's nearby stores earlier in 2007. Bettas are extremely beautiful fish as you know, and Frank's colors were amazing - he had deep reds and blues that sometimes seemed to blend into purple from the right angles. He was a cool dude. I used to always tap on his small fish bowl every morning and say, "What's up, Frank!" He would just swim over to me for a few seconds, and then drift back onto the middle of the bowl as if he was sophisticated and had better shit to do. One Friday morning, I came in and did my usual one tap on the bowl. I do not know if Frank was in a deep dream about a female fish or what, but apparently the tap startled the hell out of him because he swam back and forth faster than he ever had before. On his third trip across the bowl, he thumped right into the side of the bowl, and it was hard enough to where I could hear the actual collision. Frank appeared to be a bit sluggish the rest of the day and was not quite himself. A couple of my coworkers and I looked at him a few times throughout the day and we felt that he may have done some critical damage to himself. At the end of the workday, Frank was still sluggish so we were hoping that he would snap out of it. We were thinking that if he was not better by Monday, he might not be around much longer. Sure enough, on Monday morning when I arrived at my cubicle and looked at his bowl, he was floating motionless at the top of the bowl. Frank had perished. The lesson that you should get from this is not to tap on your fish bowl or tanks because you can really scare the hell out of your fish, which can cause them to possibly injure themselves.

Now, back to the question that was asked to me. I discussed with my coworker how I had always had dogs growing up, so at that moment I decided that I should get my own dog. I had worked at PetSmart for 2 years, so I am not sure what took me so long to come to this conclusion, but I was there now! So, later that day, which was December 31, 2007, I went on Craigslist and looked in the Pets section. The first link that I clicked on was an ad with a Chihuahua. Her coat was white and tan, and her face was that typical, funny little Chihuahua face. Her front left paw was turned slightly outward, and she was just so amusing to look at that I laughed out loud. I said to myself, "I have to go see this dog." I replied to the ad and the owner called me. She said that the dog was named Baby, and that she was really her son's dog but he went away to college, so they wanted to find a good home for her. The owner also told me that Baby broke her left paw when she was a puppy, and that is why it was turned outward in the manner that it was but she still has her full mobility, as I would see when she walks and plays. I told her that I had dogs all of my life and knew how to care for them, and that Lady would be in great hands with me. So, on New Year's Day 2008, I went down to Gilbert, Arizona and met my new dog. When I first saw Baby, she was so funny looking, and she would not come to me on her own so the owner had to pick her up and introduce her to me. She shied away from me as that was her personality - she obviously did not fool with people that she did not know. As we put her in my car, the owner gave me her kennel and a little blue blanket with some cartoon animals printed on it. She said, "This is Baby's blankie. She is super attached to it so wherever it goes, she goes." I said, "Cool. That's great to know. She'll always have that blanket then."

The owner bid farewell to Baby, and then the dog and I made our 35-minute trek back to Northwest Phoenix to my apartment. She seemed to be pretty chill throughout the drive home. When we arrived at my apartment, I parked in my space by the sidewalk that led to my building. Baby was in the front seat, and I was not thinking, so as soon as I opened my door, she jumped over me and out of the car, and darted off like gazelle running from a cheetah. I started yelling, "Baby, stop! Stop right now!" I did not realize how those words sounded so anyone that may have seen or heard this going on was probably laughing their ass off while I kept referring to my dog as "Baby."

For at least a good thirty minutes, I chased this dog around the area between the cars in the parking lot and the two apartment buildings that were nearby. It seemed almost as if she was playing with me because she would let me get somewhat near her, but never near enough to grab her because as soon as I lunged for her, she would take off for about 20 yards and then stop and look back at me. I was about to give up and said to myself, "The hell with this damn dog. If she runs off and I can't find her, at least I tried." It was at this point that I remembered her prior owner bringing up Baby's blue blanket and her attachment to it. So, I said to myself out loud, "It's worth a try." I took the blanket from the kennel and kneeled on the sidewalk in front of the car. Baby was about 20 feet away from me on the end of sidewalk that was closer to my apartment. I faced her, and I said, "Baby, look at what I have!" I held out the blanket as if she was to jump into it. Baby saw the blanket and ran right into it, and into my arms. That blanket was amazing, and Baby and I became great friends after that.

After a few days of having her, I got tired of calling her Baby so I wanted to come up with a new name for her. I felt it would be easier for her to catch on to something that sounded like her current name, so that is how she became "Lady." She was already housebroken for the most part, so I kennel trained her for a few weeks until she got used to my apartment. Then I let her roam free, and I walked her three times a day - in the morning before work, when I got off work, and most days at night before I went to bed. My brother, who I will talk about in the next chapter, used to laugh at her ears all the time. However, even though Lady liked him, she would still snap at him when he messed with her, and that is when he would always say, "Mann, that bitch is crazy!" Anyone that knew my brother can hear him saying that, and you will know more about him as you keep reading the book.

Lady was a hit in the apartment complex with her sexy self, as other Chihuahua owners that lived in the complex would always ask me about breeding her with their male Chihuahuas every time they saw me walking her. I would always say, "Lady is chillin'. She is too lazy to be a mother!" In case you did not know it, Chihuahuas are very popular dogs in Arizona, and it may have something to do with the state bordering Mexico, which is where the Chihuahua breed originated. You can even spot packs of stray Chihuahuas wandering the Phoenix streets from time to time. It was very weird to see but also cool at the same time because that is some shit you would never see in Atlanta. Anyway, I picked up Lady from her last owner on New Year's Day 2008, which was a Tuesday, so you know I was so amped to take her to work that Friday. I had been telling my coworkers about her all week, and when I finally brought her in on Friday morning, they loved her! I still have pictures from that day, and she looked a little overwhelmed but was still happy to have the attention.

Lady and I became very close. She did not really warm up to new people quickly, so when someone came around her that she had not been around before, which was basically everyone besides my brother and my coworkers, she would crouch down and put her ears back, and snap at anyone that tried to touch her. My parents came to visit us that May, and when my mom first came into my room, Lady was at the edge of the bed in her crouching pose. I said to myself, "This will be good because my momma doesn't play!" My mom said, "Hey Lady! I've heard a lot about you." As she came closer to the bed, Lady rose up and barked at my mom like crazy and went over towards her like she was about to throw them hands! My mom wound her hand back, and I was thinking, "Aww shit, Lady! You brought this on yourself!" My mom's hand came down and mushed the shit out of Lady, and Lady fell out of the bed. I laughed like hell! Lady then barked at my mom softly as she moseyed on over to her kennel that sat right outside of my bedroom door. Lady then became my mom's friend, and they never had any problems after that. As they say: "Spare the rod, spoil the child." In this case, apparently it applies to dogs, too. I guess I spared the rod sometimes, but Lady did not want those problems with my mom. I still spoiled the shit out of her though.

In July 2008, I made the difficult decision to relocate home to Atlanta as I discussed earlier in the book. Lady made this 29-hour drive with me, and she was a trooper, for real. She would look up at me with an annoyed face every time we hit a noticeable bump, so imagine comforting your dog periodically during a ride this long. When I make long drives, my ritual that I mentioned when I was courting Faithe is to drink energy drinks and eat beef jerky during the ride. I figured beef jerky would also be the perfect snack for a dog during a ride of this magnitude, but by the time we reached Louisiana, Lady was so tired of beef jerky that she turned her head away every time I tried to give her some from that point forward. I did not think it was possible for a dog to turn down beef jerky, but I have witnessed it with my own eyes.

When I moved back to Atlanta, I stayed with my parents for a few months before getting my own place in early 2009. I felt that Lady would have a better home with my parents and their miniature Schnauzer in their fenced-in backyard so I left her there, and I would come to see her a few times a week. When Faithe and I moved to the home in Mableton, Faithe wanted Lady to come and stay with us and provide a little security so I brought her on over, and she has been with us ever since. By that time, Lady had her routine down, so we could just let her outside to do her business, and she would come right back into the house. All of my close friends knew my dog, so when they would ask about Faithe and me, they usually always asked about Lady too.

Lady was one and a half years old when I first picked her up on New Year's Day 2008. I am proud to say that, as I am writing this book, Lady is still alive and doing well, and we celebrated her 12th birthday in October 2018. She has outlived some other dogs and people that I know, and she was in my life before Faithe and the child that I am going to write about in a later chapter so she definitely has a special place in my heart. If the Lord allows me to outlive this dog, I know that when she expires, I will have to take a day away from everyone and everything to reflect on Lady and the impact she has had on my life. I believe that loving her the way we do has kept her going, along with going up and down the stairs each day. Love is a powerful thing, and animals possess it too.

Now, as the reader, you may almost be at the point, or right at the point, where you are saying to yourself, "I know this joker didn't write an entire chapter on his dog." Well, yes - I did just that. Let me explain to you why. There are two main points that I want you to get from this chapter, and I will break down each one.

My dog and I have an amazing bond. She knows when I wake up each morning, and she will wait until Faithe leaves the house before trotting on down to our bedroom to get some attention from me since she does not have to share it with Faithe at that point lol. If Faithe and I have a disagreement, or one of us is going through a tough time, Lady can sense that, and she will come up to lay by us and offer comfort. I can walk Lady without a leash in our busy apartment complex because she will only go so far before she turns around and looks to see where I am. She plays with me and even cracks a little doggy smile when I am rubbing her belly. Lady loves riding in the car, and once she hops in, she will not get out until that car leaves the driveway, even if I just take her around the block and back. To us humans, running an errand is just running an errand, but to a dog with its head out of the window while the wind runs through its mouth and fur, it is like a cruise! Lady has a begging pose in which she lays halfway out of her bed when she wants some of what we are eating. When Lady does not get her way, her eyes actually tear up, and she will give you her mean look to show you that she would slap the shit out of you if she had hands and take your food. If Lady is in my lap and I am holding my phone as if I am looking at something on it, she will either lay right across the phone, or slap at it with her paw.

I say all of this to bring you to my first point:

Dogs are not humans, but they do have personalities and FEELINGS.

Therefore, please keep this in mind if you choose to have a pet, whether it is a dog or a cat. I included this point in the book because it is very dear to me. If you are considering getting a dog or already have one, and your plans for its long-term care involve leaving it outside chained up for most of the day, or you do not have the time to spend at least 10 minutes showing your dog some attention each day, you probably should refrain from having a dog. Not everyone is a pet person, so be honest with yourself because, while it is not a human life, it is still a life that you control. It is despicable when a person mistreats a dog. Imagine if you were that animal that has to endure such treatment.

The second, and more important, point that I want you to get from this chapter is the concept of LOYALTY. This applies to both animals and PEOPLE. If you are a dog owner that actually pays attention to your dog, you know how loyal your dog is to you. You know that your dog will die for you with no hesitation, and your dog will listen to you before it listens to anyone else (unless food is involved). You can discipline your dog for doing something that you do not approve of, and it may be mad at you for a short time, but after a little while, that dog will still be there wanting your attention because it is loyal to you. No matter what you have going on in your life with trials, tribulations and even people, your dog is the only thing that will ALWAYS be happy to see you when you walk through your door. I say all of this to emphasize the following point:

Just as a dog is loyal to its owner, be LOYAL to those people and things that are true to you.

This is something that we all have battled with but once we become consistent with being loyal, life genuinely gets easier. You may have temptations, and many people naturally do, but learning to be loyal to those people and things that care about you will make your relationships much smoother. This concept can be applied in so many areas of your life that it is ridiculous. For me, I spoke earlier in the book about the great job that I had at PetSmart in Phoenix, Arizona. I relocated back to Atlanta for personal reasons, but I believe that if I had stayed loyal to PetSmart and dedicated myself to the company long-term, I would likely be directing the department that I was a part of by this time in my life. This has been somewhat proven because one of the great people that I trained myself is now the manager of that same department. Since then, I have transitioned to a new job every three to four years or so, and each transition was made for different reasons but my salary has increased in turn with each position, so I have benefited from the changes. However, if I had stayed loyal to one or two of those companies and allowed more time for the company and I to adjust to our common goals, my salary would likely have increased the same amount or more over the same period through various promotions. I do not regret my professional decisions, and I learned a great deal from each one that I made, but I still cannot help but wonder "What if?" What would have happened if I stayed at this job or that job? Things are not like they used to be thirty or forty years ago when people often stayed with the same company for their entire working career, but consider this as you make professional decisions throughout your life. You still must be careful when it comes to your application of loyalty in professional and political situations. If we look at the President of the United States that is currently in office at the time this book is being composed, we can see that he has had many people who were loyal to him and his causes, and they benefited well from their loyalty during the time that they expressed it. However, when they decided to become "individuals" and be true to themselves by expressing beliefs that were different from the President's agenda, they were destroyed by the very person that they were so loyal to.

Loyalty comes into play with your family and friends as well. Sometimes friends have disagreements, and they may result in the two people not associating with each other for a short time, or a long time. I have been there myself, and I almost lost the friendship of the person that I now consider my best friend due to a disagreement that resulted from something that I said regarding his fiancé (now his wife). I did not realize how much I hurt him with my words, but I eventually heard it from other people. However, I did not practice loyalty in this situation and instead reacted with disappointment - and this resulted in me telling my other friends that were in contact with him that neither he nor his fiancé would be a part of the big event that this disagreement resulted from. When my friend heard what I had said, he reached out to me and asked if what I said about eliminating him from this big day was true. I said it was true because I had not heard anything from him, and Faithe had not heard anything from his fiancé.

We went on to talk about the situation, and it was in that conversation that I learned about how my words affected him, and I apologized. He did the same as he could have come to me earlier about how he was feeling instead of me having to hear it from our mutual friends. However, to this day, I regard myself as being completely at fault because of what I learned from that situation. My friend's reaching out to me facilitated our reconciliation, and we are great now. However, HE was the one that showed his loyalty by being the bigger person and knowing that our friendship was more important than what we were disagreeing about. I have absorbed this valuable lesson from that situation, and I now work hard to employ loyalty in all of my dealings with family and friends. I have also learned to be conscious of my words and how they can be interpreted because people do not always perceive the human language, or the world for that matter, in the same manner that you do. No one is exactly like you and you should always remember that. Also, remember that words can hurt people more than a physical blow.

Family and loyalty can be a touchy subject for many people because all families are different. I have not had many issues with loyalty when it comes to my family or my spouse, and that is a good thing. However, I have known people who have been stressed out due to their family not feeling a sense of loyalty from them when it comes to certain situations, or the situation was flipped and those people did not feel a sense of loyalty from their family. People must navigate these waters in the best way that they see fit, but one thing that I have seen some of these people do is cut the toxicity from their lives, and this allows them to function at a much higher level of happiness. In some cases, the toxicity is created by the family, and this is what they decided to cut off. In other situations, they discover that the toxicity is coming from the exact thing that their family is trying to protect them from, and once this is realized, the person can cut whomever or whatever this poison is from their life and continue to live on with grace. I will dive more deeply into the concept of toxicity in a later chapter because it was something that I had to deal with in recent years.

Loyalty among couples is also critical, but if the two people have a good understanding of each other, they can avoid disagreements about their loyalty to each other. I have learned from my marriage that, while I know my wife is completely devoted to me, she also has a certain degree of loyalty to her family. And the same is true for me. However, we also are aware that we have to make decisions as individuals and not let our decisions be made by our families. I also speak on this subject again in a later chapter as I discuss a very important decision that I take ownership for that was slightly influenced by my family. They did not tell me what to do in that situation, but I knew the decision that would make them happy, and I factored that into the ultimate decision that I made due to my loyalty to my family.

Loyalty comes in many forms and fashions. Applying this to your life in the correct manner can work wonders for you because you will always have people that will support you in return for your loyalty.

And I love L.A.D.Y. because that bitch is loyal.

INTERMISSION

S.E.G.W.A.Y.

Congratulations! You have made it to what I officially consider the halfway point of the book. I hope you have enjoyed reading about me and some of my experiences. I also hope that you have absorbed some lessons from those experiences that you can apply in areas of your life. I have made an effort to write a book that is different from anything that you have ever read. In doing that, I wanted to keep it fun and easy to read while also conveying some deep messages because I do not want you to ever reach a point of boredom on any page in this book, and I do not think that you will. I know that the previous chapter on my dog may have led you to think that you were going down Boring Street, but I hope the lessons on LOYALTY made it fully worthwhile.

You are now about to enter a different part of the book. This is an extremely deep part of the book that is filled with serious events, along with so many good lessons and advice that each reader can make use of in some part of their life. The next two chapters are based on two huge parts of my life, and I speak with complete truth in both of them because they affected my life in different ways. I want you to keep in mind that, while some names will be changed for obvious reasons, the persons that you will hear about are real people that exist. The people that know me personally will know that what I write about is real because they know "me," and the people that personally know the individuals that are characterized in this book will also know that what I write is real because they know "them." The upcoming chapters will overlap with the previous chapters as far as the time periods are concerned, and this was done in an effort to highlight each experience as they are better explained alone than in a chronological manner - you will understand this as you read further. While educating you on these experiences and how they have affected me, I also make an effort to paint a portrait of what I gained from each event and occurrence, and I hope that you can close the back cover of this book as you read the last sentence and be changed forever in some way. I hope you can also share my experiences and messages with others, and if you think that this book can help someone that you know get through a tough time in their own life or help them understand something that they may be going through more clearly, encourage them to read this book. If they cannot go buy it for some reason, *give them this book.*

Now, let me be clear - while I talk about some serious shit in the next chapters, some of which will make your jaw drop, this book is still going to be fun to read and you will enjoy it. Nothing will change as far as the entertainment value, but make sure you keep an eye on what you can gather from the content that you will read that will stick with you. You will still see "lol" sprinkled here and there, and I will still be cursing sometimes, but as you read further, you will definitely understand why I cuss, and you will likely be doing some cursing of your own as you keep reading. You will laugh aloud at some parts, and you may yell in anger or cry real tears at some other parts because I write about these events in an attempt to make you feel exactly what I felt at these moments. If you have been in situations similar to those that you will read about in the pages to follow, you will feel my words in your bones because you can truly relate to what I have gone through.

Well, go get your popcorn out of the microwave (do not go too heavy on the butter and Lawry's like I do - be better than me lol), kick back and enjoy the rest of the book.

II. LIFE TURNS

5

B.R.I.A.N.

I cannot clearly recall much of the period during which my mother was pregnant with my baby brother. However, I sure as hell remember the day he arrived. I remember sitting in the living room at our house on Dawn Court in Jennings, Missouri on February 29th, 1988, while my dad called every person that he knew and repeated, "Hello. Yep, he's here! 7 pounds, 3 ounces - with a head full of hair!" Then on to the next person, "What's up, man! Yep, he's here! 7 pounds, 3 ounces - with a head full of hair!" That continued for at least a couple of hours. Now that I am thinking about it, I was slick jealous about that boy's head full of hair because I was born with only a sprout of hair in the middle of my head and bald everywhere else, but that is neither here nor there. Anyway, what is important is that…

Brian Tramel Rounds had arrived!

And he was 7 pounds and 3 ounces, in case you did not catch that...

I remember Brian and my mom arriving at the house from the hospital a couple of days later. When I first saw him, I was intrigued because it finally hit me, and I was thinking to myself, "I actually have a brother. I'm now a big brother!" I was also intrigued because this negro was light-skinned with a bunch of hair while I was born with paper bag-brown skin and almost no hair at all. I remember looking at him and my baby pictures on the coffee tables and comparing the two lol.

I enjoyed easing into life as a big brother. I was seven years old at the time so I still did not have much of an idea about the significance of a new life coming into the world. Therefore, babies were like aliens to me, and I vividly remember spending a lot of time just looking at him because I was intrigued with such a little life that had the same blood flowing through its veins. Around the end of that year, when Brian was nearly one year old, my parents told me that we were moving to Georgia. Earlier in this book, I talked about how excited I was to make this move because it would be something new, and much of the excitement came from the fact that I had a new little brother to make the trip with us.

We moved to Atlanta and settled in the Whisperwood Apartments that are located in the suburb of Austell. It was in that bottom floor apartment that I was able to watch my brother take his first steps, and that was so exciting! I took credit for those first steps because I felt like I was the one in charge of getting him to that point - my one responsibility at that time in my life lol. As Brian grew, it was obvious that he was definitely going to be a character. When Brian started pre-school, he met his first female crush: Ms. Gatehouse, his Pre-K teacher lol. She was a tall, blond woman who was very pretty, and Brian never wanted to miss a day of school with her. She also prepared him for the testing that he would excel in and would allow him to start kindergarten at the age of four. As Brian moved into the early elementary grades, I would always hear my mom saying to my Dad and her friends, "Well, the teacher said that Brian is a talker but he does get his work done. Eventually!" Brian talked to everyone, and there was not a person that did not like him, even at that early age. My god brother Vic and my younger cousin Jazzy were around the same age as Brian so he had two good friends from an early age, and they often played together.

As Brian went into his elementary years, he was introduced to sports just as my parents did me. He played football for one year when he was six years old, but he did not quite gravitate that way. In his first and only football game that I remember, he was playing the center position. On the first play of the game, instead of snapping the ball to the quarterback, he picked up the football and took off straight up the field for 70 yards for a touchdown. What made this whole thing funny was that all of his teammates were celebrating in the endzone with him because they all believed that it was a legit touchdown lol. Brian was just that electric of a person even at that early age - if he was celebrating, you would find yourself celebrating with him with no questions asked, and this was a quality that he would always possess. Baseball was the next venture for him, and that did not quite work out either as he just had too much energy to confine him to a dugout and a particular spot on the baseball field.

Brian was then introduced to the basketball court, and that was where he found his home. Brian was pretty good at basketball and was always one of the better players on each of the teams he played for. He eventually moved into AAU basketball as he entered his teenage years. Now, before I go into that, I should mention that Brian and I were complete opposites when it came to our personalities. I was always a little quiet as a child and my personality was more laid back, while Brian was always talking, and was the one that got everybody excited about whatever he was talking about.

One thing about us that differed greatly was our self-confidence and sensitivity. When I played basketball as a child, my dad would often yell at me (out of love, of course) and tell me what I was doing or not doing right on the court. My sensitive ass would usually become teary-eyed, and I would pull my mom aside during timeouts and halftimes and say, "Momma, tell Dad to stop telling me what to do! I am trying!" Now, do not get it twisted - I was always good at the sport but I just got tired of him always finding something to get on me about. That is just what good fathers do and, in later years, I came to understand that just his presence alone at every little league game that I had was more than many other kids had as far as support. I can sincerely appreciate that now as a grown man. However, I say all of this to convey that I was an emotional and sensitive ass little boy at that stage in my life. Brian, on the other hand, used to let those yells and comments from my dad bounce right off him like, "Yeah, whatever. Watch this!" Then he would go down the court and do whatever he did, and most of the time he actually scored. I think my dad also learned a little from his prior experience with me because I do not think he yelled at Brian on the court quite as much as he stayed on me, and maybe this was also because he understood that Brian did not need it as much as I did. Do you see how that came full circle? The things you do not pick up on until you are older! This is why older people will always be wiser than younger people. Not smarter, but wiser - there is a difference. Brian had less sensitivity and always carried a high level of confidence while also being humble and extremely caring. This is an amazing combination for one person to possess, and this is what drew people to him.

In addition to sports, Brian also had a heavy interest in racecars and motorcycles. So much so that, when he was eight years old, my parents bought him a mini dirt bike. At this time, I was in the tenth grade, and we were living in a home in Austell that had a very steep driveway that extended about 30 yards out from the house. A small creek ran under the driveway at the halfway point between the carport and the part of the driveway where the sharp incline began. Even at a young age, Brian was always one to push the limits, which caused him to often take the route in most situations that would give him the most enjoyment and think about the pain later. One day, he decided to shoot down the driveway on his dirt bike at full speed. He was moving pretty fast, and as he made it halfway down the driveway, he realized that his brakes were not going to stop his bike before he reached the house. In an effort to avoid a painful crash into the brick home, he made a right turn when he was about ten feet from the house, looped around the front yard and went headfirst right into the creek, which was still painful. My mom frantically ran out to him and picked him up, and he said, "I'm alright! Let's get my bike so I can get back on it!" My mom said, "You're not getting back on that bike today." At that point, we thought that Brian avoided injury aside from some small scratches until my mom went to dust some dirt off his shoulder, and he yelled, "Ouch!" My parents took him to the emergency room, and it turned out that his collar bone was broken. It healed, and if you knew Brian, you know he was right back on that bike faster than a groupie on a professional athlete.

Brian continued to play basketball throughout his middle school years while also staying engulfed in his hobby of watching or reading anything that dealt with fast cars and motorcycles. He developed some good friends during these years and they followed each other into high school. Due to the school district lines, our god brother Vic ended up going to Douglas County High School in Douglasville while Brian attended Lithia Springs High School. However, they still saw each other often at basketball games, at the mall, and at parties. Brian first played on the freshman basketball team at his school, and in his sophomore year he went up to varsity. The varsity team made the state playoffs that year but was put out in the first round by Cairo High School, a small school in South Georgia and coincidentally the same school and town that my first ex-girlfriend that I spoke about briefly earlier in the book is from. My parents and I, as well as Brian and his teammates, were laughing at the Cairo players when they first ran onto the court because they looked so country and plain with their mini afros and snug uniforms. We were joking and saying that those boys looked like it was their first time leaving Cairo. However, we all learned that day not to judge a book by its cover because those boys mopped the floor with my brother's team on that cloudy evening in Macon, Georgia.

Brian simultaneously played AAU basketball for a team called the Etowah Stars that was ran by a former NBA player. In case you are not aware, AAU basketball is big all across the country, but it is especially popular in Georgia, and many great players have come out the state to go do big things at the college and professional level. Brian was not too serious about basketball but he just had a love for the game, and he was naturally good at it so he continued to play at both levels. When he was not playing basketball, he was either hanging out with his friends or watching something on television about souped-up cars or motorcycles. Oh, I cannot forget - he spent a lot of time on the phone with the girls as well lol.

As Brian ended his junior season at Lithia Springs, he was not happy with how the coach was playing him as far as playing time, and my parents were not happy about it either. Therefore, they transferred him to Chapel Hill High School in Douglasville for his senior season. Brian embraced the move because he wanted to play more, and he knew he would still see his friends since they started to drive cars around that age. The Douglasville and Lithia Springs areas are not that big, so all the schools were close to each other. Therefore, it really did not matter which high school you went to because all of the teenagers generally congregated at the same places when they were not in school. We found out that the grass was not as green on the other side as we thought because it was expected that Brian would receive more playing time at Chapel Hill. However, it turned out to be a situation where the head coach believed that his son should be on the court more than some other players on the team that were obviously more talented than he was, and this interfered with the desire that those other guys had for the team, including Brian. This caused Brian to slowly back away from basketball as that season progressed, and since he was at the age where he wanted to make money so he could put it towards the purchase of a car, his attention shifted away from organized basketball. That senior year marked the end of his basketball career.

Brian graduated with his high school diploma at the end of the school year in May 2005. That was a great day in our lives, and I enjoyed watching him celebrate with his friends that graduated with him. Vic was a year older than Brian, but due to my mom starting him (and me as well) in school when he was four years old instead of at the traditional age of five, they both graduated that year. At this point, Brian was more focused on cars, motorcycles and girls, and less on continuing his education. However, my parents are sticklers for education so he had to go somewhere. He had applied to Georgia Southern University down in Statesboro, Georgia back in the fall of his senior year. He was accepted, and this is where he would end up going in the Fall of 2005.

Brian went down to GSU and had fun while he was there. He went to class, but it became obvious that college really was not his thing, so he spent a lot of time playing PlayStation with his friends in the dorms and going to parties. Vic ended up going to Savannah State University so Brian would go down and hang out with him sometimes, and vice versa. The schools were only an hour from each other so it was a quick drive between them. I went down to visit Brian one weekend and there was a pajama party going on. I went with him to the party, and he was having fun introducing me to his friends. However, being seven years older than him, I felt a little like a college boy at a middle school pep rally so I just kicked back and sipped my adult beverage while Brian worked the room. I noticed that, no matter who Brian was talking to, he always stayed within a distance where he could see me. I really appreciated that because Brian always showed me, as well as other people, that he cared about what his big brother was up to and how he was feeling.

Brian attended GSU for a year before returning home, as he just was not interested in going the college route. We knew that his passion was motorcycles, so my parents worked with him to find a job that would allow him to earn money and transition him into the field of mechanics. At first, Brian claimed that he could not find a job. He was a little spoiled but my parents were not having that. They had some work done to one of their vehicles by a collision body shop owner named Dexter. He was a cool guy, and he mentioned to my parents that he could use some help around the shop, so this seemed like a good way for Brian to start learning more about cars and work his way from the exterior of vehicles to gaining knowledge about the mechanics under the hood. My mom told them that Brian would come and do whatever they needed to be done because he was about to be homeless lol. Dexter laughed, and he told them that Brian could start the next day. Brian was excited about the opportunity and he went to work with Dexter. He was able to gain some good experience in preparing cars for painting while also learning about the body components of many types of vehicles. They loved Brian at the shop because of his funny and wild personality, and he would clown with them all day while he worked. They even let Brian paint his own car - the 2000 Nissan Maxima that our family still owns and drives occasionally today. While Brian loved cars and basically anything with a motor, he could not shake his love for motorcycles.

Brian graduated from high school right before the summer of 2005, and I had left to take my new job with PetSmart in Phoenix in early 2006. I had visited home a couple of times after settling in Phoenix during that year, and Brian was always excited to see me when I arrived. I would usually go with him to one of the 21 and under clubs where he and his friends would hang out. When he introduced me to his friends that I did not already know, he would always use the phrase that became his trademark for me, "What's up, y'all. This is my brother, Mann. He lives in Phoenix and he works in real estate. He got money!" Or, if he was introducing me to female friends, it was, "What's up, y'all. This is my brother, Mann. He lives in Phoenix and he works in real estate. He got money and his own place out there! Better tell your sister about him because these women are on him!" That was my brother - always looking out for me.

During my visits, we would chat about his plans to buy his own motorcycle one day and the different avenues that he wanted to explore in that industry, such as starting his own bike club and owning his own motorcycle customization shop. I loved that Brian dreamed big, and he never had any doubts, but I will admit that, at times, I honestly wondered how he would reach those dreams. Brian had introduced me to some of his girlfriends that he had during his time at GSU, and they were all very smart, focused, beautiful young women. And academically, quite the opposite of Brian, ha! However, I looked back on that years later and understood that sometimes women are drawn to the guys that they would have the most fun with, despite whatever else the guy had going on. Brian understood that earlier than I did, hence the women he was able to date. My parents and I joked later that Brian always came across the women that were going to be lawyers and doctors (some of whom have actually gone into those same professions), and he would end up marrying a rich woman who would buy him a motorcycle and everything else he wanted, while I always came across the attractive, but broke, dysfunctional women during my high school and early college days before I entered my first real relationship towards the end of college lol. I did meet some good women over my lifetime so it was all in fun.

In early 2007, while I was in Phoenix, Brian called me up one day. We were chatting, and I was asking him how things were going down in Atlanta. He said that they were going good. Then he said to me, "Mann, you know I'm all about motorcycles. I want to come out to Phoenix to attend MMI because that will help me launch my career in motorcycle mechanics." MMI sounded like a school, and Brian was not dumb by any means, but he did not quite have the best reputation when it comes to higher institutions of learning due to him being "Brian." Therefore, my next two questions to him were "What is MMI?" And after he answered that, "Things didn't work out for you at Georgia Southern. What makes you think it would be different here in Phoenix?" He replied, "Mann, you know motorcycles are my heart, and that's what I love to be around. If I get the chance to do what I really love and what I'm interested in, I know without a doubt I'll make it work. Just trust me." At this point, I had been in Phoenix for a year, and I was honestly considering making the move back to Atlanta because, while Phoenix was a beautiful place, I was just feeling like the South is where I needed to be. However, at that moment, I thought about my brother and his dedication to me, and I knew without a doubt that if the roles were reversed, he would stay in Phoenix and let me come pursue my dream with no further questions asked. So, I said "Yeah, bro. Let's do this. Tell me more about this school and I'll help you with your application."

As I did my research and Brian worked on some things on his end, I found out that the Motorcycle Mechanics Institute (MMI) is regarded as the top school in the country for those who wish to pursue careers in motorcycle mechanics. Therefore, if Brian came out to Phoenix and handled business, he would be qualified to work on motorcycles in some great facilities anywhere in the country. Brian applied and was accepted to MMI, and my parents brought him out there in February 2007. In preparation for his arrival, the property management team for my apartment complex worked with me and allowed me to switch from my one-bedroom unit to a two-bedroom unit a couple of weeks before Brian arrived. They did not seem to care much about me switching units as long as I was ready to pay the difference in rent. I liked the setup of the two-bedroom unit because I had one side of the apartment to myself with my own bathroom in my room, and he had the same setup on the other side of the apartment, with our living room being in the middle of our domain and serving as our common area.

The apartments were set up in a "motel style" - at least that is what I call it - where there were four apartments in each building, and the front doors for each unit were all on one side of the building. Each building had two apartments upstairs and two downstairs. Our apartment was upstairs on the left side if you were facing the front of our building. The bedroom on the right side of the apartment had its window right by the porch that led to our front door, while the left bedroom had a window that could not be accessed without a ladder because the porch stopped at the front door. Since I was paying the rent and bills, I put Brian in the room with the window by the porch because I did not want to be that accessible to people who may come on the porch. I loved my brother, but he was living virtually rent-free so he could take on the risks lol.

Brian started school at MMI in February and he was enjoying it. I could see that he was entering a different phase in his life because, while he still took time to enjoy himself, he appeared to have a focus that I had never seen him possess before. While he was staying at home in Atlanta, either my mom or I was waking him up almost every day reminding him not to miss something that he was supposed to be doing, whether it was work or another kind of appointment. Aside from two or three days where he may have stayed out late or had a little too much to drink, I really did not have to wake Brian up for school in Phoenix, or really get on him about anything. Brian's expenses were not high. Actually, they were nearly non-existent due to his living rent-free with me, and my parents sending him money here and there. This allowed Brian to focus solely on school. He would come home and tell me about some of the things that he was learning, and he knew that I had no clue about any of the technical stuff, so he was good at not really going into the minute details while still explaining which part of the motorcycle he was currently learning about.

At least every other week, Brian would also come home and tell me about a different student that passed away in a motorcycle accident, and it was at that time that I became aware of how dangerous motorcycles could really be. It was also during this time that a neighbor and good friend of my parents in Atlanta named Darrell, who had spent a considerable amount of time with my brother, passed away on his motorcycle after running into a car that pulled out right in front of him on a busy street in Douglasville, Georgia. When I asked Brian how he felt about Darrell passing away on his motorcycle, he said that he was sad about it but he still loves motorcycles, and then he said one of the things that I would never forget: "I love bikes, but if that's the way that I go, that's just the way that I go." At that moment, I learned something about human beings: *if there is something that a person loves about as much as life itself, and they are extremely passionate about it, you cannot keep them from it.* Moreover, if you attempt to keep them from it, *they will never be truly happy until they can have it.* This applies to many types of people and passions, so remember that. One other thing that Brian said shortly after that is, "Once a rider stops respecting his bike, he needs to get off of it." If you are not a rider, you may not understand that. If you are a rider, you know exactly what he meant.

Brian was good about saving his extreme fun for the weekends, so he would hang out with guys that he met at MMI. He made some good friends such as Marc, Avery, and Cam - these were the names that I heard the most and the only friends that I actually met. He also had another friend named Ivan that he was cool with, and this friend caused what I consider to be the only real issues that my brother and I had out there in Phoenix. As I have mentioned previously, Brian has a big heart. He came home from school one day and walked into the apartment with a friend who had on the same school uniform as he did. Brian said, "Mann, this is my friend Ivan. He moved from out of town to come to MMI just like I did." I said, "Oh ok, cool. Nice to meet you, Ivan." When Ivan left, Brian told me, "Ivan is out here staying with another guy from the school. He doesn't really have his own place and he thinks the guy he's staying with now may ask him to leave soon. Do you think he can stay with us for maybe a week or two while he finds another place?" I was not too keen on having people reside with me that I did not know well, so I was about to say "No," but since I believed that Brian saw something in this guy, I agreed to let him stay as long as he contributes something to the apartment, whether it was food for the kitchen or cash for the utilities.

Ivan did not have many belongings so he slept on the couch. After about a week and a half, I could see why Ivan could not stay in someone else's residence for too long. During this time, Brian and Ivan would go to school, and then come back to the apartment. They would play the PlayStation, eat and go to sleep. This was cool since they were young dudes. However, I did not see any movement on Ivan's part as far as him seeking his own place to live. There were a few days when he would be there laying on MY couch watching TV, and eating up MY food while Brian was out looking for a part-time gig just to make a little cash. Now, Ivan was of Latino descent so he had long, wavy hair that he kept in a ponytail, and he was a good-looking dude so I am sure the women noticed that. I think these features also allowed him to garner a little sympathy for his financial situation, or lack thereof, and persuaded people to lend him aid. He was very mannerable, but anyone that knows me knows that I do not like to be taken advantage of.

I asked Brian after Ivan's first week with us when I would receive something from him on the bills or food, and Brian said that Ivan would give us something soon because someone from his hometown was sending him some money, but in the meantime, Brian was willing to cover Ivan's portion. I told Brian, "No. That is Ivan's responsibility, and he needs to tell me what he has arranged instead of it coming from you." However, during this period, Ivan never offered anything. A few days later, I asked Ivan when he would drop something on the bills. He said he would have something for me soon, but he really gave no explanation on his status, or what he was working on as far as securing his own residence, or his next residence. I did not want to be rude with him because I know that he did not have a true support system as Brian did, so I just said "Ok" and went on about my business. I asked Brian to come to my room that evening while Ivan was out at the store, which was a place that he could still somehow manage to go, and that was part of my problem with him. I told Brian that I had been observing Ivan and his habits, and from what I was seeing with him going to the store and other places that required money, I felt that Ivan had enough money to contribute something to us but I believe that he is taking advantage of the situation because he knows you two have a good friendship, and that you have a good heart. I then told him that I am like Mom and Dad – I am not with someone staying around here who I feel is intentionally not giving us anything, and I feel he will do it as long as he can. I told Brian that Ivan needs to give something on the bills and explain what his plan is within the next few days or he will have to find somewhere else to stay immediately. After this, Ivan still stayed with us for about another week and a half but he was not around the apartment as much. He eventually left our residence but I do not recall where he went.

Ivan seemed to be a good dude but I brought up this story for a couple of reasons. First, if Brian believed in you, he would give you the shirt off his back, no matter how long he knew you. He demonstrated this with Ivan. My other reason for talking about this story is to illustrate that while someone may seem like they are taking advantage of you in a financial or inconveniencing situation, take a moment to step back and try to find out what is going on with that person that is causing them to be in the situation that they are in. I speak about this topic again later in the book, but I never really sat with Ivan and attempted to find out how things were back where he was from, and how his experience had been since he moved to Phoenix. I never asked him about how he felt being in a new city alone, and the hardships that come along with that. People deal with a lot of emotions and things that you may not be aware of, and often we only see the results of how they deal with things, but not necessarily the root cause of it. Keep this in mind if you encounter similar situations throughout your life, and also remind others of this if they find themselves trying to figure out why someone in their lives act the way that they do.

Now, Brian and I had some fun times together while out in Phoenix. One of our funnier moments happened when Brian, a good friend of mine named J.V. that I met from PetSmart (who was also originally from Georgia), and myself decided to drive to Las Vegas for the 2007 NBA All-Star weekend. I was driving my car, with J.V. riding shotgun and Brian in the back seat. As we were leaving the Phoenix city limits, we stopped by a gas station. J.V. got some Bud Light to sip on. Brian's crazy ass went straight for the tall can of Steel Reserve 211. If you do not know what that is, go online and look it up, or ask somebody. Keep in mind that it was around 10:00 a.m., so I said to Brian, "Dude, I don't remember seeing you eat anything this morning. You sure you wanna do that 211?" Now, if you know about 211, you are probably saying to yourself, "Aww shit! This dude may not wanna do that on an empty stomach." And, of course, Brian responded, "Man yeah, this ain't gonna do nothing. I'm gonna be ready for another one before we get to Vegas."

We had driven a little ways and were cutting up, talking about how many women would be in Vegas and how we would have so much fun. After about a couple of hours, we had just crossed the Hoover Dam and I noticed that Brian had gotten a little quiet. I said, "Bro, what are you up to back there?" J.V. and I glanced in the back seat, and Brian was holding his stomach. He said, "Man, this shit is tearing my stomach up. Ugh!" He was back there in pain! J.V. and I were laughing while telling Brian that we tried to warn him. I felt bad for him because he was almost in labor pains until we reached the hotel in Vegas lol. When we got there,

I said, "Dude, lay down and get some rest while we go to Wal-Mart and get a cooler to load up with beer for the weekend. I'll bring you back some Tums and something to eat because that's probably all you need." We went to Wal-Mart, and then stopped and got some food on the way back to the hotel. When J.V. and I walked back into the room, Brian was up and looked as fresh as some Krispy Kreme donuts coming off the line. We were like, "Dude, you bounced back quick!" He said, "Yeah, I just went and took a dump. I'm good now. Gotta get out here and get on these girls. What's the plan for the evening?" That's one thing about Brian - no matter what's going on with him, he's always going to find a way to not miss the party, even if he is in there sick lol.

We went on to enjoy Vegas, but it was not as much fun as we thought it would be because it was entirely too crowded to do anything, and any club that was a club on or near the strip was charging at least $150 per person for admission. You know that three guys staying in a motel off the strip with a cooler full of beer in the car that they were walking back and forth to the whole weekend to avoid having to buy drinks were not doing any of that shit. Hell, all of our food and beer for the whole weekend did not even come to $150 so it was a cheap trip for us. The best thing to me was seeing how tall many of the NBA players were in real life.

It was cool to see my brother grow during his time in Phoenix. He would hang out with friends that he met out there, and of course, the girls would come into play eventually. Brian was able to see, as I did when I arrived in Phoenix, that the color lines are a little more blurred out on the West Coast than the dating segregation that we experienced in Atlanta, where ethnicities tended to date within their own races for the most part. Therefore, it was nothing for a Latino, Caucasian or Asian female to approach you and talk to you just like a woman of your own race. That amazed Brian at first but he quickly got used to it lol. Sometimes Brian's friends from MMI would let him borrow their bikes, so he would ride around the area wearing a helmet that had a blue mohawk attached to it because that was a trend that started around that time. He would always say that it was so easy to meet girls out there because they would just walk up to the bike and ask him to take them for a ride, and once they saw that gold pop-out grill that he had in his mouth, it was a wrap. Yes, they love hood boys out on the West Coast too. Brian did have one female friend named Renee that he spent a considerable amount of time with, and she was the closest thing to a girlfriend that he had during his time in Phoenix. She was a pretty girl with a light complexion (because Brian liked them light-skinned thangs), and relatively soft-spoken compared to his talking ass. Whenever I was at the apartment with them, he would always crack jokes to make her blush in light embarrassment. He cared a lot about Renee, and they had fun together.

During our time in Phoenix, I was also able to see my brother's admiration, respect, and dedication to me. One experience that will always stick in my mind and heart that showed my brother's love for me occurred one Saturday night. It was a clear, beautiful night in Phoenix, as most nights were, and I was about to go out and hit the streets in Scottsdale to see what I could stumble into. Brian came into the apartment while I was mixing up some E&J V.S.O.P. and Coke so that I could pre-game before and during the drive to Scottsdale. He was holding a Nike bag and he said, "Mann, I copped some new kicks today." I said, "For real? Let me check them out." He took them out of the box and they were a pair of brand new, snow white high-top Air Force Ones. I said, "Damn, bro. Those are hard as hell! The chicks are gonna be all on those." He replied, "Thanks man. You know how I do. You like 'em?" I said, "Hell yeah. Those are clean." He saw that I was about to ride out for the night, so he said, "Go ahead and wear them tonight." My feet were a shoe size bigger than his so he knew that I could fit into most of his shoes, but I did not have any intentions on ever asking him to wear those shoes, especially a pair of brand new, white tennis shoes, so I said, "Naw bro, I can't do that. You just bought those shoes and you haven't even worn them yet." He then replied, and I will never forget him for this: "Mann, I'm out here in Phoenix living life and it is all because of you, my big brother. I'm seeing things and places that I would have never seen if you didn't make it possible for me to be here. Go ahead and wear them. Let me know how they feel. Have fun tonight, bro." And then he just walked into his room. I stood there shocked because he did this with no hesitation or selfishness at all, and it seemed like it was almost nothing to him. What makes this memory so powerful to me was that Brian could have been going out with some of his friends that night, and he may have even had an outfit that he got that week to match those Air Force Ones. However, he asked ME if I wanted to wear them first.

Now, I have to be completely honest - I would have hesitated a little to let Brian wear him some shoes that I had not even worn yet, and this is not because I did not love my brother, but because I had myself in mind first, and I know that many other people in the world would have felt like me. However, when he saw that he could provide something that brought me joy, he never hesitated to do it. He did what made me happy without a second thought. What is even more powerful is that if you are reading this book and you spent time around Brian, you probably have a similar story of his generosity towards you or other people. While I am a man of integrity, I still struggle with stubbornness at times. Therefore, I try to live my life with a generosity similar to what Brian displayed every single day. You should also keep this concept in mind because I believe that you will be eventually rewarded for what you give.

Oh yeah, after Brian told me I could wear the shoes and walked into his room, he did pop his head back out of the room and say, "Don't worry about scuffing them Forces. I got some white polish so I'll get 'em back right and still go out and catch something with 'em." That was Brian. And he did catch a chick with them shoes that next week.

2007 was a very important year in Brian's life, as well as mine. We bonded during this year and I do not think could have happened in any other situation. We did not have any family or childhood friends around while we were out in Phoenix - it was just him and me. We were all each other had in city that was 1,845 miles from everything we grew up around. We would take drives through the city on Saturday afternoons with the sunroof open in his car or mine and look at the desert sights. We were able to experience this together, and that is something that I will always cherish. We drove to Sedona (the place you see on postcards with all of the red rocks and canyons) a couple of times and talked about our dreams on the way up there and back. He would talk about his desire to riding through the desert and see the entire state of Arizona from end to end, and I would talk about just loving the freedom of the desert and my dream to own a home on a small desert mountain, like the one in Waiting to Exhale where Angela Bassett burned her husband's car.

On a serious note, the cool thing that makes me tear up as I write this paragraph is that I have the satisfaction of knowing that my brother did get to realize his dream. His friend Marc allowed Brian to use one of his motorcycles, and this is how Brian was able to learn how to ride a motorcycle at a very high level. This generosity of his friend allowed Brian to ride with other guys on trips where they would travel through the desert to the northern border of Arizona, and also ride down to the southern border of the state. I can cry tears of joy as I type this knowing that my brother was able to achieve his dream of seeing the entire state of Arizona from the highway, and I can tell that it changed him because he would then start talking about how he wished that everyone that we knew back home could experience what he had seen. My brother truly did more living in that year of his life than many people do in their entire lives. I get goosebumps every time that I think about Brian's experience because I had a front row seat to watch my brother live his life to the fullest.

I was able to see my brother be completely free and happy.

Most importantly, I was able to watch Brian grow into a MAN.

Earlier, I spoke about wondering if Brian would come out to Phoenix and do what he needed to do to succeed at MMI. Initially, I did not believe that he would succeed, but I still wanted him to come and get the experience of living on the West Coast and seeing the desert that had changed me. Well, truth be told, Brian worked his ass off that year and focused on school like never before. When he came home one day in March of 2008 and told me that it was official - he would be graduating as a certified Suzuki mechanic, I was so proud of my brother! He proved me wrong. My brother had grown up, and while he was still the same old Brian, he was also a new "Brian." This Brian knew that in order to achieve his dreams, he would have to work towards them because he had to earn them. And he did just that.

My parents were very proud of Brian - so proud that after holding out during an entire year of him attempting to persuade them, they bought him a 2006 Suzuki GSX-R1000 that month. Brian had a couple of his friends drive him to a point in Texas where my parents met them with the motorcycle strapped to my dad's pickup truck. They transferred the bike to the truck that Brian and his friends rode down in, and then my parents drove back to Atlanta while Brian and his crew headed back to Phoenix. My parents told Brian to wait until he got to Phoenix before he rode the motorcycle in case anything needed to be adjusted on it before he pushed it to the limit as they knew he would. Brian was already tired from waking up early that morning and he had a long day, but once they made it to Tucson, Brian had his friends help him take the motorcycle off the truck. This tired ass dude rode that bike from Tucson all the way back to our apartment in Phoenix, which is a one-hour ride.

This occurred in the evening, and it was on a Saturday night, so of course I was out at somebody's club or lounge hanging as usual when he made it back home. I did not get into anything while out that night, so I came back to the apartment around 1:00 a.m. As I opened the front door, I saw the funniest thing that I ever laid my eyes upon. Brian was laid out on his stomach on the carpet a few steps from the door. This dude was knocked out while still fully dressed in his motorcycle jacket, pants and shoes. He even still had his gloves on. Brian was so tired that he did not even make it past the couches in the living room, ha! He just had to ride that motorcycle that same day he got it. What made this moment even funnier was that my dog Lady was sitting a few feet away on the couch looking down at him, and then she looked back at me like, "This nigga here...." I started to nudge him and say, "Brian, get up and get to your bed so you can be comfortable." Then I saw how peaceful he looked on that floor. So, I just stepped right over him and grabbed Lady, and we went to my room. I woke up the next morning and went into the kitchen to see what I could fix for breakfast. Brian was still on that floor lol. He did eventually wake up that morning, and he spent an hour rambling on about his ride back from Tucson, and how much he was loving that bike.

Brian spent the next couple of months worshipping that GSX-R1000. He showed it off to his friends at school. His friend Marc had a customized Yamaha R6 Raven so they would swap bikes sometimes just to ride something different. His motorcycle was already a beast, but he would take it to MMI and do stuff to it to make it even faster, such as dyno fuel mapping. He did other stuff to the bike but I am not really a motorcycle person so I do not know the lingo. He was in love with his motorcycle, and I pretty much never saw him until night time after he got that bike because after he left the school, he was riding with friends or gone somewhere.

Brian's friend Marc told me one particular story about Brian that will always be in his mind. When Brian finally got his own motorcycle, he and Marc would roll out around town and parking lot pimp, trying to come up on some females to hang out with. One Saturday morning, they decided to get some gas and then go post up at the Metro Mall by Castles and Coasters, which was close to where we lived. They were young guys so they were just looking for fun, and they noticed a group of cute girls that were sitting on the curb by the mall, pointing at them and smiling. Marc and Brian liked the attention, so they decided to show out by revving the engines on their bikes up so they were really loud, sounding like fire-breathing beasts. They then took off hard and left the lot. Marc said they felt so cool at that moment! When they finally got to their destination and got off their bikes, Marc looked at Brian's motorcycle. There was a large, heavy-duty trash bag stuck in his bike's swingarm, and it was waving like a flag. He said they both started laughing their asses off, and they cracked up for at least a good 15 minutes. That bag is the reason the girls were pointing at them, not because they looked cool lol. I love hearing this story because that was Brian all the way, and his other friends from Phoenix have endless stories about Brian and his bike.

Brian's time to graduate came in May 2008, and my parents made the trip to Phoenix to see it because they had anticipated this day for a long time. MMI has training programs designed specifically for different motorcycle manufacturers. For example, a person can become certified as a Harley-Davidson motorcycle mechanic, a BMW motorcycle mechanic, or become certified any of the other popular motorcycle manufacturers that they offer programs for. Students also have the option to become certified in more than one manufacturer if they wish. Brian had always been a Suzuki guy ever since he became very serious about motorcycles, so on this day he proudly graduated as a Certified Suzuki Mechanic at the top of his class. That was a proud day for us all. My brother actually set his mind to something and finished it.

And he did not have to marry a rich chick to do it.

While Brian thoroughly enjoyed his time in Phoenix, he was ready to get back to the South with his friends and his motorcycle, so my parents loaded up his bike and his belongings that they were able to fit onto the truck, and they drove out the same day he graduated. As they were about to leave, Brian gripped me and hugged me, and he said, "Thank you for everything, bro. See ya when you come home to the A. Love you, Mann." Then he hopped into the truck, they drove off and that was the last time Brian saw and breathed the dry Phoenix air.

As you already know, I followed suit and relocated back to Atlanta a couple of months later. I was already homesick after nearly two and a half years in Phoenix, and with Brian leaving and taking that little bit of "ATL" with him that kept me going each day, I was ready to go home. Therefore, I sold all of my furniture and my big screen television, packed up Lady and hit the road for the long journey back to Atlanta. Brian had time to get settled back in Atlanta so he was glad to see me, and since I did not have a job when I first got back, he spent a few days catching me up on what was going on with his friends and the Douglas County area. He also told me about how he had ventured downtown a few times to check out the Atlanta motorcycle scene and how it moved versus the Arizona bike culture. One of his observations that I found interesting, and let me clarify that this was HIS observation so I do not want you to take this personal if you are a motorcycle rider, is that bikers in Atlanta ride more for show and attention, and are not as skilled in riding as bikers on the West Coast. The riders out West seemed to take better care of their bikes when it came to the vital components, while it seemed like the Atlanta riders were more focused on the exterior parts of the bike that people will see. He also learned how to do wheelies while he was out in Phoenix, so he would do them in Atlanta, and he made videos of himself doing wheelies for nearly half a mile on I-20 East in front of Six Flags. He said that if he was going to ride in Atlanta, he would rather start his own bike club instead of joining another one because he was just so used to the West Coast riding culture that he felt he would not quite fit with an Atlanta club.

When Brian was not riding his bike around the city, he was either hanging out at home with my parents or going to parties and clubs with Vic, his friends Mycal and Roland when he was in town, and other people that he knew. He also hung out with Ieesha and Kelvin, the son and daughter of my parents' next-door neighbors. They were close friends of the family, and Brian was very close to them. He also spent time with our cousin Tiffany, who came to Atlanta to attend school at Clark Atlanta University. She and Brian were around the same age so he would go down to the Atlanta University Center to hang with her and meet new people, and he would bring his friends down there to mingle as well. They all had good times together.

Brian seemed to know someone at just about every place that he went so he did not come across many strangers. He would often be the life of the party, and he would always find a way to get some attention on himself and his fellas. Brian was always going to stunt whether he had it or not, and Vic and Mycal have talked about how Brian would buy a bottle at the club with all of his money (he was not 21 at that time but they were), and then turn around and ask them for money to put gas in his car so they could get home. One time, he told them when they pulled to the gas pump after leaving the club one night, "I don't have enough gas for us to get home, so if y'all don't wanna give me any money, we ain't going home. We're gonna be sleeping here at the pump!" That was Brian for you. And he always got that gas money from them. When Brian was at home, he was just being Brian - eating sunflower seeds, drinking green tea and tripping out with family and friends when they visited the house. I think he got his love of sunflower seeds from me, but I do not know where he got that green tea addiction. I think that is why my mom still keeps a fridge full of it now.

My cousin Geneva would come over to our house with her daughters LaNia and LaZandrea to hang out, and sometimes my mom's friend Shirlene would come over with her daughter Kala to visit. My sister would also bring her two daughters over along with my nephew. As soon as those kids got to the house, they went straight for Brian. Brian was like a kid magnet - children were magically drawn to him, and we have never really seen a person that kids liked as much as Brian. This was mostly because he liked entertaining kids just as much as they liked playing with him. My mom would joke and say that when the kids came by the house, I would walk by and pat them on the head, and say, "Hey," and keep walking lol. Then Brian would come along, lightly hit them on the shoulder, and take off running, and they would light up and yell, "Brian!" and take off chasing after him. Those last two sentences pretty much sum up our personality differences. Brian and my dad would also spend some evenings in the garage working on his bike, doing things such as changing the tires or adding components to it. Brian was the expert now so he liked showing my dad what to do, but my dad had been a motorcycle rider for years so he knew some things as well. It was a good relationship, and they both were able to spend some great quality time together on these nights that I know neither would forget.

One Wednesday in mid-December, my parents and I were at the bowling alley doing what we do on league night. Our team consisted of my parents' friend Jimmy, my mom, my dad and me. We were halfway through our second of three games, and I happen to be looking towards the front door of the alley when I saw Brian walk into the building. This is significant because Brian had never come to the bowling alley to watch us bowl. He simply was never interested in bowling. I said, "Bro, you've never been up here. You came to watch us?" He said, "Yeah, I came to watch for a little bit. And get some money from mom or dad. You know how I do." We laughed a little and I said, "Yeah, I do. Well, Dad is having a good night on the lanes so you may wanna try him first." He said, "Say no more." He then walked towards my dad. I am not sure which of my parents he got money from that night but he watched us bowl a game, and then he went home to get ready to go out.

On Wednesday nights, Brian and his friends would often go to a club that was then called Savoy, located on Campbellton Road near Greenbriar Mall in East Point. The club was promoted by Kelvin, the oldest son of my parents' neighbors that I mentioned earlier. I went with Brian once after returning to Atlanta, and I was impressed by the nice

18-and-up crowd that Kelvin was able to muster up on Wednesday nights. I cut my own hair most of the time when I lived in Phoenix because I did not really know where to find a good barber when I was out there, so I became decent with my trimmer skills, and I would line up Brian's hair and mustache in between barber shop visits because he would only go get his hair cut about every three or four weeks. When I got home from the bowling alley on this particular Wednesday night, Brian was already dressed for his night out. He said, "Mann, I need that good ole' line up before I ride out." I said, "I gotcha, bro." We went into the bathroom, I grabbed my clippers from under the sink, and he sat on the toilet while I lined him up. He asked me how we did at the bowling alley, and I told him that we took all three games so we had a good night. I asked him if they were riding out to Savoy, and he replied, "Yeah. Gonna see what we can come up on tonight." When I finished, he put on his trademark white wave cap, tied it tight and rolled up the back of it because that is how he wore it. He said, "Thanks, bro." I followed him back to the living room and I watched him skip down the stairs and out of sight.

I had started my Lease Administrator job at Aaron Rents in October of that year, so on that next day, December 18th, I had arrived home from work. I did my usual routine of ironing my clothes for the next day, and then chatting with my mom in the kitchen. I had been dating a woman named Trease for a few months, and she arrived at the house around 6:00 p.m. My mom had cooked so we ate some dinner, and then my mom and dad went down to rearrange some things in the garage while Trease and I watched TV in my bedroom.

Around 8:30 p.m., I heard some loud thumping coming up the stairs. I heard my mom and dad yelling my name,

"Mann! Mann!"

As soon as I heard the tone of their voices, I immediately knew that something was not right. My dad opened the door and said,

"Mann! One of Brian's friends said he was killed in a motorcycle accident!"

My dad was in a state of shock, so I knew he did not know what to do, and my mom was standing there with the same serious look. She was in shock as well, and I do not think that it had quite hit them yet because this is something unlike anything they had ever been told. I think that I had to get validation before it would hit us all. Therefore, I jumped up and ran down the stairs with the quickness of a cheetah, and out through the open garage doors. Brian had been riding with a friend named Wendell, a fellow rider that he met when he first got back to Atlanta. As I ran outside, I saw Wendell standing at the end of the driveway while another guy was sitting on a motorcycle about 10 feet away on the street.

I ran up to Wendell and said,

"Is it true?"

I saw one tear roll down from his left eye as I watched this man do what was probably one of the hardest things he ever had to do in his life…

"Yeah. Brian is gone."

Gone.

My mom immediately collapsed. All I heard was "No! Not Brian! He can't be! Not my baby! No!" I heard my mother yell out in a pain that was indescribable, and it is taking everything that I have not to cry as I type this because, while I had just heard that my brother was dead, hearing my mother in that kind of pain was the worst thing that I had ever experienced in my life. No son ever wants to see or hear his mother endure this type of pain. My dad lifted my mom up from the ground and helped her walked back inside of the house. At that time, I could not really focus on details and I just wanted to be near my mom and dad, so I looked at Wendell and said, "Man, I can't believe this. Thank you for coming to tell us yourself." I turned around and walked back into the house.

Everything was a blur, as if my life had gone out of focus. As I walked up the stairs, I could hear my mom sobbing and calling Brian's name repeatedly, and it hurt my heart. It really hurt me. All I could do was pace back and forth in the living room because I was lost. I did not know what to do or say. As it slowly sunk in that Brian would not be coming home, I saw police lights flashing outside. I think my dad saw them too because he looked at me as if he knew someone was outside since their bedroom window overlooked the driveway. I told him, "I got it. Stay with Mom." I walked back downstairs and out of the garage because that was the way that we often came in and out of the house. There were two Atlanta Police cars parked along the curb, and an officer got out of each car. I walked out to meet them at the end of the driveway, and the one that drove the first car walked over to me. I said, somberly, "Hello. We have heard about my brother Brian." The officer looked at me and said softly, "Yes. I'm sorry to inform you that Brian was officially pronounced dead at 7:49 p.m. in the City of Atlanta." The officer then said a few more things and gave me his card, and said that the city coroner's office would be in touch with us in the next day or two to discuss where Brian's body would be delivered to after the autopsy. He then gave me a few of Brian's belongings that he was able to hold in his hand. These belongings included his Nextel flip phone and his wallet. I thanked the officer and walked back towards the house. As I stopped for a second and looked at Brian's phone and his wallet, the tears were streaming down my face as they are now as I write this because, at that moment, it hit me…

Brian is not coming home again. I will never see him again.

Man, it was hard to go back up those stairs. As I walked back up, I vividly remember Brian's phone ringing nonstop. I was amazed then and now at how fast news travels, especially this type of news. I believed that some of Brian's friends knew about his death even before my parents and I did. I flipped the phone open and turned it off. I could not deal with the constant ringing because I knew why they were calling. I did not want to talk to anyone at that moment. I resumed pacing back and forth in the living room for a few minutes, and then I heard the doorbell ring. I went downstairs to the front door and opened it. There was a young man there that looked to be around the same age as Brian. He said to me, "Hey Mann. My name is Danny. I am a good friend of Brian's." Brian had mentioned Danny many times and spoke very highly of him. Danny was very independent and had been raised by his uncle, and he was supporting himself and was doing well. Brian said that he was a laid-back guy and a very cool person to be around. His story and how he was raised really intrigued and inspired Brian, and I am not sure where they first met but he spent a lot of time hanging out with Danny. He then said, "I heard about what happened to Brian and I am so sorry. I can't believe it myself, and I know this is very hard for you and your family to deal with. I just wanted to come and see if y'all needed anything, and please know that I will always be here for y'all." Danny had to be a strong man to come do that at that moment, and I really appreciated it. I replied, "Hey Danny. I know who you are because Brian talked about you a lot, and he had a lot of admiration for you. Thank you for coming by. When things are better, we'll sit down and talk." He said that would be fine, and he left.

I went back to my pacing in the living room. That was all that I could do at that moment. Every minute or so, I would stop and stare at my parents' room. Their bed faced the door, so when I looked in there I could see my mom on the bed crying. I just could not go in there at that moment because I felt like I would break down, and I believe I needed to be strong at that point for my mom and dad. My dad was walking back and forth around their bed, keeping a close eye on my mom. People were calling his phone, and he was answering. I cut off my phone when I cut off Brian's because I just could not deal with anyone outside of my home at that moment.

I had left the front door cracked, and as I was again staring at my mom from the living room, I heard sounds of sobbing coming up the stairs. My cousin Geneva and her two daughters had run up the stairs, and straight to my mom's room. All I could do was stand there while they rushed to the bed and cried along with my mom. It all seemed to happen in slow motion, and the world was still blurry as I struggled to find focus on the situation. This death really hurt many people, and at that moment I saw that they were feeling the pain right along with us. My cousin's husband Melvin was also there, and he had tears on his face as he sat at the dining room table because Brian was close to him as well. After about an hour, the pastor of my parents' church arrived at our home. I walked him up the stairs and over to my parents' room. He had been a good friend of our family for a while since he used to live right across the street from us. I can see that his presence brought my mom a small bit of relief, and he kneeled by the bed and led everyone in the room in prayer. I still stood in the same spot in the living room. The pastor sat by my mom's side for about thirty minutes to comfort her as best as he could. He then left, and my cousins stayed for about another hour before they left.

After I closed the door and came back upstairs, I realized that it was just us. We had to continue to deal with this while everyone else went home. For my parents and I, there was no "going home" – this was our reality. I heard my dad still talking on the phone while my mom cried and cried. I walked over to their room and quietly said to him, "The police brought Brian's phone and wallet. I think you may want to stop answering calls and console Mom because she needs you right now." I knew my dad did not know how to react in this situation because he had not dealt with anything like this since his brother Brian had passed away many years ago, and I was struggling with this myself, but I appreciated him saying "Ok," and then doing what I had suggested. He closed the door a little and went to lay with her. I walked back and forth for a little while longer, and then a rush of rage hit me out of nowhere. I ran and punched the wall that bordered the kitchen and my fist went right through the drywall. I was extremely mad, as you can imagine due to the circumstances. It did not hurt me physically, but at that moment, I thought about my brother losing his life, so it did not make sense to inflict any more pain on myself.

After another thirty minutes, my friends Todd, Tate, Devonte, Levi, and Leroy came over to check on me after hearing the news. We all just stood outside in a circle in the driveway. They asked me how I was doing but they did not really know what to say because none of them had lost a sibling before. How could they? We were outside for about an hour, pretty much just staring at the ground for most of that time, and then I told them I was tired and needed some rest. They all hugged me and said they were there for me, and to be strong. I went back into the house and went to bed. I was petrified at the thought of facing the next day without Brian, but I found a way to go to sleep.

The next day was a hard one. I woke up and went to check on my mom. My parents have always been early risers so I do not know how much sleep my mom got, but as I walked into their bedroom, she was sitting up in her bed with her back against the headboard, where she would end up spending most of the day. She had pictures of Brian laid out on the bed on each side of her legs, and I know that was her comfort at the moment - seeing his smiling face. I gave her a hug and told her that everything would be all right. She kissed me on the cheek and asked me how I was doing. I told her I was doing ok, and that I would be all right. I knew that my cousin Geneva and her family would be coming over soon, and that they would be caring for us and make sure we were all fed that day, so I told my mom I would keep an eye on everything else, and if anyone such as the police or any other authorities that are handling Brian's death contacts us, I will handle it until I needed their input. My sister and her kids also came, and it was a tough time for us all.

There were many other people coming in and out of the house so I do not recall who all came by that day because, while I was gaining a little focus back with every passing hour, my mind was still in somewhat of a blur. My mom called me back into their room. I closed the door until it was cracked a little bit so no one could really hear us. I am still not sure how it happened or how they found out about what was going on, or who even called them, but my mom said that a funeral home director would be arriving at the house in about twenty minutes to discuss arrangements for Brian. Damn, that was fast! Who calls these folks and tells them when people die? That was one of my thoughts at that moment.

The director arrived right as scheduled and was directed to my mom's room where my parents and I were. He was a tall black man, about my height (I am 6'4", in case I have not mentioned that yet), somewhere in his late forties or early fifties, and was a nice guy. He gave his condolences to us, and then my mom talked about Brian a little bit and gave him a picture for the obituary. It was our favorite picture of Brian - his senior picture from high school where he had his biggest, brightest smile on. The director looked at it and dropped his head a little, and shook it softly from side to side. He had an expression on his face that was one of sadness, as if he knew Brian. At this moment, I realized that he must have seen Brian in his post-mortem state and his face likely looked a little different, and that they must already have the body. I remember thinking at that moment that these funeral folks move too damn fast for me. They are just doing their job, I guess. But still. The director then confirmed that Brian's body was at their funeral home, and we could come to view the body the next day if we wanted to since he knew we would need this day to deal with the reality of our situation. We said we would come tomorrow and discuss any other arrangements then.

The director left, and I remember my cousins and other people that were at the house giving him a stern look as he walked out because, at this moment, everyone was protective of my mom and our family, so strangers were not quite the most welcome at a time like this. This may be something that many families feel when losing a loved one. One other feeling that arose in me on this day was anger because I needed validation that no one purposely caused Brian's accident. His friend and fellow rider Wendell, who had witnessed the accident and delivered the news to us the night before, arrived at our house that afternoon to check on us. After he gave his condolences to my parents, I walked with him outside as he was leaving, and then I had to ask him, "Wendell, did anyone that was there at the scene cause this accident? Brian was too good of a rider for this to happen. It just doesn't make sense. I need answers, bro. I need them now." Wendell replied, "No, Mann. No one caused it. It was just a freak accident. I saw it all and I can assure you of that." I asked, "Bro, what happened out there? I need to hear it from you since you were there with him in his last moments."

Wendell then began to speak:

"We were riding over in the warehouses off Fulton Industrial Boulevard and Boat Rock Road. We were on this street back there where a lot of guys go sometimes to run their bikes at high speeds. It is about a quarter to a half-mile long, with a slight curve to the left towards the end. It was me, Brian and two other guys that I ride with sometimes, and he also rode with them before as well. Brian was trying to show those guys how to do wheelies since he had learned how to do it out West and they wanted to learn, but they couldn't quite get it. Brian had a 2006 GSX-R1000, one of the guys had a 2007 model of the same bike and the other had a 2008 model. Therefore, since they all had GSX-R1000s, they decided to just run them against each other a few times to see how each model performed against the others before we left for the evening. So, they ran them one time down the street, and then they ran them again. Brian and the guy with the 2008 GSX-R1000 had just about tied on those first two races, so Brian said, 'Let's run them one more time before we get outta here since it's getting kinda dark.'

I served as the starting line for each race at the top of the street, so they lined up with me. I gave the motion and they took off. The riders usually end the races right where the street starts to curve to the left, so this is where they normally start slowing down. When they got to this point, I could see the bikes but I couldn't make them out as clearly as I could if they were closer. However, I could tell that Brian was in front of the other two riders. I noticed that the two other guys slowed down, but Brian's bike appeared to still be going full speed and right into the curve without turning. Then a second later, I just saw his taillights and headlights flashing and exchanging places, and that's when I could tell that his bike was flipping end over end and something had gone really wrong. He was going so fast, so I bugged out and hopped on my bike, and rode down there to where he was. When I got to the grass where Brian had landed, he was lying in a messed up position and wasn't moving. I saw a little blood coming from the back of the helmet, and the face shield had come off so I could see his face. He was gone before I got to him."

I asked Wendell if there were many people around when it happened.

"There were some workers that came out of the warehouse across the parking lot from the grass area where Brian laid at, but it was only about 7 of them aside from us riders, and the police that arrived shortly after they were called."

Then Wendell said this:

"I will say this - those other two guys that were riding with Brian were hurt to the core. They said after experiencing that, they were retiring their bikes and will not ever ride again. It's going to be hard for me to ride for a while myself."

At that time, that was a powerful statement. After looking back on it years later, I saw that my brother's tragedy might have saved the lives of two other people. I have not spoken to Wendell since Brian's funeral, and I do not know if those other two guys ever rode again (maybe I will find out once this book spreads around the world), but I pray for all of those men and I know they had to be praying for my family as well.

To provide clarification on what happened as we received more details in the weeks after his death, as Brian was going into the curve, he somehow lost control of the motorcycle (something that I will add to in a little bit as there is a good possibility that it was not his fault), and he was thrown from it. He was going around eighty to ninety miles per hour at this point, so his body was flying at this high speed once the bike came from under him. As his body flipped, the back of his head hit a curb, and the rear of his skull shattered. We believe he died instantly, and this happened with his helmet still on his head. After he hit the curb, his body flew around another 30 yards before coming to rest in a grass lot.

The next day was Saturday. My parents, my sister and I went to the funeral home off Cascade Road in Atlanta to see Brian's body. We pulled up outside, and we all got out of the car. We took about five steps towards the door of the funeral home, and something told me to look back over my shoulder. I noticed that my dad was still at the car. I turned around towards him, and he said, "I can't go in. I can't see this." My dad has been strong and had held up pretty good until this moment. This is when he realized that he was not ready to see the son that he had raised from birth to a young man dead on a table. Everyone deals with death differently, and everyone has a breaking point during the grief process. It may hit some people right away, and some it will not hit until days or weeks later. My dad has reached his point, and it was his time to let it out. We all hugged him as he softly wept and kept repeating that he could not go into the funeral home, and we told him that he did not have to. He stayed outside resting up against the vehicle while the rest of us went inside. The director greeted us, and then directed us back to the room where Brian was. We paused for a second when we were right outside of the room and held each other's hands because this would be the first time that we saw Brian in his post-mortem state. We mustered up all the courage and will that we could at that moment, and then we walked into the room together.

Brian was laying on a table, with his upper body exposed and everything below his waist was under a white sheet. He did not look nearly as bad as we were all probably imagining he would look. He had some scratches on his arms and shoulders, and a few on his chin, but his face was largely unscathed. His eyes were closed, but his face still had the expression that he likely made when his head hit the curb at his last breath - a look as if someone threw a basketball and hit you in the side of your head, and you flinched. We observed him for about ten minutes, and we all talked about how he looked good. My mom then went back outside to check on my dad. My sister and I looked at Brian up close, and then we looked at his head. The back of his head was resting on a headrest so we could only see the sides of it along with a little of the rear. We could see some red crust around the edges of the headrest which was dried blood, and it looked like there was a very little gap of space between the headrest and his head, so I think that the damage to his skull happened in that area that we could not see without moving him. We never touched him, but my mom did kiss him on the forehead before she went out to be with my dad.

My mom came back into the funeral home, and the director went over casket options with us. It was a surreal moment because here I am picking out my little brother's last bed, and it felt so weird. We finalized the funeral arrangements, and then we went to a suit warehouse to pick out his last outfit. This was a tough moment for me because I never thought in a million years that I would be selecting a suit for my brother's funeral. Of course, I knew the dangers of motorcycles, but you do not imagine yourself having to go through such a situation until you find yourself in it. Brian loved the color blue, so the suit we went with had a royal blue jacket with blue pants, and a sky blue shirt accented with a royal blue tie. As we gathered these things for Brian, I can tell that all of us were trying to figure out how to cope with what we were doing. We had not experienced a death so close to us, and in our case, it was Brian, who was the last person we would expect to be doing this for. As the day went on, we talked about good memories and kept our minds off the negative. We knew that the toughest moment would be the funeral, so we just mentally leaned on each other and geared up for that day.

Brian's funeral took place on the next Wednesday, which also happened to be Christmas Eve. Despite the holiday, the turnout for his service was incredible. We had just about all our family present from St. Louis and Houston, and many of Brian's friends and former teachers also attended the service, along with motorcycle riders that he met in Atlanta so there were at least 200 people at his funeral. It started with people viewing the body at the front of the church that my parents attended, and some of his friends broke down and cried loudly as would be expected. My parents then viewed his body, my sister next and then myself. I put a brown paper bag in the casket by his chest that contained a bag of sunflower seeds and a Mix CD of his favorite songs. I wanted him to be buried with two of his favorite things

The pastor preached a sermon, and since it was a tough day for me, I do not remember much of what he said. However, I do remember one thing very clearly that was remarkable. At the end of the sermon, the pastor asked for anyone in the audience that wanted to give their life over to God to come to the altar. It started with about three of Brian's friends, and after about a minute, there were nearly 30 young people at the front of the church lined up in front of his casket. Brian touched all of these people during his lifetime, and it was heartwarming to see his death lead to such positivity when it came to these people seeking to spiritually improve their own lives.

The next part of the service was the hardest for my family and me. As the service ended, the funeral staff turned a crank that slowly closed the lid of the casket. I knew that this was the last time that I would ever see my brother's body, and it cut me like a knife to where I cried harder than I had ever cried in my life. This hurt. It really hurt. At the time, I remember thinking that this situation was not fair to my family, but I had to deal with it. It was hard seeing my parents cry at this moment because this was the last time they would see their youngest son in the flesh, and I am glad they had each other to lean on at this moment.

Brian's casket was loaded into a hearse. I had emailed an Atlanta-based motorcycle club a few days before the funeral and told them about my brother's story, and asked if they could come out to do some kind of tribute for Brian. I never heard anything back after my request, so I was pleasantly surprised when twelve members from the club showed up at the church, and they led the caravan over to the cemetery in Mableton where Brian was to be buried. Every car within view that was not part of the caravan pulled over at the sight of the procession because the motorcycles and the vast number of vehicles involved were beautiful.

There were so many cars in the procession that they were lined up for about half of a mile as everyone parked at the cemetery, winding up the hilly road that goes through it. The pastor said a few words, and then Brian was lowered into the ground. As the burial ended, the bikers lined up in two rows on both sides of the cemetery driveway and revved their bikes as loud as they could go. It was ground shaking and amazing, and I really appreciated the love and support they showed for a fallen rider that they did not even know, on Christmas Eve! I pray that all of those riders that showed up are alive and well today, along with their friends and family. People that attended the funeral service on that day talked about how amazing Brian's home going celebration was for years after that. Some of them have told us that they believed there were over three hundred people at his service, and most of those people came over to the cemetery after the church service, even with it being on Christmas Eve. That is how much my brother was loved.

In the weeks following Brian's death, my parents and I were extremely dissatisfied with the lack of information we received from the authorities regarding his death. This prompted my mother to conduct some research, and she connected with a law firm that specializes in wrongful death situations. My mom met with two lawyers from the firm. They all discussed the details of the night of the accident that we were able to obtain, and then the firm flew in a private investigator from Florida that they regarded as one of the best in the business, who would help gather information on the accident and try to figure out exactly what caused it. His name was Mr. Hillbender - I do not think I ever knew his first name because he dealt mostly with my mom, but he was a retired detective who now made a living conducting private investigations for this law firm as well as others. He met with my mom and I, and we told him all that we knew about the accident. He then spent roughly a week doing very rigorous investigating that involved him retracing Brian's steps for that entire day on which he died. Mr. Hillbender went out to the accident scene to gather whatever evidence he could, as well as retrieved every record that he could get his hands on from the police department concerning Brian's death.

At the conclusion of his preliminary investigation, Mr. Hillbender compiled all of his findings into a thick binder that he gave to my mother. This binder included a lot of stuff, including photos of Brian as he laid dead in the grass. I was not present when he discussed his findings with my mom, but he brought some interesting things to light for us. First, in January 2009, not even a full month after Brian's death, Suzuki issued a recall for its 2005 and 2006 GSX-R1000 model motorcycles due to possible fracturing of the bikes' frames. A motorcycle's frame essentially serves in the same capacity as a human skeleton does in a person. Per the company's statement, when these motorcycles are rode aggressively, the frame is susceptible to cracking. Aggressive riding is not clearly defined, but it could include doing wheelies on a bike, which Brian did from time to time. The issue with this is that his motorcycle was two years old at the time of his accident, which is still fairly new for a bike. The other issue is that if this recall would have been issued a few months earlier, things could have been different. This does not mean that Brian would have stopped riding that motorcycle, but he would have been made aware of the issue and, in turn, could have examined his own frame closely. The frame of Brian's motorcycle essentially broke apart in a few pieces as he was riding at a high speed, so he literally had no control over the outcome.

Mr. Hillbender stated that we would have a good case to take to Suzuki if we could gather most of the frame, and at least seventy-five percent of the total motorcycle. The problem with this is that the towing company that gathered the motorcycle, which is a popular company that had a contract with the City of Atlanta at this time, did not have much of the bike left in their possession. Mr. Hillbender believed that some of the employees might have sold off the back tire and other parts of the motorcycle on their own because the company could not, or would not, provide any details on why so much of the bike was missing. This pisses me off to this day because there should be stricter policies and procedures put into place when a company tows vehicles that have been involved in accidents that result in serious injury or death. Mr. Hillbender said that we could investigate the towing company and possibly track down most of the motorcycle, but it will be very expensive and would take months to complete, and that is before the case is even brought to the motorcycle manufacturer, which would require further litigation and would cost even more money.

I sat down with my mom and we discussed everything after reviewing Mr. Hillbender's findings. We agreed that if we were to spend all of our financial and emotional resources pursuing this case, when it is all said and done, none of it would bring Brian back to us. No apology or any amount of money will result in Brian walking this Earth again. We felt we were in a good place and were slowly healing as a family, so we decided to move on with our lives and honor his memory in other ways instead of putting ourselves through further pain and possible disappointment that Brian would not want us to endure.

My mom later told me that she threw the binder that Mr. Hillbender had compiled for us away because she did not want to relive the accident again. I told her that I wish I could have seen it because I wanted to see a picture of Brian as he lay in the grass. I felt that this would be hard for me to see without getting emotional, but I also believe that this is something that would bring closure to me because I did not get to see my brother at the moment he perished. I may never get that closure now, but I spent a lot of time thinking about it early after the accident because, at times, I wonder if Brian felt like he was alone for any moment when he came to rest in the grass, or if he was gone before he came to a stop. I know that if he had any breathing moments as he laid there, he spent it thinking about my parents and me. From time to time, I think about that, and I hope that he never felt alone at that moment. However, a part of my soul often rubs me on my back and whispers in my ear that by the time Brian was in his final position, he was already making his ascent to Heaven.

Living life without Brian was a huge adjustment. Going into his room and seeing his helmet and framed Suzuki mechanic's shirt from his graduation made my heart sink every time I entered. It is during this time that I asked myself and God, "Why?" So many other people could still see and hug their siblings, but I cannot. During the next few months after his death, I continued to go out and hang wherever my car took me, on my own. I would go to different bars or lounges and have drinks, and listen to the music that would be playing wherever I was because, at that time, music had more meaning to me. It was soothing because I had more difficulty dealing with my feelings in a quiet room. Music was a quick escape, and each three or four-minute song was like an hour drive through a clear, beautiful desert for me. I listened to every song that I heard and tried to see how it related to my situation with Brian. Some songs had nothing to do with my situation, and some hit my feelings right on the head. I continued to go out instead of sitting at home in a shell because I felt that was what Brian would have wanted me to do. I believe that he wanted me to live life as I lived it before him, so I did what I thought would get me as close to "happy" as I could be at those moments.

Part of the reason that I wrote this chapter on Brian is to talk about how I handled the grief process, and how I am still handling it. I know that many people have lost siblings and other family members, as well as friends, and you may have wondered if you have grieved or are grieving in the correct way. Let me take a quick moment here to discuss the first and probably the most important advice that I can offer for someone that has lost a loved one or someone very close to you:

Never let anyone tell you how to grieve.

Many people that you will encounter will not be able to relate to how you feel after losing a loved one because they have not experienced it. Some people may have lost a loved one that was as close to them as yours was to you, and they may feel that they can relate, but they are not YOU. They will never be YOU because no one else can be YOU. Therefore, you handle your grief in the manner that best puts you at ease. If you want to be alone and read or listen to music while you figure out how to continue your life without your lost loved one, then you do that. If you want to go visit the cemetery every day to see the grave of your loved one, you do that. If you want to go out and have a drink each night or every other night, you have the right to do that. However, if you choose to consume alcohol or other substances to put your mind at ease during a tough period in your life such as dealing with a death, and we are grown folks so I will speak on it because it is reality, please do not do it in excess because this could cause further emotional issues for you and your family.

The point that I want to make is to do what makes you comfortable during your period of grieving. You may feel like people are judging you and how you are coping with your loss, but at the end of the day, you have to deal directly with your feelings while they do not. I continued going out not only because I felt that my brother wanted me to live my life, but because I just liked the freedom of driving somewhere and being in a physical space that was not the home that so often reminded me of Brian's presence. The sounds of people enjoying themselves at the different spots that I went to were bittersweet because, while it was good to hear people living their best lives, it also reminded me that these were times that I would no longer get to have with my brother for the rest of my life. The fact that he passed away a little over two months before his twenty-first birthday made it even rougher on me when I thought about it. Sure, we drank together on occasions since I was old enough to buy liquor, but I will never be able to experience walking into a bar with my brother and legally ordering a Crown & Coke or Long Island with him. I will never again have the chance to smoke a cigar with him, and talk about work and life. I will never be able to see him get married and have kids. If you have a grown sibling that is alive and you are in regular contact with them, you can put down this book and go do all of the things that I just mentioned with them right now, if they are physically able to. Imagine NEVER being able to do this with a sibling that you had known for most of your life! This is my reality. These are things that I will have to spend the rest of my life wondering about. The rest of my life regarding my brother will always be "What if?" Even if your sibling is incarcerated, which I know is not an easy situation for either of you, at least you can still see this person and hear their voice. I no longer have the ability to do that, either.

I began keeping a journal after Brian's funeral in which I talked to him with my pen. This was therapeutic because writing has always allowed me to escape and go to a place where I can express myself completely. I believe that I have always been able to express myself better with the written word that I could verbally. This is just something that I have accepted about myself, and having the ability to write beautiful things is a blessing. Therefore, I would use my journals to tell Brian how I was doing, and to let him know how much I missed him. I also talked about many other things that were going on with me, and I felt like he was right there watching me write to him. I wrote consistently in my journals for about two years straight, and I eventually moved to an online journal that made it easier to write because I could pull it up anywhere, and I could type faster than I could write with a pen. It has been over six years since I last wrote in any of my journals, but I feel that writing this book is an extension of those journals in a way. If you are a writer like me and are dealing with the loss of a loved one, consider escaping by writing to the person that you have lost. It will make you feel good, and that loved one will be looking down on you and smiling as well because they would want to see you feeling good. If you do not consider yourself to be a good writer or speller, it does not matter - you can still do this because your journal belongs to only you, and it is just for YOU. Write what you want, how you want.

Another point that I would like to make in reference to grieving is:

Only time will heal your aching heart.

I tried so hard to repair myself in the weeks and months following Brian's death. After the first year, I realized that there is no On/Off switch for grieving. I could not just say, "I'm over it now. I'm ready to live life as it was before I lost my brother." It just does not work like that. What I can say is that, as time went on, coping with Brian's death got easier. When he first passed away, I visited the cemetery every day, and if something kept me from going out there, I became filled with rage because I felt as if I was not doing what I was "supposed" to do for my brother. After a month of visiting the cemetery every day, I started going two to three times per week. After the first year, I started going every one to two weeks. After the second year, I would go out there monthly. As the years progressed up until the writing of this book, which is over ten years since his death, I now go sporadically. Sometimes I may go three or four times in a month, and sometimes I may not go for two or three months. I let my soul tell me when to go visit my brother's grave, and sometimes I will just drop by when I am driving through Mableton and I know that I will pass the cemetery.

I also like going out to Brian's gravesite for the scenery. His grave sits at the edge of a lake that is in the middle of the cemetery. The lake sits in a valley and is surrounded by hills on all sides so you can get a clear view of the sky as well as half of the entire large cemetery from his grave. When the weather is nice, I will pull my folding chair out of the trunk and sit right next to the grave. When I first started to visit Brian's grave after the funeral, I would sit next to his grave and talk to him aloud the entire time, as if he was sitting on the grass right next to me. Now, I go out there when things are going well in my life and I just want to tell him about it, and I go out there when I am going through a rough patch and I just want to talk to him while crying it out. In the next chapter, I write about some of the most difficult moments in my life resulting from a situation that commenced about a year after Brian's death, and I was definitely putting in time venting at the cemetery because of that shit, and you will definitely see why lol. However, on most days, I just sit in my folding chair, say a few words to Brian and God, sit and enjoy the scenery and peacefulness for as long as I feel like it that day, say parting words to my brother along with a prayer to the Lord, and I leave. Time has changed the way I grieve, but my brother will always be near and dear to my heart.

One other main point that I want to make about the grieving process is:

Talk to your surviving loved ones if they are available.

Brian's death was a tragedy, but one thing that it did was bring my surviving family closer together. My parents and my sister spoke more often than they did before Brian's death, and my sister and I were in contact more as well. We spent most of our time talking about happy memories that Brian created for us. My dad and I have always had a good relationship but we spoke more after Brian's death, and we have maintained good communication to this day. As a momma's boy, my mom and I spoke daily, but she was also my best friend when it came to dealing with Brian's death because we both shared many of the same feelings and grieved in much of the same way, except her and my dad were not hitting the streets like I was. We talked about how we felt Brian's spirit lingering around us and in the house after his death.

My mom and I also talked about the dreams that we had when we slept. My mom would dream about him often. While I thought about Brian constantly in the months following his death, I did not dream about him as often as I thought I would - maybe once a month or so during that first year. My dreams often involved him and I doing something together, like riding in the car or walking - nothing really out of the ordinary. He would talk to me and I would talk to him.

I told my mom about one particular dream that I had that was very powerful. It occurred about 3 months after Brian passed away. Brian and I were walking through an outdoor basketball court at a park that was filled with people. We were talking and laughing about something as usual. We walked out of the gate that led to the sidewalk near a large street. I said, "Time for us to get outta here bro." Brian said "Yeah, Mann." He then paused for a moment and looked at me with an expression of slight surprise, as if he had just figured out something. I believe that at that moment, wherever Brian's spirit was resting in the Heavens, he then realized that he could not physically go with me, and that this was something that was bigger than the both of us. He shook my hand and hugged me, and then he gave me a look that said, "I'll miss you, but I will see you again." He then turned around and walked away silently.

I told my mother that I believe that, although Brian did not speak when he walked away in this moment, he was saying to me, "Mann, you'll be all right. I know I left you sooner than we all expected but I'm resting now, and I am at peace so don't worry about me. Let go and let God take over. Live your life the fullest. I'll be watching." I woke up from this dream with tears streaming down my face because, while my brother was not saying goodbye, he was saying, "Goodbye." This was the turning point that I needed because I felt that my brother's spirit has also grasped the reality of the situation, and now he is telling me how to deal with going forward. He was always one to not show weakness when it came to his emotions, and I am amazed at how he was still able to do that after he had transitioned.

My mom and I have talked about many things over the years regarding Brian's accident, and this has helped us both heal. She also talks to my dad, as her job has always been to help him heal as well. She and I feel the same way from many perspectives. One thing that we agreed on was that we felt that if Brian had to perish, it was better for him to have died instantly as he instead of having to suffer from the pain and anguish of tragic injuries that would change the way that he and our family would have to live our lives forever. Due to the severity of his accident, if Brian had survived, he likely would have been in a state where he would not be the same person that he was before the accident, and it would have been even harder to see him in a vegetative state where he could not move or speak.

We also felt that it was easier for us to deal with Brian's death because he was doing what he absolutely loved to do when he perished, and he had always said that if he was to die, he would rather it occur while he was riding. This forced us to think about all of the families that had to deal with losing loved ones in intentional incidents such as murders or executions. We could not imagine the pain that a person and a family feels when a loved one is taken from them intentionally, and our hearts go out to families that have had to endure these types of tragedies. Most people do not, and will not, comprehend the pain endured in these situations until they have experienced it themselves.

Just a nugget of advice for you - when you are attempting to console someone who has recently experienced the death of a loved one, in many cases, the worst thing that you can say to them is, "*I can relate.*"

While you may feel like you can relate because you lost a sibling or parent like this person has, your relationship with your loved one will never be identical to the relationship that this person had with theirs because you both lived different lives, and you do not know what this person has been through with the person that they lost. If the person asks you if you have experienced something, or if they ASK you if you can relate, then it is acceptable to say yes, and then you can elaborate on your experience because this particular person may need that kind of conversation to help them understand why they are feeling the way that they feel. However, other people will not need this. They just need YOU.

I would advise that if you are not sure what to say to a person that has just lost a loved one, do not say anything. Just be there. Sometimes just your presence is the best support that you can give a person, and they will eventually thank you for it.

My mom and I discussed going to counseling to help deal with the situation. I had never considered counseling for anything, but at this moment, I thought that it could be something that might help us deal with Brian's death, and that it would probably benefit my mom more than me. She looked up some counseling options online and came across a group called Compassionate Friends. It was a grief counseling group that met on the second Tuesday of each month at a church in Tucker, Georgia, which was east of Atlanta, about 40 minutes from where we lived with traffic. They now have other sessions that meet at different chapters throughout the metro Atlanta area. Compassionate Friends has a popular group for parents that have lost a child, so my mom went to a session. The next day we talked, and she told me how that one session really helped her, and that she had met a new friend named Tina at the group that had also recently lost a son that was a few years younger than Brian in a freak accident at his high school - he punctured a lung and later passed away at a hospital. Of course, talking about the loss of a son is never easy, but my mom was very excited about going to more sessions, and she informed me that they also have a group for people like me that have lost siblings. I found this interesting so I decided to go with her when she went the next month because I was curious as to what I could get out of it.

When the day came, my mom and I rode out to Tucker together. The session started with all of the people present joining hands and being led in prayer by the director of the chapter. Then we broke off into the groups - the parents stayed in the main sanctuary of the church while the sibling group went to a classroom. There were eight of us in this session, and we were all at different stages of the grief process. One woman had lost her brother seven years prior to that day. I had lost my brother about four months before this day, and there was even one woman that had lost her sister just a couple weeks prior to that session. Her sister was to be the Maid of Honor in her wedding, and she was getting married in a few weeks. She was doing well despite the circumstances, but the rest of us in the group had all been through the grief process so we knew that, while we had our own issues, she needed our support and our ears to listen to how she was feeling because we knew the kind of "new" pain that she was dealing with.

We all talked about our experiences and how we have dealt with our grieving, and while no one told another how to grieve, we talked about things that worked for us. I would have to say that being around other people that had also lost siblings really helped me because it made me realize that I was not alone - everyone in this room had been through the same thing that I was dealing with. It felt good to have other people to talk to that had similar experiences, and it also felt good to have these people listen to me because they were truly absorbing my feelings and ways of dealing with grief that could help them. Realizing that I was not alone when it came to losing a sibling helped me to overcome another barrier on the road to healing. My mom and I felt that my dad would also benefit from coming to the group. He was hesitant at first because that is just how we men are, but with some nudging from us, he finally went to a session, and it helped him as well. This helped us all see that our family was not alone when it came to losing a son or a brother, and it allowed us to continue to heal and move forward together.

The message that I want individuals and families to take from the last paragraph is to seek counseling if you are feeling lost after the loss of a loved one.

Many communities, especially the black community and black men, in particular, do not feel like they need counseling for anything. I would encourage you to be open to counseling because it can benefit you in ways that you may not be aware of. This is true not just in grief counseling, but in marriage counseling as well as mental health counseling. One aspect of counseling that is beneficial is that you can have someone listen to you that is knowledgeable about what you are going through, and they can give you a perspective of your situation that you cannot see because you are "you."

Sometimes you need light shed on you from someone that is on the outside looking in because you cannot see yourself as others see you. I speak about this more in the next chapter as I encountered someone in my life that I believe could use some counseling because I do not think this person understands how others see them, or understands that others can actually "see" who they really are. You may have a sweater that you think you look great in, but sometimes you need that person that can tell you, "That sweater is way too tight on you," without worrying about repercussions. You may think you are completely right in how you are handling a situation with a girlfriend or spouse, but you may need that person that can sit you down and say to you, "You're really being an ass, dude," without fearing retaliation. Well, maybe not in those words, but you get the gist of what I am saying. You may be on the verge of having a mental breakdown, or possess a mental illness that you are not aware of, and you may need that person that can tell you, "I believe you have some issues that you need to work through and I can help you," or "I believe that you have bipolar disorder. Let's talk more about it and discuss treatment options that can help you improve your quality of life."

Sometimes you must realize that the problem is bigger than you. This is where counseling can help you or your family. Always keep this in mind.

There was one very remarkable thing that my mom and I were able to get out of the counseling experience. My mom became good friends with Tina, the woman that she met at her first grief group session. As they talked and got to know each other, they noticed that there were some similarities in the actions of Brian and Tina's son in the days before their deaths. My mom mentioned to Tina that Brian had never come to see us bowl, and on the night before he passed away, he came to the bowling alley to watch us for the first time ever. Tina told my mom that, before her son passed away, on Saturdays, her normal routine was to leave in the morning and spend most of the day shopping at malls and the grocery store before heading home in the late afternoon. Tina's son always stayed at home on these days and played his video games or hung out with his friends all day because he never wanted to spend his entire day shopping. The Saturday before her son passed away, Tina was preparing to leave in the morning to start her day of shopping when her son stopped her and said, "Mom, I want to go with you." Tina was shocked because that was the last thing that she was expecting to hear that day, but she was still excited and said, "Sure, let's go, honey!" Her son spent the entire day with her at the mall and the other stores that she stopped at, and he spent the entire Sunday with her as well. He had never done that willingly until that weekend, but Tina spent those moments enjoying her son and he did the same, just as we enjoyed Brian coming to see us that Wednesday at the bowling alley for the first and only time.

Both Brian and Tina's son had no clue, to our knowledge, that those would be their last days walking this Earth, but they were subconsciously being prepared for their transitions by spending some memorable moments with the people that they loved, and God was showing them the way. At first, it seemed like a coincidence, but after doing some research, I found that many people that have lost loved ones have shared similar experiences in which the person that died did things a little differently in the days before their death, such as spending more time with loved ones. This was very interesting to us because both Tina and our family were able to see our loved ones enjoy their last moments with us.

The point that I want you to get from that last concept is:

Enjoy and LOVE your loved ones while they are here because you never know when it will be their time, or your time, to leave this Earth as we know it.

As this chapter is long enough, I want to move towards closing it. There are a few things that I want to leave you with, and I have touched on all these points throughout the chapter. First, if you have lost a loved one, never let anyone tell you how you should grieve. Do what you feel is best for you. Every situation is different, and every person is different. People are unique, situations are unique, and everyone's way of grieving is unique. Next, allow time to help yourself heal. You can control how you grieve, but you cannot control how long it will take you to get to a better place in the grief process. Give it to God or the Higher Power that you believe in, and let life take its course. You can keep your lost loved one in mind every day for the rest of your life, but also remember to continue to live your life.

It is perfectly fine to seek counseling if you are not sure of how to deal with the death of a loved one. Counseling can help with grieving, but it can also help you in other areas of your life such as relationships and mental health. Some people fear being judged for seeking outside help, but people will respect a person that makes an honest attempt to improve their mental health and well-being instead of just doing nothing at all. And remember to love and appreciate your loved ones while you still can, and allow them to love and appreciate you as well. Do not make it hard for people that love you to be in your life if it is reasonable and within your control. I understand that this can be more complicated than it sounds as I discuss in the next chapter how it is currently hard for someone very dear to me to be in my life, and me to be in their life, due to very tough decisions that I had to make for my own well-being as well as that of my family. Therefore, I know that it is not always reasonable.

In closing, as I write this passage, it has been a little over ten years since Brian left us, and I can say that my family is doing very well. We have had to endure another tough situation that the next chapter will cover in extreme detail, but Brian's situation has prepared us to deal with anything, and the strength we gained as a family from that ordeal allowed us to effectively deal with the next situation that essentially spread over the next ten years of our lives.

We vowed to keep Brian's memory alive so we came up with a wonderful way to carry on his legacy that he would make him proud. Brian used to tell us about how some of his classmates at the Motorcycle Mechanics Institute struggled financially with traveling out to Phoenix to attend school, as well as putting a roof over their heads and food in their mouth when they got there. Therefore, in 2009, we established the Brian T. Rounds Youth Association (BTRYA) to award travel grants to deserving students who wanted to attend MMI and needed financial assistance. We have awarded multiple scholarships since BTRYA's inception, and we will continue to give more money to students who desire to attend and excel at MMI in the future. Our organization now operates with this purpose, as well as assisting underprivileged kids with preparing for careers in the mechanical trades. In 2013, we officially became a 501(c)3, not-for-profit organization and we are proud of this accomplishment. My mother, Janice Rounds, is the Executive Director of BTRYA. I serve as Program Director. While we work to raise funds for our causes, we have held an annual toy drive each December since 2009 that has grown each year. We have helped over 200 families since that first year, and we will continue to give back to make the holidays easier for those that are less fortunate.

You should know that, to this day, sometimes when we enter my parents' house from the garage, we can actually hear sounds of someone walking upstairs as clear as spring water.

Even in the afterlife, Brian Tramel Rounds still raids the fridge looking for his green tea.

6

D.A.L.I.L.A.H.

This is the chapter that you have been waiting for. The chapter that will get your mind moving. The chapter that contains the situations that ultimately inspired me to put my story on paper. I am sure that the last chapter on my brother Brian touched you, but this chapter will leave you in awe. There will be some moments in this chapter that will literally make you laugh out loud, and there will be others that will make you want to punch a wall. But hey – that is what a good story should do to you, especially a REAL one. I want people to understand that this is a true story and this is real life, and that you never know what people are dealing with, whether they are good things or bad. I say this because I want people to know my story, and this is the transparency that may lead others in the world to fix their own situations. I want this book to be part of the legacy that I leave for the world, my family and someone very dear to me that you will get to know through this chapter.

So, kick back and enjoy it, but you still want to buckle your seatbelt because you are in for a ride…

A few months into 2009, shortly after my brother Brian passed away, the romantic relationship that I was in at that time ended. I believe that God puts people in your life for a reason, and while I was not with this person for a long time, I believe that her purpose was to help me through that tough time involving my brother's tragedy because she had experienced the deaths of loved ones as well as others in her community where she was raised, and some of these happened at a young age. Therefore, yes - I was single again and ready to fucking mingle! Lol. Throughout that summer, I hung out with my friend Todd, as well as my friends Levi and Tate. Todd was the explorer like me so he would be my guy for hitting the city with, and we would check out clubs and lounges in downtown Atlanta, Midtown and Buckhead. Levi and Tate were my fellas that I hit the local Cobb County parties with since we resided in that area. I always say that those cats do not believe in going inside of I-285 lol.

In early August, a friend of mine named Harry invited us to a party at his home in Powder Springs. Harry stayed at the home with his girlfriend Cheryl and a roommate, and they had a nice-sized house for a young couple that also happened to be a great place for parties so we were hyped about that. It was a Saturday night, and we pulled up out front of Harry's home. I drove my car while Tate and Levi rode together in Levi's car. On nights when we rode out, our routine was to meet at one of our homes and start sipping our alcoholic beverages (which is known by the term "pre-gaming" that I mentioned in the last chapter), and then make a cup for the road and throw the rest of the liquor in the trunk so we would have our own stash for the party. I do not encourage drinking and driving by any means, but back then we could not hit the road for a party without a cup in the car and a bottle in the back seat or trunk. Needless to say, we were feeling pretty damn good when we got to the party.

After we found somewhere to park, which is always a challenge at a good house party, we went in and posted up downstairs in the den for about fifteen minutes. Harry's house was a split-level home, and the den contained a pool table and a foosball table so that is where many folks had congregated. We mingled with the people that we knew for a little bit, and then we went back upstairs to get some ice for our drinks from the kitchen. There was a dining room area that we had to walk through to get to the kitchen, and there was a patio door behind the dining room table that led out to a large deck and the backyard. After we got our ice, Tate and I posted up on a wall in the kitchen because it was a good spot with lots of traffic, and this traffic included females. Tate then pointed at the patio and said, "Hey Fleezy, ol' girl been lookin' at you, bro." I looked out on the patio and saw a woman who was looking at me while she was dancing by herself. As men, you know we have to size up a female to see if she is worth the effort of talking to before we make a move and lose our spot at a crowded party. I looked at her for a few seconds - she was somewhat tall for a female but was not exactly my type, and it looked like an "easy kill" so I decided to go take a shot.

Yeah, I know it sounds ruthless, but that is how we men think when we are young and single - a woman is either girlfriend material, or "I'll hit it a few times and quit it" material, or just "something for the night" material. Those are the main three categories, with some subcategories sprinkled in between those but breaking that down could be an entire book in itself, so I will stick to the story. I was seeing this woman as "something for the night" material, and I was officially in tipsy stage, so I went out on the patio and introduced myself. She said that her name was Emily, and that she was from Huntsville, Alabama. I do not recall how she met Harry's girlfriend Cheryl but they had known each other for a little while, and she said that they allowed her to come to stay with them as a roommate. She told me that she was twenty-two years old, and that she had come to Georgia to enroll at Clark Atlanta University. I assumed it may have been for graduate school due to her age but I do not think we ever spoke about education again after that. We talked a little more after that, and then did some dancing. Tate was tipsy by this time so I remember tripping out with him and Levi while they were messing with me and saying, "You caught one, didn't you?" I said, "Yeah, I may have." We partied for another hour or so before leaving, and I got Emily's phone number. Nothing happened that night.

I saw Emily twice during that next week. I will not elaborate on the details of what happened when I saw her because I do not want this to become that kind of book, but I will say that we did grown folks' stuff, and you can use your imagination with that one. After seeing Emily the second time, I pretty much had no intentions on ever seeing her again, and I was ready to leave that experience behind and "move on to the next," as they say. A few weeks went by, and I had not heard from Emily, which I was more than fine with. Around the end of August, I received a text message on my phone. When I picked it up, I saw Emily's name so I did not really plan on responding but I opened the message. It said, "Hey Floyd. We need to talk about something. Call me when you can." Now, when a man gets a message like this from a woman out of the blue who he has not seen her for weeks, certain thoughts run through his head, and you can bet that those same thoughts were running through mine. I thought to myself, "It was only two times, and it didn't really even happen like it was supposed to for something like that for something to happen. So, it shouldn't be anything like that." After I finished going over those thoughts in my head, I called Emily. I said, 'What's up?" She then said,

"Floyd, I'm pregnant."

In my mind, I was saying, "Shit. I really didn't want to see this girl again and now she's telling me that she's pregnant? What the fuck, man!" I was in shock, as you could imagine, so the first question that I could think to ask was,

"Are you sure?"

She said, "Yes, I'm sure. I took a pregnancy test."

My next question was:

"Is it mine?"

"Yes, it's yours."

"And you haven't been with anyone else?"

"No. I haven't been in Atlanta that long so I don't really know anyone else besides the people that live in this house and the people I work with. And you."

We talked a little longer, and I was not going to pressure her either way, but I asked her, "Do you plan on having this child?" She said, "No. I'm in school and I don't need a child right now, and I know we aren't going to be together so there's no reason to keep it." In my head, I am thinking, "Fucking right. Abort that thang. Mission aborted. That's what I'm talking about! You go, girl! High five!" However, my actual words were, "Yeah, you're right - you're young and have your whole life ahead of you, and so do I. And we're not going to be in a relationship so I totally agree." She then said she would research some abortion clinics and let me know which one she will go with.

One thing that I want to mention before I continue, and I feel it is important to break from the story to state this because this is something that I had to give much thought to, is that some readers may not be comfortable with the previous paragraph due to your personal or religious beliefs, and that is perfectly fine because we are humans and have our own opinions. I completely understand that. However, please also understand that I am not writing this book to make everyone happy because that is impossible, and I cannot restrict my creativity and talents in an attempt to do that. My purpose for writing this book is to tell the world MY story, and how "I" felt as I went through the things that I had to endure at the time in my life that I had to endure them. This can only be conveyed in the manner that my heart leads me to, and that is the way that I will write my story, as I have done throughout the book. Use this paragraph to realize that, when observing something that we may not necessarily agree with, we should try to understand its purpose and origin from the perspective of the person or thing that created it, and be able to look beyond our own interpretation of what we see.

Ok, back to the story now.

The next day, Emily identified the clinic that she wanted to go to and said she would head out there in a couple of days, and that it would be five hundred dollars for the procedure. You know that I was at her house with that five hundred before she could put the phone down lol. I asked her if she wanted me to take her, and she said that her older sister Cerita would come down from her home in New York to be with her, but she would call me after it was done and let me know how it went. On the day Emily was supposed to go, I got a call from her. She was crying, and she said, "My sister came down to go with me, but when I got there, I just couldn't do it! This is a tough thing to do and I just couldn't go through with it." She said a few more things to that point, but I could not really say anything. I was just thinking that I was going to be stuck with her and this baby that would be coming. Emily had not really spoken about going to school since I first met her, so I was not sure if she was really in school, or even had an undergraduate degree, so I was wondering what her plans really were. I started asking myself at this point, "Who is Emily, really?" I had no answers other than what I had gotten from her thus far.

Now, I really did not want to start discussing the negative things about Emily this early in the book, but for relevance, I must put things where they fit:

I later found out from someone that Emily talked to that she never intended on going to get the abortion. *She put that money towards her rent and bills.* Why she would tell someone that instead of keeping it to herself is beyond my logic, *but that is Emily.*

Like I said, buckle your seatbelt. There is PLENTY more…

But yeah, there it is. I guess ol' Fleezy has a baby on the way.

I kept all of this to myself for a few days while I processed it. I thought about my future, and how this baby would affect everything that I still wanted to do with my life. The baby itself was not what scared me, and a part of me actually wondered what my seed would look like, and how much like it would be, so I subconsciously embraced that. What scared me were my thoughts about how this woman Emily was still a sort of a stranger to me, and how I would have to find a way to make room for her in my life. I hardly knew anything about her, and she says she is now carrying my child. Wow. I thought about how my life as a young man enjoying all that the world had to offer would be over in nine months. I knew that this was not the end of the world for me because I was aware that many other people in the world were raising children with others that they were not in romantic relationships with, so I never had to be in a relationship with Emily and that brought a little peace to my mind that was so scattered at that moment from the news. My situation was different because I had never been in a relationship with Emily, which made this whole scenario a bit awkward.

The first person that I told was my mom, who was naturally the first person that knew about anything and everything that was going on with me. Well, not "everything," but I digress lol. I remember sitting in her living room with her as she talked about possibly getting a foster child so that her and my dad would have someone else around the house because it felt empty without my brother Brian. As she finished talking, I said to her, "Well Mom, you may not have to worry about getting a foster child now." She said, "Why not?" I said, "Well, I found out a few days ago that I have a child on the way." My mom made the funniest face at this moment, and I could read her feelings from her expression - it was a look of her being shocked because she had never imagined me saying this to her on that night, but she was also a little happy because she could now take her mind off of Brian. Then after a pause, all she could say was "Huh?" Lol. I said, "Yep, your son is going to be a father in nine months." She said, "Wow. Really, Mann?" I said, "Yes, Ma." I told her about Emily and how I had met her a few weeks back, and that we had hung out a couple of times. I elaborated on the phone call that I had with Emily a few days earlier, and how she had told me the news. My mom said, "Well, you need to start getting ready, then. And I guess we should meet her as well."

Emily did not have a car, so I picked her up and brought her to my parents' home the next week. I introduced her to them, and she sat down on one of the couches in the living room. My dad never really says much until he gets to know someone so he spoke briefly, and then he and I went out on the back deck to hang out with their dogs. Emily and my mom stayed inside, and they chatted for about forty-five minutes before I took her back home. I asked my mom the next day how their conversation went, and she said it went ok. She said that she asked Emily the normal questions that the mother of a son would ask a woman that is having his baby. She also said that she asked Emily if this baby could possibly be another man's child, and she said Emily responded, "Oh, no ma'am! I hardly know anyone up here because I haven't been in Atlanta for long." My mom also said that she knew that I was not into Emily like that, but her and my father would help me out with the child, and that after losing a dynamic life such as Brian's, they were looking forward to having a new life enter the family. I said, "Yeah, I guess that is a cool way to look at it." I sure was about to see all of the things that were to come with this new life, both good and bad.

Going through a pregnancy with a person that you have never been in a relationship with and do not have romantic feelings for is extremely weird and awkward, and I would not wish that scenario on anyone, not even my worst enemy. People that have gone through a pregnancy with a significant other or spouse probably could not imagine having to experience this, and if you are currently in a relationship and are expecting a baby, cherish every moment of sharing this beautiful experience with your mate because I definitely did not get to experience any of that. Emily was young as she was twenty-two years old, so she did not really experience much sickness during her pregnancy, if any. I would check on her periodically and ask if she needed anything, and then drop it off where she was staying on my way home from work. Aside from that, I did not really spend any real time with her.

I slowly started to tell my close friends that I had a baby on the way. Their questions were basically the same as my questions to Emily when I found out she was pregnant:

"Is it yours, dude?"

"Yeah, she says it is."

"And she hasn't been with anyone else?"

"She said she hasn't been with anyone else since she hasn't been in the A that long."

"Oh ok. Well, congrats, I guess."

My friends all asked me one particular question: "How do you feel about this?" I honestly could not tell them how I felt because I did not really know what to feel. My thoughts were what I said above - a new life was coming into the family, but it is coming from a person that I really do not know and really care to know. I felt like it was not fair for a good man like me with so much ahead of him to be stuck with a baby from a woman who really did not have anything to offer me at that time, and that I did not want to be with. This may seem harsh to you as the reader, but that is genuinely how I felt. I also realized that I created this situation, so I could not truly blame anyone but myself. I just had to deal with it, and that is what I did.

Five months into the pregnancy, Emily told me that there was too much traffic coming in and out of Harry's house, so she moved to her uncle's home in Mableton. However, after a couple of weeks at this residence, she had worn out her welcome there due to various reasons so she needed another place to live. Now, by this time I had paid her portion of the rent for Harry's house for four months, so I was looking forward to a break from that. Therefore, I was not really happy when she wanted to end her stay at her uncle's and asked me to help her find her own place because I knew I would end up footing some or all of the bill for it.

I was renting a small home in Lithia Springs that was not too far from my parents' subdivision, so I asked my landlord if he knew of any rental properties in the area because I wanted to help find a spot for

Emily to move to. He said that he had another house about a mile down the road from my home that was available, so I met him there one day to look at it. It was a very small house with two small bedrooms, one bathroom, and a living room that connected to the open kitchen. The house had a nice-sized front porch, and overall it was small but would be good enough for Emily and the baby. I worked out the financials with the landlord and moved Emily into the house the next week.

As I mentioned earlier, Emily did not have a car to drive. My parents happened to be visiting my family in St. Louis, and they came across an older Toyota Corolla in great shape that one of the residents at my grandmother's senior citizen apartment building could no longer drive due to his health condition. They bought this car for less than one thousand dollars and drove it back to Atlanta for Emily to drive. However, Emily did not pay attention to the oil light that came on in the car after she had it for a little while, and after a few months of driving it, the engine locked up and made the car undriveable after that. I am stating all of this to show that Emily really did not have much to worry about except for having the baby. I even covered the rent at her new residence because I knew she did not have it, and I still have these records. I was not with Emily and never had intentions on ever being in a relationship with her, but this woman was having my baby so I felt that it was my responsibility to keep her comfortable at least until this happened.

Emily's pregnancy was without complications for the most part. However, about a month out from the anticipated delivery in May 2010, she started to experience some very sharp pains so my mother took her to the hospital because I could not make it due to an obligation that I had. The doctor told them that everything was fine so my mom took her back home, and then she called me afterward. She said that they examined Emily and told her that the baby was just shifting (I am not an OB-GYN so please do not ask me anything else about what the doctor said because I could not tell you), and that it was not a serious issue. However, my mom told me that the doctor asked Emily if she ever had an abortion, and she hesitated a little before saying, "Yes." I found this a little odd because this was never mentioned when she decided not to abort this baby. I am not saying that this was necessarily my business because I had no intentions of being with Emily aside from co-parenting, but it did further support my theory that she intended to have this baby from day one because she had the option to choose the path that she went down previously.

The doctors set May 25th as the date that labor would be induced if it did not happen before then. Despite everything that I had done for Emily during the past nine months, in the back of my mind I still had plans to have a DNA test conducted after birth to confirm that this was my child. I did not bring my thoughts to Emily because I really did not plan on telling her about it, but I could tell that she sensed that I still had my questions. Emily was not a dumb person (we can revisit this notion later in the book as you may have a different opinion after hearing more of the story), and as I got to know her during the pregnancy, I knew she could read people and choose her words based on what she observed. Therefore, she was smart not to add fuel to any doubts that I may have been having about the paternity of this child, and she was good at distracting me by talking about the new baby, and how exciting it would be for my family. I did not consider Emily as "family", but she was trying hard to sell herself as such, and due to the situation she was in at that time, I see why she wanted to latch on to us. Even after nine months, this whole situation with Emily and this baby was just as weird as the day I found out the baby was coming. However, we all just continued to roll with it. Life happens, I guess.

Oh yeah – here is a fun fact for you: I found out as I was writing this book that Emily was actually telling her family that we were engaged to be married during her pregnancy, and that my mom was helping her with wedding plans. That could not be further from the truth because I had no romantic interest in this woman whatsoever outside of the actions that took place back in the previous August.

Yeah, it gets better as I have not even scratched the surface on Emily. Keep reading.

The doctors did induce labor on May 25th, 2010. Dalilah Rounds entered the world! She was a beautiful baby and was very healthy when she was born, and as I looked at her, I saw my mother's lips. When my parents first came into the room a few hours after the birth and saw her, I told my mom, "Those are your lips." She replied, "You know it!" During those first few days of Dalilah's existence outside the womb, I would just look at her and think, "Wow. This is my child. I have something here on Earth that will be living for me. I need to make sure I give her the world." The birth of this child changed my entire outlook on life, and anyone that has had a child can understand that shift in mindset. Once you are living for another individual that you created and not just yourself, you change as a person. Even if some people do not change their negative habits, you will change if you intend on being in your child's life. I signed the birth certificate, so Dalilah was cemented with my last name from that moment forward.

Dalilah was now officially my child.

The first weeks after birth went pretty smooth. Emily's sister Cerita and her husband Justin came down from New York a few days after Dalilah was born to see her and provide some support. They stayed for a few days and were very helpful. They were genuinely nice people, and Cerita seemed to be very different from Emily. Cerita was very laid back and genuine, while Emily's personality was loud, both literally and figuratively, and you never really knew where her words were coming from or what their intent was. This was what made it nearly impossible for me to connect with Emily on a level higher than that of which I currently dealt with her.

Justin and I rode to the store to pick up some things one day during their visit, so we had a chance to converse with each other. He told me a little about Emily's history, and how she and her mother had a great relationship that became somewhat strained as Emily entered her teenage years. My conversation with him explained some things about Emily, but she was still something of a stranger to me because I felt like I still did not really know her. During Emily's pregnancy, she had spoken to her father that resided in North Carolina, who she had not seen much in the years prior. He informed her that she had an uncle that lived in Mableton, and it was through him that she was able to meet a cousin of hers named Ethan, who was a few years older than me. He had a wife named Morgan who was pregnant with a child, and they had two other girls together. Ethan and I had become good friends towards the end of Emily's pregnancy, so he and Morgan also provided some support during this time. They were a great couple that had been married since college, and their kids were wonderful and well-mannered as well. Again, Ethan was related to Emily, but he was nothing like her. None of her family members that I met were anything like her.

Once the hype of the new baby had calmed down, it was just me, Emily and Dalilah. And the weirdness of this situation continued to linger. For the first couple of weeks, I stayed at Emily's house. She would sleep on one couch with Dalilah while I would sleep on a couch that was perpendicular to theirs. I spoke earlier in the chapter about how it is awkward to share the experience of a birth with a person that you are not emotionally attached to, and the awkwardness definitely continued into these days because Emily seemed excited about Dalilah's existence, as she should since she is her mother. However, although she never verbalized it, this excitement seemed to lean towards the inclusion of me as us being a "family" when I clearly could not fathom this. Emily would refer to Dalilah as "our" child, while I could only relate to Dalilah as "her" child and "my" child. It actually made me uncomfortable to say "OUR child." How could I use the word "ours" when there was emotionally no "we?" There was simply no emotional connection. However, I knew that in order to raise this child together, I had to embrace the fact that "we" would be involved in decisions, and that there was no "I" or "me" when it comes to that because it would cause issues when it came to decision making. As you read further, you will see that this exact concept became a serious issue down the road for "us." Emily seemed to be extremely good at blocking out the reality of the situation and speaking as if this was a completely normal scenario, and I started to think that this trait of hers would keep me from knowing what else she was blocking from me and everyone else. The couch arrangement continued for the first three weeks, and then I started staying back at my home again. While I loved being around Dalilah with her beautiful self, I loved being back in my own house because it was more inviting and familiar to me than Emily. I do not want to say that anything was wrong with Emily, but I think I actually liked my house more than I liked her.

Emily tried to breastfeed Dalilah and pump milk for her. That lasted about a month and a half before she decided to switch to formula. She insisted on Similac soy formula because she heard that was better for babies, but she never really presented any evidence on the validity of this. However, since I had neither the knowledge nor a reason to object, I rolled with it. Emily did not seem to really connect with Dalilah and have the bond that most mothers have with their children at this early age, so at about the two-month mark, I found myself with Dalilah most of the time once Emily was healed up and back to normal. Therefore, this Similac formula became a significant cost that I ended up covering for most of that first year until Dalilah was able to start eating baby food. I was buying the ready-made formula that was four dollars a bottle, times seven bottles a week, so you are familiar with this kind, you know my pockets were feeling this lol. However, I found a way to get over by reusing coupons a few months after Dalilah's birth so I was getting the formula for the low until the self-checkout people started to catch on to me lol. They hurt my poor feelings when they shut my formula operation down. Back to full price, Fleezy…

Anyway, back to the story. Ethan's wife, Morgan, was a stay-at-home mom, so she agreed to babysit Dalilah during the day at their home in Austell while Emily and I worked, and I would pay for it. The routine became as follows: on the weekday mornings, I would drop Dalilah off with Morgan. She would watch her during the workday, and when I got off from work, I would swing by and pick up Dalilah. On most days when I picked her up, I would drop her off at my parents' house while I would tend to anything that I needed to do in the evening, or if I just wanted to have some "me" time. They would enjoy Dalilah for a few hours, and my mom would bathe her and get her ready for bed. Then I would stop back by their house around 8:00 p.m. to pick up Dalilah. I would take her home, and she would spend the rest of the evening with me. On some evenings, my mother would keep Dalilah until the morning, but most days she would come back with just me.

Dalilah was such a funny baby. We did some great bonding during those nights together, and she became so attached to me. I knew her so well since she was with me so much. When I would bring her back to my house, I would spread a blanket on the floor in front of my flat screen television and turn it to the Sprout channel for young kids, and place her down there with her toys. She would play with her toys and look up at the television periodically, and then look to see where I was. I would take the moments when she was looking at the television to do the things that I needed to do, such as get my clothes ready for the next day or talk on the phone. Whenever she looked back and I was out of her sight, she would immediately start crawling towards the back of the house to see where I was. As long as she could look back and see me, she would turn around and resume her playing and TV watching.

Sometimes, while Dalilah's eyes were glued to the TV, I would tease her her and go hide in my bedroom, and peek around the corner at her. I would see her turn around and look for me, and as soon as she realized she could not see me, she would immediately take off in a fast crawl looking for me. I would wait in my bedroom doorway until she crawled in front of it, and then I would yell, "Here I am!" Each time I did that, she would smile and laugh as if it was the first time. Even as she grew into a young girl, she always possessed that trait of not letting me out of her sight. When it was bedtime, I would sit in my rocking chair in front of the TV and rock her until she went to sleep, then I would take her to the bedroom and place her in her bassinet. I would then either lay in the bed until I went to sleep myself or go back to the living room and watch TV, or play with my phone until I fell asleep. Dalilah would wake up sometimes in the middle of the night, but this was an easy fix – I would just put her in the bed with me, pat her back softly and she would fall back to sleep instantly. At first, I was nervous about rolling over on her delicate frame and hurting her while sleeping during the night because she was so young. However, as I got more comfortable with it after a few weeks, I eventually slept as if I was in the bed by myself. I would wake up in the morning, and I would be on one end of the bed while Dalilah was at the other. It was every man and woman for themselves in that bed, and Dalilah quickly adapted lol.

During those early months, Emily would get Dalilah for about one or two nights during the week, and occasionally on the weekends. However, during that entire first year, Dalilah spent roughly fifty percent of her time with me, around twenty-five percent with my parents, and the other twenty-five percent with Emily (with me crediting some of Emily's twenty-five percent to Ethan and Morgan because they watched Dalilah for Emily on numerous occasions outside of the normal babysitting hours). We were originally supposed to alternate every other weekend with Dalilah, but when it came to Emily's weekend, she would often have something that she wanted to do, and Dalilah would end up with my parents. On my weekends, I would generally spend some time with my parents so Dalilah would be with me, and sometimes I would let her spend the night with my parents so they would end up with Dalilah most Saturday. So, it is safe to say that Dalilah spent many weekends with my parents, whether Emily had her or I did.

To touch on the point that I mentioned earlier, most mothers are virtually inseparable from their offspring for at least the first year of birth, and they can barely go more than a day or two without seeing their child. Emily was not quite like this, and after the first couple of months following her birth, sometimes I would have Dalilah for three or four days straight and maybe receive only one or two calls or texts from Emily asking about Dalilah. I am not sure why Emily was like that, or if it had something to do with her own upbringing, but it seemed like the loose bond went both ways because Dalilah did not seem to be particularly eager to go with Emily either, and maybe this was because she spent more quality time with me and my parents than she did with her mother. This also continued into later years as I will discuss later. Emily's past could possibly have clarified some of her actions, but she never really discussed it with me, and I actually learned more about her history from her relatives and other people than I did from her. However, I do not believe that anyone really knows much about Emily's past, neither personally nor academically, other than her long-time friend that resides in Alabama, who also happens to be Dalilah's godmother. Emily is a master at dodging conversation on these subjects so I doubt that anyone will ever truly know much about her past other than the people who were directly involved in it.

My parents and I talked about how we would have liked Emily to keep Dalilah more and bond with her, but as we began to notice certain things, we started to question the care she was giving Dalilah when she had her. These concerns started when Dalilah was around six months. I dropped Dalilah off one morning with Morgan and went to work, and Emily agreed to pick her up that evening, which she did. She dropped Dalilah off that next morning with Morgan, and I went to pick her up that evening. When I walked into Morgan's home, Dalilah gave me that big smile and mumbled her baby talk, and then reached for me from her playpen. As I picked her up, I noticed that she appeared to have on the same clothes that I dropped her off in the day before. I asked Morgan, "Are these the same clothes that Dalilah had on yesterday?" Morgan replied, "I believe so. I washed them and put them back on her." I said, "Thank you. Do you think her diaper was changed while Emily had her?" Morgan said, "Honestly, I'm not sure but I can't say either way." As I knew that Morgan and Ethan did not want any drama with Emily, and I knew they were family, I did not want to involve them in how I was feeling at that moment because I truly believed that Emily might have had Dalilah for a whole evening and night without changing her diaper.

The next morning, I dropped Dalilah off with Morgan, and I marked the inside of a few diapers that I left in her bag with a faint blue marker because I knew that Dalilah would be wearing one of them home with Emily since she was to pick her up again on this day. Emily may have noticed the mark on the first day because after I did this, Dalilah had on different clothes on the days that Emily dropped her off with Morgan, so I could not really prove at that time that she was keeping Dalilah overnight without changing her diaper or bathing her. I did not believe that Emily would tell me the truth if I asked her about this so I just kept an eye on it myself. However, after noticing this, I could not help but wonder exactly what Emily was doing with Dalilah when she took her home, and this led me to actually being ok with the fact that I will likely have Dalilah with me most of the time because I knew that she was in great care with me and my family. I also did not have to wonder where Dalilah was, or if Emily was dropping her off with someone else when she was not with me.

My cousin Geneva and her family loved Dalilah just as much as my family did, so they would watch her sometimes on Saturdays and overnight into Sunday as well. Geneva changed my diapers as a baby so I knew that Dalilah was in excellent care with her, and eventually Emily got to know Geneva and her family a little bit, which led to her also dropping Dalilah off with Geneva on some Saturdays. When this happened, I usually did not know about it until Geneva communicated this to my mother, who would then let me know. While Emily was a great communicator and spoke fairly well, I often would not hear back from her when texting or calling to find out where she and Dalilah were if they were not at home, or if someone else had her.

While I paid for Dalilah's babysitting expenses most of the time during the week, Emily would sometimes ask Ethan and Morgan to watch Dalilah along with their own kids on the weekends. When I would pick up Dalilah from them on some of these occasions, Ethan would tell me as we prepared Dalilah to go, "Emily told us when she dropped off Dalilah that you would pay us." I would be thinking in my head, "This girl would really arrange this with them without telling me?" Morgan was a good woman and Ethan had become a good friend of mine, so I paid them without hesitation. However, this would make me furious because I knew that Emily knew that I would pay them, and as soon as I would get in the car and try to call Emily about it, of course she would not answer or respond to my texts. When she would have to see me again to exchange Dalilah, she would carry on as if nothing ever happened. Sometimes, when I called her on it after she did this, she would say, "I'll give you the money back if it's a big deal." And she would say this like it is nothing, like I owe HER or something lol. Hell yeah, it is a big deal to obligate me to financial shit without telling me!

This happened a few more times until I told Morgan not to accept this explanation from Emily without calling me first. I know that Ethan and Morgan are about their money, and they had only known Emily just as long as I had, so on days when she was dropping off Dalilah and picking her up, they made sure to tell her that she needs to pay because I said that I was not covering it. Of course, Emily would sometimes find a way out of this by telling me that she had something to do after work, and then have me or one of my parents pick up Dalilah. In this instance, we would have to pay Morgan, and collecting the money back from

Emily could be troublesome as she usually had a purse full of excuses as to why she did not have cash on hand. Sometimes you just could not win with Emily. The dangerous thing about her is that she knew that, too.

Aside from my spending more time with Dalilah than Emily did, things went somewhat smooth during Dalilah's first year of existence. Dalilah spent her first Halloween with me at the age of five months, and she would continue to spend most Halloweens with me in the years to follow. I dressed her up like a pumpkin, and she was the prettiest thing! My cousin Zaire, who is also Dalilah's godfather, would hold her while I gave out candy at the front door, and the kids and their parents all loved her costume. She looked like a piece of candy corn with those huge cheeks, and I still look at those pictures from that day from time to time just to be reminded of those earlier days with Dalilah. I did not really have any major complaints during this time in Dalilah's life other than the concerns that I described above. I met Faithe when Dalilah was ten months old, and she interacted well with Dalilah. Dalilah also liked being around Faithe at this early age.

Next came Dalilah's first birthday party, and this is where Faithe finally met Emily for the first time. Faithe is more soft-spoken and laid back like me, while Emily is the total opposite - constantly loud and seeking attention - so their first meeting was a little awkward but it was cool. Due to the personality differences, the co-parenting situation and age gap, it was obvious that they would not ever be close friends or anything, but they got along for the most part. Dalilah also enjoyed this day, and it was nice to see much of the family and friends come out and enjoy themselves as well. We also saw how much she loved icing as she made a mess with her small, personal birthday cake. That little girl was something else!

As we went into Dalilah's second year, things were still going relatively good. Faithe was coming down to Atlanta on the weekends to see me, and while she was here, she would clean Dalilah up very well and put nice clothes on her. I loved seeing that because I knew that when Faithe and I have kids of our own, they would be the cleanest, happiest and prettiest things on this Earth. I am not sure if it was because Faithe's presence was becoming more prevalent to Emily, but she slowly started keeping Dalilah more, which was nice to see because it gave Faithe and I more alone time to bond. Emily was also working full-time so she was providing for herself, but I still paid the rent at her home as well as provided diapers and other necessities for Emily when she needed them. However, they always say that some things are too good to be true. Little did I know how bad it would get.

One evening in October 2011, Emily called me. She asked a few things about how my job was going and talked about some other miscellaneous stuff for a minute. As we never really spent much time doing "small talk" due to me just not wanting to talk to her much due to our co-parenting situation, which was still somewhat awkward, she then went into the reason for her call. She then told me she was having trouble paying her bills, and that she needed additional money from me to cover her expenses and take care of Dalilah's needs. Emily was working and had been for some time, so I told her that she is a grown woman and her bills are not my responsibility, and that my money should not be used for that. However, if she needs more necessities for Dalilah at her home, such as baby food and diapers, I will purchase them and give them to her so she could spend less time worrying about Dalilah's expenses and focus on her own. Emily then said that my providing of necessities for her would not be enough and that she needs a monetary lump sum each month from me.

Then she said to me,

"If you don't work something out with me, I'll just put you on child support and I'll get it that way."

Bitch, what?

Did this woman really just say this to me when I have this child with me as much as she does, AND I cover all of the child's expenses? AND I am already paying five hundred dollars per month for HER rent? Really? It took everything that I had in me not to go off at this moment, so I took a deep breath, and then I told Emily that my obligation is to support Dalilah, and that she needs to cover her own bills and personal expenses. I also told Emily that she needs to put herself on a financial budget because she should be able to maintain her own expenses since she is employed full-time and claims to be working many overtime hours, and she even has another vehicle now for transportation that MY parents put the down payment on. Keep in mind that I was already providing formula and diapers for Emily when she needed them, in addition to providing formula and diapers for the sitter and paying weekly babysitting expenses. I pretty much had to start covering these expenses because, as I mentioned earlier, Emily would sometimes short pay

Morgan or not pay her at all sometimes. At this point, I was pretty much done with the conversation because, after all that I had done and was doing for this woman, she actually had the audacity to come at me and threaten to put me on child support. The thing that was fucked up about this was that, up until a few weeks before this call, I had Dalilah with me more than she did. After I hung up the phone, I said aloud to myself:

"Ok. I'm not sure why she would push me this far, but she crossed the line with that shit. It's on."

I knew that after that conversation, things would no longer be as they were before it took place.

I analyzed at my situation, and then looked closely at Emily's situation. I concluded that I was basically being threatened by a woman that I was partially supporting. I knew it could be a tough road ahead, but I knew at that moment what I had to do. I sat down with my parents the next day and told them about the conversation, and that I had decided to file for full custody of Dalilah. I do not know if Emily's threat to put me on child support was empty, and it may have been just to see if I would give her the money, but it was just flat out disrespectful to allow this young woman to come at me like this without some repercussions after all that I had done for her. Who does that? I know that, as the reader, you are probably saying aloud, "Is that bitch stupid or something?" She may have been. I guess that remains to be seen, as I mentioned earlier in this chapter.

Financially, I knew was extremely more stable than Emily, and due to the wise counsel of some of my close friends that were co-parenting and raising children of their own, I had kept good records to show how much support I had provided for Dalilah and Emily. I also knew that I could obtain written validation from everyone that had been involved with Emily or the baby to confirm the financial expenses that I had shelled out to cover her rent, as well as the babysitting and other related expenses.

Sometimes people can take your kindness for weakness. Emily had barked up the wrong tree with this shit.

Nearly a week after my dreadful conversation with Emily, I reached out to a friend that I graduated from high school with named

Lena. I saw from her social media profile that she had gone on to receive a law degree from the University of Georgia and was now a practicing criminal lawyer. I asked her if she knew of a good lawyer that specializes in family law. She said that she had a good friend named Rachel that she met in law school that practices in family law, and she gave me her phone number. I called Rachel and introduced myself, and told her that Lena had referred her. Rachel said that she and Lena were good friends, and that Lena told her that I was "good people" so to take care of me. Rachel was nice and inviting, and could relate to me as we were around the same age. She told me about her education and experience, and then I gave her a brief overview of the situation with Emily and Dalilah. She said that she could come out to Buckhead to meet me at the Starbucks near my lease administration job at Aaron Rents, and we could discuss the situation in detail during my lunch break. I agreed.

We met at Starbucks the next day. I went over every detail of my situation, from the day I first met Emily all the way up to the conversation where she threatened to put me on child support. Rachel asked me if I had records to support all that I had done for Dalilah and Emily, as well as receipts for the financial expenses that I put towards both of them. I told her that I had just about everything, and that I had already spoken with some of the other people involved in the situation and they agreed to provide signed statements validating everything that I had paid for rent and childcare. Rachel said that, while the State of Georgia tends to lean heavily towards mothers in custody battles and Emily technically had sole custody of Dalilah since we were not married, if I had all of the records in my possession that I claim to have, it sounded like I still had enough to put me in a good position to have a chance at obtaining full custody through the courts, or at the very least equal, joint custody. I told her, "Let's do it!"

Rachel then asked me, "Have you had a DNA test conducted to confirm that Dalilah is indeed your biological child?" I said, "No. I was considering it during the pregnancy, but when Dalilah was born, she had Emily's distinct nose while her other features looked so much like my mother." Then Rachel said something that I would never forget: "Well, you know what they say - if you feed someone long enough and they are around you long enough, eventually they start to look like you!" We both laughed aloud. I said, "Yeah, that may be true!" We laughed again, and then she said, "It will be ordered by the court, so you should definitely get a DNA test." I agreed.

Rachel asked me to gather everything that I had to show what I did for Emily and Dalilah, as well as any records of communications with Emily and any evidence showing actions of hers that were detrimental to the proper raising of Dalilah. I gathered everything that I could get my hands on - phone and text records of communications between Emily and I, pictures from her Facebook page of her in lingerie for everyone to see, printed bank statements with copies of the rent checks that I paid for Emily when she was staying at the home in Powder Springs and at the current residence that I helped her get into, and other supporting documentation. I scanned all daycare, formula, diaper and clothing receipts that I had into electronic files so that I could print them out and neatly place them into a binder. I also had a signed statement from Cheryl confirming the rent and that I covered for Emily at Harry's house, as well as a statement from the landlord of my house and Emily's current house validating what I had paid. When I said I was ready, I was ready! I still have all of this information saved online and in a binder as I write this.

I presented all of this information to Rachel, and she told me that she appreciated all of the work I had done in gathering these items for the case, and she was starting to prepare the petition for custody. Aside from exchanging Dalilah when we had to, Emily had gone somewhat silent after that last conversation because I believe she felt that she had pushed me further than she intended to and was unsure of what I was doing. She did not have to wait too long because, after a couple of weeks, I informed Emily that I was petitioning the courts for full custody of Dalilah. After nearly a year and a half of me supporting this child and her, she simply said,

"Ok."

And that was it. I believe a part of her did not mean to push me as far as she did, and the other part of her had too much pride (and maybe stupidity - I will let you be the judge of that as we have discussed a couple of times already) to just hit me up and agree to whatever I wanted regarding Dalilah. However, she was able to dodge the process server for a few weeks so I knew she was trying to figure out what she was going to do on her end.

After being officially served regarding my petition for custody, Emily went and retained a lawyer to represent her. I am not sure who was advising her, but I am sure she talked to someone who told her that it may be a good idea to get her own counsel. Rachel began corresponding with Emily's attorney, and she said that he appeared to be an affiliate of one of those lawyers that advertise on the radio, so Emily likely got him at a low fee and would receive the kind of service that she was paying for. This would be good for my case. However, the sour part of this is that after I told Emily that I was seeking full custody of Dalilah, she stated that she was going to keep Dalilah with her from now on, and that she "might" let me get her on the weekends because she felt that Dalilah was no longer "safe" with my family and me. And no, I am not making this up – this woman actually said those words lol. You have read everything that my family and I have done for Emily and Dalilah up until this point, so you can see the problem with this. You are probably getting frustrated yourself as the reader, but guess what? There is much, much more! Keep reading.

Emily was now playing that card that some mothers in this situation often play - using the child as a pawn. This was kind of fucked up, and it hurt me because for the next few weeks I only saw Dalilah a few times through my mother since Emily would deal with her and not me, but I felt that I would have full custody of the child soon so I dealt with it. However, it still hurt because I was able to confirm through the marking method that I described earlier that during that period that I was not seeing Dalilah, on at least two occasions, and probably more, that Dalilah did go an entire evening and night without having her diaper or clothes changed by her mother. I also later found out some other horrible things from people that watched Dalilah over this period regarding the care, or lack thereof, that she was receiving from her mother, but I am going to omit the descriptions of those details because it would make you very angry, especially if you are a mother. Therefore, I knew that Dalilah was not getting the proper care that she should be getting, and much of this was also noted in my Child Care Journal that was submitted with my petition for custody.

I want to take a quick break from my story to speak to the fathers, and even the mothers, who may be at the end of the stick that I was at this time. Sometimes the person who currently possesses custody of the child will use the child in an attempt to hurt you. If you are currently going through a court battle, you must be careful to keep your cool during this period because any negative or hostile actions that you show towards the party holding the child can be used against your case in court. On the other end, if you are a mother or father that is keeping a child or children from their other parent in an attempt to hurt them, and this not being done for a valid reason such as the child's safety or a special needs situation, then yes - you have likely do what you have set out to do: hurt the other parent. However, what you may not be aware of, or may be aware of but still choose to ignore it, is the fact that you are hurting your child much more than this other parent by causing them to be without a parent that they know and love.

Yes, you have a child, bills and many other things that make up your daily life. However, what you do not understand is that you and the other parent that you are alienating from your child ARE your child's entire life, especially at the younger ages. Therefore, by keeping a parent from a child who has been active in a child's life, you are essentially hurting a large part of your own child's emotions. What is even sadder is that, in these cases, many parents actually see their child hurting right in front of them but refuse to do what is right for the child because they choose to put their own developed feelings first over a child that is still developing emotionally. If the other parent is not a physical or emotional danger to your child, my message to you is:

Put your pride aside and do what is best for your child. You may not realize it, but you are the one that is going to have to deal with the consequences once your child gets older.

Over the next couple of weeks, Rachel organized all of the documents that I gave her, and she corresponded with Emily's attorney when necessary. As she did that, the DNA test was ordered to be administered by a reputable lab company. I had to go to an office in Austell to give my sample, and Emily had to take Dalilah to the same office to get hers. I went and gave my sample the same day that Rachel gave me the instructions. I texted Emily and asked when she was taking Dalilah. She said she would take her the next day. This turned into three days, and as I asked Emily every day when she was going because she seemed like she was dragging her feet, she seemed to joke about it, saying things like, "I took her yesterday. Nah, I'm taking her today, for real!" After those three days of staying on her, she finally took Dalilah to give her sample.

I was so focused on getting full custody of Dalilah and ensuring that Rachel had everything that she needed for the court case that I literally forgot that we had taken the DNA test. This was probably because Emily was not really giving me a hard time during the nearly two weeks that it took for the results to be mailed back, and she even offered to let me get Dalilah for a few days. I figured it was because she was feeling like I may actually get full custody, and was trying to butter me up before she pulled an attempt to sit me down and work out some sort of agreement. However, after dealing with her up to that point, I was ready to take my chances in court because I needed to bind her to a legal agreement due to her talking reckless about child support.

I saw the envelope from the lab company when checking my mailbox one day, so I grabbed it and walked back to the house. I had never seen a DNA test up close so I was intrigued to see what it looked like, and see how my numbers compared to Dalilah's since she had my blood in her. I opened the paper and unfolded it. It had my name and Dalilah's name at the top, and below there were two tables. Each table had ten columns that were headed with a combination of letters and numbers, and below the heading rows, there were two additional rows with numbers in them. Some of the columns had the same numbers in them but many of them did not. I kept reading down the paper since those tables looked like another language to me. As I got to the bottom of the paper, I saw a line that said:

Combined Paternity Index: 0 to 1 | Probability of Paternity: 0.00%

In my mind, I was thinking that, in statistics class, I learned that a 0% probability meant no chance. Hmmm…

I read the next line, and I will never forget it as long as I live:

These results indicate that FLOYD ROUNDS JR. is <u>NOT</u> the father of the child, DALILAH ROUNDS.

Wow.

I remember sitting in a state of shock, with a warming feeling taking over my body that felt almost like the moment I was told that my brother Brian had passed away. The feeling that you are feeling right now as you read this. My thoughts slowly started to verbalize in my brain…

This is not my biological child.

This is not my biological child.

DALILAH IS NOT MY BIOLOGICAL CHILD.

Oh, my God. What the fuck.

My next thought was…

THIS BITCH LIED TO ME ABOUT THIS CHILD.

ALL THIS TIME.

As you can imagine, so many thoughts ran through my head at this moment. I first felt stupid because I believed that Emily knew that this child was not mine from the day she texted me back in 2009 and said that we needed to talk. How could a woman do that to a man? Especially a man that had never done anything wrong to her? Then I thought about all the shit that I had been through with her up to this point. It was just mind-boggling to me how someone could give a person so much difficulty, and then you find it was all based on a lie at the end.

I know that, as the reader, you are still saying to yourself, especially if you know me personally, "Wow…Wow….Fucking wow, Floyd." I was, too. That is an emotional atomic bomb, isn't it? My next thought was, "How do I move forward from here? What is the next step?" I knew that the next thing that I had to do was confront Emily but I needed to do it in the right way because I felt that if I flew off the handle, she would bombard me with lies and shut down on me, and I may never get the answers that I needed from her, which would further strain things even though I considered this to be her fault. Easter Sunday was coming up in a few days so I decided to confront her about it then, but I would have to do it in a way where it was just us two. I had discussions with my mom and Faithe about the faint possibility of this child not being mine before the test was taken so I was slightly mentally prepared for it, but when you actually see a piece of paper that is telling you for sure that a child is not yours, the moment is still surreal.

The first person that I called was my mother. As soon as she answered, I simply said,

"Mom, Dalilah is not mine."

"What? Are you serious, Mann?"

"Yes."

She then said, "I'm so sorry. I hate that this has happened to you. I know this is tough to hear. Do not feel like you are alone in this because this has not happened to just you - this has happened to all of us. Emily clearly lied to you, and there is no excuse for her actions, but she also lied to your father and me because we asked her if that child was yours and she said yes with no hesitation. Therefore, she lied to you, she lied to us, and she lied to everyone in the family that has been involved with Dalilah. Now you need to go talk to Emily." I said, "Yeah, I plan to. I need some time to process this so I'll talk to her this weekend because if I go over there now, I feel like I might physically hurt her. And Dalilah doesn't need to be around either."

After I finished talking to my mom, I saw the sun beaming in from outside, and I just needed to be in an environment that did not feel confined like the inside of my house did at that moment, so I shot to my favorite escape, and the only place I knew to go at that moment: my brother's grave site. As I set up my folding chair next to Brian's grave, I sat down, and my feelings, or lack thereof, caused me to feel like I was melting into the chair itself.

I was in a state of numbness as I pulled out my phone and called Faithe, who was back in Chattanooga. She answered and asked how I was doing. I said, "I could be better, I know that." Faithe immediately knew what was up.

"No, don't tell me it's what I think it is!"

"Yeah. The results say that there is no chance that Dalilah is my biological child."

I could hear the hurt in her voice as she responded, "Floyd, I am so sorry. I really am. You are a good man, and you have been so good to Dalilah and that woman. And for her to put you through this crap all of this time knowing that Dalilah wasn't yours is despicable. There are no words for what she has done to you and the family. She knew Dalilah wasn't yours from day one. There is no excuse for this crap. You need to talk to her because she knew what the results would be, and that's why she was beating around the bush when it came time to take the test. I'm here for you. You can talk to me about how you're feeling because I know you may want to vent."

We went on to talk for about ten more minutes. I just vented about how stupid I felt not getting a test right away after Dalilah was born, and how Emily put me through all of this bullshit knowing that this child was the seed of another man. I just could not comprehend how a woman could do this to a man. I know that this has happened to other men, and I had seen talk shows and heard stories about situations like this, but I never, in a million years, thought that it would happen to me. And now, here I am. I had never done anything wrong to Emily, so why could she not tell me that she had been with someone else when I asked her? And I asked her more than once if she had been with someone else. The fucked up part of this was that Emily knew that my family and I were vulnerable because we had just lost Brian about eight months before I met her, so she had the perfect recipe to slide herself right into our lives, and Dalilah was that missing ingredient. She took advantage of us, and it was intentional.

There were so many thoughts going through my head at this moment. Any man that has been in my position can relate to all of those thoughts. It is a tough pill to swallow. I then told Faithe that I really appreciated her support at this moment, but my mind was very tired so I was going to go back home and get some rest since I had to work the next day. Yes, I still had to go to work the day after finding out this shit so imagine how hard that was going to be. I sat and looked blankly at the cemetery lake for another twenty minutes, and then I drove back home. I spent the rest of that afternoon and evening literally walking around my house, both the inside and outside because I simply could not sit still, and I did not know what else to do. As the night fell, I took a shower because I believed that would make me feel a little better and refreshed, but I cannot say that it did. I put on some basketball shorts that I usually slept in and finally sat on my couch. As I sat there, the emotional numbness started to set back in. I eventually went to lay in my bed, and that is when I let it out. I literally cried myself to sleep.

I want to take a moment from my story to talk to the readers because I want some things to sink in. Yeah, I know you are in suspense and are like, "What the fuck! What happened? Hurry up and get back to the story!" Well, I am doing this to you on purpose so roll with it – this will not take long, and I want to see you squirm in your seat like a dog that is been in the house all day and is ready to go outside. First, if you are a man that has been through a similar situation where you found out that a child that you are currently raising or have raised was not your biological child, then trust me - I feel the emotional pain that you felt. I know how it hit you in the gut, and how it hurts. I understand that feeling because you know your child is completely innocent, but the mother of the child is the person that caused this pain due to her dishonesty. You felt some anger, and this is natural because you were lied to. If you asked the child's mother if she had been with anyone else, and she said "No," and she led you to believe that the child in question was your child when she knew that it was a possibility that the child could belong to another man and did not disclose this to you, then yes - you were lied to. Even if you did not ask her if the child was yours or not, the mother still had an obligation to tell you that it may not be yours, no matter how this may affect your relationship because once that child is born, the union between mother, father, and child cannot be completely solid until the truth has been confirmed.

Now, to speak to the mothers that have created similar situations, I will keep it real with you because I have been the man on the sharp end of the sword - if you told a man that a child was his without disclosing to him that there is a possibility that the child could belong to another man, then you have intentionally misled him because he needs to know the circumstances under which he is about to dedicate a large part of his existence to. The only way you are not at fault for confirming the paternity of your child is if you told him that the child may not be his and he says, "Well, if that's a possibility then I don't even want to know. I just want the child." This does happen, but it does not happen often, and for men that respond in this manner in situations such as this, I commend you for WANTING to be a father because we have millions of men out there with kids, but not nearly as many FATHERS.

Last, but not least, if you are a person that is the child in a situation such as this, and you are at an age where you can comprehend this book and what I have written above, try to talk to both parents about the situation and how you feel about it because their emotions could cause one or both of them to lose sight of the important piece of this equation: YOU. If your father had been an active part of your life up until this moment, he may have emotions of sadness and anger after being misled that are not directed towards you, and you may not understand it. Your mother may have refused to talk to you about the situation, or tell you the truth, and it may be tough to understand why she is acting in this manner. There is no easy way to navigate a situation such as this, so just remember that, no matter how alienated or confused you may feel or have felt at this moment, you are loved. Prayer also can help the soul navigate troubled waters, so stay close to God while things work themselves out because He will provide comfort, and He will not leave you.

The next day after I found out the truth about Dalilah, I called Rachel and told her the results of the test. She was hurt by it because she did not want that to happen to me, and she assured me that everything would be all right. She also admitted that she had a feeling that Emily was not being truthful because she had seen this sort of thing before, and she saw from Emily's actions during this process that her pride was leading the way because Emily really did not know what to do once I filed for custody and the DNA test had been ordered. Rachel brought up a solid point - the test was one of the few things in Emily's life that Emily could not talk her way out of. It was simply a fact – Dalilah is not my biological child and Emily knew that.

Rachel suggested that I first talk to Emily to get some answers. She also suggested that I talk to my family and think about the situation, and then decide how I wanted to move forward. Once I had a good handle on the situation mentally and emotionally, we could talk and see if anything further needs to be done legally. I agreed and thanked her for the sound advice. I also told Ethan and Morgan later in the day that I had found out that Dalilah was not my biological child. They were hurt for me, and I knew that they did not know Emily much better than I did because they had just met her after I did so they could not foresee her doing something like this. However, as Emily is related to Ethan, I made a promise to myself not to involve him or Morgan in any further discourse that I may have with her as a result of what I had just learned because I would not want to make life awkward for them since they would still have to deal with Emily going forward.

Easter Sunday came, and we had some family over at my parents' house. Emily had brought Dalilah to the house after they went to church. Dalilah was so beautiful that day with her bright yellow Easter dress on! She was a bubbly child, and she always wanted everyone's attention. I loved that when I came around her, she would instantly move towards me, no matter who was trying to get her attention or restrain her. She knew who Daddy was! She was the apple of my eye, and I was the apple of hers. Every time I saw Dalilah, it was weird to see her mother's distinct nose on her because it made me feel like I could never really get away from Emily. However, the child was beautiful. Now, I can say that things were different this day because when I looked at her, I knew for sure that she had none of my blood in her veins. I know that at this age that did not matter to Dalilah and probably never will, and it did not change the love that I had for this child, but finding out that a child is not yours biologically when you were told that it was yours slightly changes the way that a man looks at a child because you now have the knowledge that she was produced by another man. I still loved this little girl with all my heart, and she was still "my" child, but things were a little different now.

I told Emily to come with me to the den downstairs because I needed to talk to her about something. She followed me into the room, and once we got in there, I took a folded copy of the DNA results and gave it to her. I said, "Take a look at this today, and come by my house tonight because we need to talk about it." She did not look at the paper right at that moment because she probably knew what it was, and she simply said "Ok," and walked back into the living room. As I went back into the living room to enjoy the rest of the day with my family, Emily prepared to leave, as I believe she had an idea of what was in that folded piece of paper and probably wanted to get away before I began to talk about it in front of the others that were at the home. As Emily was leaving to go back home, she asked if I wanted to keep Dalilah that night. I said, "I'll have my mom watch her because you and I have some stuff to talk about." She said that was fine, and she went home. My mom agreed to keep Dalilah and said she would drop her off at Morgan's in the morning, and that I could come by the next day and talk about how my conversation with Emily went. I told her that I would do that, and I went home.

I was hungry that evening, and all I had at my house to eat were boiled colored eggs from earlier, so I was in the kitchen peeling a few of them when I saw headlights coming up my long driveway. I knew it was Emily, so I had a feeling of numbness because I was not sure what I was going to hear when she came into the house. I knew that whatever it was, she had thought it out weeks before this day. I opened the door as she walked up, and she came into the house. I sat in my rocking chair, while she sat on the couch. Her demeanor was quite surprising because she sat down and looked at me as if we were about to talk about the latest episode of a reality show – showing no stress at all. She then said, "I saw the results of the test. I thought she was yours." I said, "I asked you on multiple occasions if you had been with someone else. Why did you lie to me about this?" Emily dodged this question like Neo from the Matrix, and said, "I really thought she was yours until the doctor told us the date around which she was conceived." The problem with this response was that we were told this damn near nine months before

Dalilah was born, so she still knew all that time that the child was not mine. That did not make any damn sense at all. After nine months of pregnancy and eleven months of us co-parenting, this was all that Emily could come up with?

Then her next statement was:

"Well, we were only together two times so..."

Then this bitch had the nerve to LAUGH.

As if I told a joke. Yes, she really did. I cannot make this up.

At this point, I really just wanted to punch her fucking face through the window that we were sitting in front of. And if you do not like the cussing that you are reading, I am sorry, but I am going to keep it one hundred percent real in this book so the words that were in my head at the moments I discuss are what you are going to read on these pages. I am sorry for the disclaimer because this probably is not the time for it, but back to the conversation.

I sat in shock at how Emily seemed to have no empathy for my feelings, and she did not seem to take any of this seriously. This moment also allowed me to see early on that this is how Emily handles difficult situations, and this is a trait that she has never shed. However, as she saw how pissed I was, she straightened up a little. I said, "This shit isn't funny, Emily." She said, "I know." I then asked her, "So, who is Dalilah's father, since we now know you lied about that?" She said that it was a guy named Reggie, who was her ex-boyfriend that lived in Alabama. I asked her if he knew about the child, and she said that he did not. She then told me that Dalilah loves me with every cell in her body, and that no matter what, I am still her father and that I should still raise her. Emily also said that she was not close with her own father, and that she hated having to go through the things that she went through with him not being around much, so she did not want Dalilah to experience that. At this point, I really did not want to hear much more from Emily so I told her that I needed time to figure all of this out, and that I would call her when I was ready to talk to her again. She said, "Ok," and then she left.

As I sat alone in my house at that moment, I had to make some difficult decisions. This was a pivotal point in my life because however I decided to proceed at this moment would be the decision that I would have to live with, and I would have to be able to accept my decision for the rest of my life. There were two options that I was faced with at this moment. I could go to Emily and say, "This isn't my child. Fuck it, and fuck you," and then completely walk away from the situation. I then thought about how Emily spent some time in foster homes, and with the care, or lack thereof should I say, that she was providing to Dalilah, I thought about how I would handle it if I was to walk away from the situation and something was to happen to Dalilah, or if she was to end up in foster care and is treated badly. I truly believed that, at this point, Emily did not have the ability to care for this child on her own because I had Dalilah in my care more than she did before the custody discussions started. Therefore, if I was to walk away and something was to happen to this beautiful child when I could have prevented it, I felt that it would affect me for the rest of my life, and it would be a deep regret that I would have to stomach.

This leads to the other option, which would be to stay in this child's life because, while she was young, she only knew me as her father. My family and I could give her a beautiful life. However, that would also mean that Emily would be a part of my life in some form or fashion for the foreseeable future. When I first talked with my mom after I found out the truth, she had told me that her and my dad would support me and help with Dalilah if I decided to raise her. And while we were only two months into our new relationship, Faithe had also told me that she would support me in whatever I decided to do, and that if I decided to continue raising Dalilah, she would still be with me and help me with that. I thought about my options all night. Wrestling with these thoughts eventually put me to sleep.

Oh, and in case you are wondering,

Emily never apologized for the situation that she formulated. Never.

When I got off work the next day, I picked up Dalilah from Morgan's house and went by my parents' house. Dalilah was her same bubbly self - she did her baby talk as we rode over there, and she always made me laugh because she would try to have actual conversations with me with her baby gibberish, and I would act like I understood her. I would then respond to her in plain English, and she would sit there and listen to me as if she knew what I was saying, and would then wait until I was done talking before she responded lol. When we went into my parents' house, my dad picked Dalilah up and played with her. She loved seeing him nearly as much as she loved seeing me. My dad took her into their bedroom, and I sat down with my mom. I told her what I had decided to do, and that I needed her to watch Dalilah because I needed to go talk to Emily. She said that was fine, and to let her know if I needed her to watch Dalilah for the rest of the night. I told her that I planned to come back and get Dalilah when I am done because I needed her innocent energy in my presence that evening, and she said ok.

I told Emily earlier in the day that I was coming by so she was expecting me. As I walked into her house, I realized that this was the only time that I had seen Emily actually appear a bit nervous. This was understandable because she knew that this could be the moment that I walk out of her and Dalilah's lives forever and take my family with me, and the past twenty months would simply become a memory. I told Emily that I would stay in Dalilah's life and raise her, but from that point forward all the bullshit is going to come to a halt. I would pay for Dalilah's daycare and the things that I keep for her at my house, and from that moment on Emily would be responsible for all of her own bills as well as Dalilah's belongings at her place. I then reminded her again that I was not dealing with any of previous shit that we had been going through any longer, and if she ever made it hard for me to be in Dalilah's life at any time in the future, I would not be in it at all. From that point, we were simply co-parenting, and that is it. She said that she understood, and that she would not give me any problems going forward. We also agreed that at the beginning of each week we would determine who would get Dalilah on which days, and that we would alternate weekends.

I made it clear to Emily that once Dalilah gets to an age where she can understand the situation, we both need to sit down with her and tell her the truth about me not being her biological father because I believed she has a right to know. Emily said that she agreed, but I honestly do not believe she ever wanted to tell her daughter the truth, and that became more apparent later down the road as you will see. However, I knew that we would have to deal with that bridge at some point in the future. I left on a decent note with Emily and went back to my parents' home. I told my mom about the conversation and that it went well. She was very excited because her and my father did not want Dalilah to exit from their lives, and she reassured me that her and my dad would be there for me and the child whenever we needed them. I thanked her for her support throughout the entire situation, and then Dalilah started demanding my attention in her cute pajamas so I picked her up. She had been given a bath, and I loved smelling her fat cheeks afterward because there was nothing like that powder-fresh baby wash scent. I buckled her chubby self into her car seat in my vehicle, my parents waved to us from their porch and we went home.

When we got to my house, I put Dalilah on the floor on her blanket in front of the TV. She did her usual thing - watched the toddler shows for a few minutes, turned around to see if I was still sitting there, and then turned back around and kept watching. Rinse and repeat lol. As I stared at her on this particular night, I realized that I had been through a lot mentally and emotionally since her birth, but I felt a sense of relief because I had finally made this tough decision, and I was ok with it. Dalilah turned around and smiled at me again - I smiled back, and then stuck my tongue out at her while I made a funny face. She laughed and then turned around and finished watching TV.

As she turned back around, I whispered with a mixture of relief and joy:

"Yes baby, your daddy is here."

The next day, I stopped by Ethan and Morgan's home. I told them how I had decided to proceed regarding the situation with Dalilah. I felt good after talking to them about it because they praised me for deciding to stay in Dalilah's life, and they said it would be nice for Dalilah to continue to be able to interact with their three daughters as they all grow up since they were cousins. I agreed. I also called Rachel that day and told her that I decided to raise Dalilah, and I discussed the arrangements that Emily and I agreed upon. She commended me on stepping up to the plate to raise the child when I could have easily walked away.

I told Rachel that while Emily and I were on better terms, I still did not trust her and probably never would due to the lie that she told me about Dalilah, so I wanted to be protected from child support because I felt that it was not beyond Emily to still try to get money out of me in the future, even after this huge lie. Rachel told me that I would not have to worry about a judge agreeing to an order to put me on child support due to the circumstances of our situation and the proof of the past financial support that I had already provided. However, if I wanted complete reassurance, Emily and I could sign a Consent Order

Rescinding Paternity Acknowledgement, which would remove my name from the Georgia Putative Father Registry. This would guarantee that I would never have to pay child support on Dalilah and close the custody case. I said, "Yes, let's do that."

I printed and signed the document as soon as Rachel sent it to me, so once we got Emily's signature on it, the document would be official. Emily tried to hide it, but I noticed some hesitation on her end when it came to signing the document. I do not believe that the hesitation came from her not wanting to sign it, but more so because she was not exactly sure of what she was agreeing to, or how it would affect her leverage in our situation in the future as she always had to be a step ahead of whoever she was dealing with in any given situation. She did eventually sign it, and it was submitted to the courts by our attorneys so it is now public record in the State of Georgia that is accessible by anyone. However, there was a disadvantage that I was faced with after executing this document, and I did not realize how severe it was at the time - this document stated that it was now up to Emily and I to work out all future issues regarding Dalilah on our own, and while it was up to us to decide when we each would get Dalilah, this document also legally declared Emily as the *sole custodian* for Dalilah. This would come back to bite me in the ass as you will later see.

Now, I want to speak to you as the reader. There was a lot that happened in the first part of this chapter, huh? Well, believe it or not, there is MUCH more to my story. As I mentioned when I started the book, and a few times since, these are the actual events that took place in my life and I have documents to validate all of it. So yes - I still have that DNA test, as well as documents that I signed acknowledging paternity when Dalilah was born and the documents that I signed rescinding paternity to protect myself from child support, which you can actually go see for yourself online because it confirms what I said above. I still have everything that I compiled for the custody case before the truth came out and much more.

I used to wonder what made me save so much stuff regarding my association with Emily back then and during the time I have raised Dalilah, but when I started writing this book, it became clear to me that God had a bigger purpose in store for me. As I started to refer back to my repository of things that I had saved, I saw that He knew that I would one day use this information for a higher cause, and that would come in the form of this book. It is amazing when you finally understand why you were led to do some things in life.

There are some very important nuggets that I want you to take away from this chapter because this is one of the most critical parts of the entire book. The first item that I want to discuss deals with fathers who have found out that a child or multiple children that they have raised are not biologically theirs, as well as fathers who may suspect that a child or children that they are raising may not be biologically theirs. As I spoke on extensively earlier in this chapter, I know the feeling of finding out that a child is not yours, especially if it has happened in a situation where you were misled by the mother of the child. You may now find yourself at a point where you must make a decision on whether or not you will continue to be a vital part of this child's life. When making this decision, I advise that, while you should think about the child's best interest, you should also consider what is best for you and what you can live with.

Every situation is different, and I realize this, but you must consider all variables when making a tough decision such as the one that we are discussing. You may be finding out the truth right after the child has been born, which means the child has not developed an emotional connection with you. This makes it easier to walk away from the situation if your connection with the mother is weak or non-existent, and you may choose this path, or you may not. However, you may be in a romantic relationship with the mother, and this news may ruin that relationship, as well as the chances of you raising this child.

You may be in a situation where the child is older and has a close bond with you, so you must also consider this when making a decision on staying in this child's life. You may not be on good terms with the mother and may never be, but I encourage you to be a part of the child's life if possible, whether you see the child every week or every other month, because he or she needs you. Now, I know that sometimes a mother can make it hard for you to stay in the child's life due to her actions or feelings towards you, and I definitely understand this because I will speak on it more later in the book as it relates to my own situation. However, if you feel that you have done everything the right way when it comes to the child and the mother continues to make things difficult for you, you do not have to feel bad for stepping back from this child's life for a little while or permanently because, as a man, you can only tolerate so much drama or disrespect. I will say to the mothers reading this who are in similar situations, and please hear me loud and clearly:

If a man has decided to continue to raise your child after finding out that you misled him about paternity, there is no way in hell that you should make it difficult in ANY way for him to be a part of your child's life.

Some mothers forget this concept and can get too comfortable with a situation, which can cause them to ignore or forget the reality of the situation, as I will demonstrate later in this chapter. This can and will have consequences that ultimately your CHILD will have to deal with.

You may also be a man on the front end of this scenario who is wondering if the child or children you are raising are your biological kids, and you may be thinking about doing DNA testing to find out the answer for sure. To you, I would ask the following question: what would you do if you found out that the child is not yours? If your child is at an age where he or she clearly knows you as their father and has a bond with you, are you going to walk out of that child's life for good and leave them wondering if you ever truly loved them? If the answer is no, then you should consider if you even really want to know the truth. If you feel that you will still want to be a part of this child's life regardless of the results, then you probably should not get a DNA test and just continue to live your life with this child. However, if you feel that not knowing for sure will continue to bug you, then you should get a test and find out for sure to put yourself at peace. You can get one through a doctor's office, and many drug stores now offer DNA testing kits that you can administer at home.

Another reason to confirm the paternity of your child has to do with health reasons. If there are some traits that run in your family such as heart disease or sickle cell anemia, you may want to confirm if your child has your genes because they have a right to know their biological family's medical history, which allows them to conduct themselves accordingly when it comes to their health as they grow into adults. Most importantly, while I say that some men may not want to get a test if they plan to stay in their child's life, I believe that every child has the right to know who their biological father is, and they should meet him.

I did not mention this earlier, but a couple of years after I found out the truth about Dalilah, I sat down with Emily and told her that Dalilah needs to know who her biological father is. Emily told me that she did tell this person about Dalilah, and that he said he did not want anything to do with the child if he could not be with Emily as well. Neither my family nor I truly believes this, but I can live with the fact that I made an effort to push Emily to tell this person about Dalilah, although I doubt she ever will if she has not told this person about his biological daughter yet. However, I still plan to make sure Dalilah knows who this person is whether he is alive or not because she has a right to know unless she tells me she does not want to know, and I do not think it is right for any mother to ever keep this information from their child if they are seeking it. However, I do live in reality, and I realize that this is something that has happened for years and years, and will continue to happen for as long as humans walk this Earth. I know some mothers reading this are like, "Why is this dude opening this big ass can of worms? My co-parenting relationship with my child's 'father' was just fine before this." Well, I am doing it because I have been the father on the short end of the stick that I have talked about, and I want to be a voice to speak for the other fathers out there who have gone through similar situations or may be going through them now, as well as be a voice for the child.

Next, I want to briefly touch on the concept of making your OWN decisions. When faced with the option to stay in Dalilah's life or walk away, I was the person that ultimately made the decision to continue to raise her and I elaborated on the reasons why. While I was considering my decision, I knew that my parents also wanted me to stay in Dalilah's life for her well-being, and because they had so much love for the child just as I did. Now, my parents never told me what to do or how to decide, but I knew the decision that they wanted me to make. They never pressured me to make a certain decision, but they did voice their desire that I stay in Dalilah's life.

I say all of this to bring you to my point that I somewhat spoke about a little earlier: when making a major life decision as a man or woman, *always make the decision that you feel is best for YOU, and not someone else.* Do not let someone else make the decision for you. The reason why is simple: YOU are the one that has to live with it, and you must be ok with that. Now, I do not want people to think that I made my decision strictly because of my parents because I did not, but I did have them in mind when I was considering my options. Sometimes other people may influence our decisions, and that is fine because we are humans. We naturally want to do what is pleasing to those that are close to us. Just be sure that the major decisions that you make are done by YOU.

The last thing that I want to discuss before moving on with my story is the legitimation of a child. If you are a man, please pay close attention to this section. Legitimation is a procedure in which a father claims legal parentage of a child that is born out of wedlock. Each state has its own laws when it comes to establishing paternity so you can research this further as I am not a legal professional, and nothing that you read in this chapter or book should be interpreted as legal advice. However, I can speak on what I know about legitimation in Georgia. Establishing paternity in the State of Georgia gives a court the power to enforce a father's duty to support a child financially, while legitimation gives a child the right to inherit from a father and grants the right to obtain family medical history on the father's side. If something happens to the father or mother, legitimation grants the right to place the child in the home of a relative on the father's side in the event that the mother is not able to care for the child. Legitimation also works in the reverse by giving the father the right to inherit from the child. Most importantly, it gives the father the right to petition the court for custody or visitation.

I am separating this sentence so you can hear this clearly if you are a father:

Without legitimation, only the MOTHER of a child born out of wedlock has custody rights.

When I found out the truth about Dalilah not being my biological child, I executed a Consent Order Rescinding Paternity Acknowledgement because I wanted to protect myself from any financial recourse that Emily might try to attempt in the future. I did this for my piece of mind. However, what I did not think about back then is that this document also voided the Paternity Acknowledgement and Acknowledge of Legitimation that I signed back when Dalilah was born, which essentially eliminated all legal rights that I had to Dalilah. This means that all decisions regarding Dalilah from the date that document was executed by all parties legally rest solely with Emily. Basically, I had no legal rights to Dalilah from that point forward, and I still do not. However, I do not want any father to find himself in the same situation as me, so if you are a man with a child that has not been legitimized, I encourage you to complete this process as soon as possible. There are multiple ways to do this so I encourage you to research the laws in your particular state so you can initiate this process, and if you have difficulty understanding what you need to do, hire a lawyer to help you because the cost will be worth it in the long run. Trust me, it is not a good feeling to know that you have no legal rights to a child that you played a huge role in raising. That is the reality that I currently face.

LIFE GOES ON

Things calmed down considerably after the custody case was closed. Emily cooperated with me for the most part and did not really give me any issues when it came to Dalilah. Other than the occasional paying the babysitter when she did not and a few other irritating things that she would do here and there, I had no major problems with Emily right after the dust had settled.

The first few years after that were somewhat smooth. I moved Faithe down to Georgia with me at the end of 2011, became engaged to her on Thanksgiving Day in 2012, and married her in August of 2013. She helped me with Dalilah during all this time, and she was great. Dalilah pretty much had her way when it came to me because she was a daddy's girl, of course, and you know Grandma and Grandpa (my parents) gave her whatever she wanted. Faithe balanced Dalilah out because she was that one disciplinarian that kept her in check. The cool thing about observing this was that I noticed that Dalilah loved that discipline, and she needed it. She was not a bad child by any means, but she was an attention seeker and had a lot of energy like her mother so she had to be calmed down at times, and Faithe was good at doing this.

Emily got a job with a large hotel chain, where she served as a host at a restaurant in one of their hotels. This required her to have to be at work very early in the morning, so on most days she would drop Dalilah off at my house in Mableton around 5:30 a.m. I would go out into the driveway to get her from Emily's car and bring her back into the house, where I would put her back to bed for about an hour until it was time for Faithe and me to get up for work. It was annoying to have to get up so early, but as long as Emily was working and did not ask me for money, I did what I had to do lol. It was also annoying because Emily would pull up early in the morning with the music blasting while Dalilah was sitting in her car seat in the back. This was not good for the neither the neighbors nor Dalilah's hearing so I told her not to ride with high volume like that, as the motherly instinct to preserve Dalilah's hearing probably never crossed her mind. She did turn it down after that day, but I am not sure what she did with her volume when she was not at my house.

When we moved to our house in Lithia Springs in 2013, Dalilah started to attend a daycare center in that area. It was a good daycare ran by a black woman from New Orleans, and the staff consisted of all black women who gave good care to the children, so this was a great place for

Dalilah. I enjoyed dropping her off and picking her up, and sometimes Emily would pick her up on the days that she kept Dalilah in the evenings. Of course, I was still caught off guard occasionally when I would pick up Dalilah, and whatever staff member that happened to be working at the front desk on that particular day would say to me, "Mr. Rounds, are you paying the balance for this week today?" I would reply, in surprise, "No, her mother is taking care of the rest of this week. We discussed it earlier this week." The attendant would then say, "Well, when she dropped off Dalilah this morning she said you were paying it." This irritated the shit out of me because, while I know Emily was good for doing this from time to time, she would always dodge me when I try to call and text her to find out why she told them I would pay when she knew she was supposed to. I laugh as I write this because if you are reading this and you personally know "Emily," she has probably done this to you or someone that you know as well.

One thing that I noticed when picking up Dalilah from daycare on days when Emily dropped her off, as well as when I met Emily on days when I was getting Dalilah, was that Dalilah's hair often was not kept as nice as it should be compared to the other kids, and sometimes her clothes were not up to par either. However, Emily often seemed to keep herself done up. It seemed as if she cared more about her own appearance than Dalilah's. Now, if you are a mother, I will say that your child should always look just as good as you do or better when you leave the house. You may think you are getting over by half-stepping with your child while you tote the full package, but people do notice when you look good and your child does not. You can fake the funk, but actions and visuals speak much louder than words.

I want to give Faithe much credit here because, on the mornings when we had Dalilah, she would wake up and make sure that Dalilah had something clean and nice to wear, and she would make sure that Dalilah's hair looked good before one of us took her to daycare. My mother kept Dalilah some nights, and she also made sure Dalilah's clothes and hair were clean and looking good. Any member of the daycare staff could come to work and look at Dalilah, and always know whether she stayed with us or my parents, or with Emily. I know because they told me this on numerous occasions. I would laugh at this, but when I think back on it, it really is not that funny.

It was tough to work with Emily regarding Dalilah's clothes because when we would let Dalilah wear something home, we often would not see it again, and this bothered Faithe more than me because she did not like spending money on clothes for Dalilah that we likely would not see again. However, she still did it out of love for Dalilah and me. I do not think the clothes situation bothered Emily as much because instead of trying to keep up with clothes, she would just go buy new stuff once she ran out of clothes to put on Dalilah, or if all the clothes she had were dirty. Emily did give back our clothes about half of the time so I will give her credit for that, but there were many times where we did not get things back. On most occasions, we gave clothes that Emily purchased back to her but we would lose some things here and there as well, so we were not exactly batting 1.000 either but we were up above .800. If you are in a similar situation where your child regularly lives between you and the other parent, try to work together as best you can to exchange clothes because it can be tough if both parents are not on the same page. If you currently deal with this, you can probably relate.

Dalilah graduated from her first class at this daycare when she turned four years old, and that was a proud moment. She looked great in her blue cap and gown, and she loved having all of us there to watch her graduate. Emily and I decided to move her to a daycare a few miles away in Austell for the next year. Faithe and I dropped Dalilah off for her first day of Pre-K, and she looked like a little woman that day with her shorts and sandals! I still look at those pictures to this day. This was a good daycare and was well ran like the previous one that Dalilah attended. I mentioned that Faithe and I were there for her first day. We actually had Dalilah on many important days in her life, such as each Halloween, Christmas Day, and the first days of school as she transitioned into kindergarten and first grade. Emily would get her on Christmas Eve and the day after Christmas most of the time. I felt that Emily was ok with this because she knew that Faithe and I, along with my parents, would buy Dalilah a bunch of stuff, and we always did. As Dalilah got older and was able to talk, I would ask her if her mother got her anything, and she would say that her mom got her a few things. I was ok with that because I just wanted to make sure that her mother got her something. However, if Emily did not get her anything during one or more of those years, I do not think Dalilah would tell me because she knew it would cause friction if I went to her mom about it. Now, let's be clear - I am not saying that Emily did not get Dalilah anything for Christmas in a particular year when she was young – I am just saying that if this did happen, I probably would not know about it until Dalilah gets older.

I would always try to keep an eye on Dalilah's well-being and her care when she was not with my parents or me. However, I felt that Emily still was not giving Dalilah the proper care at all times when she had her. One day, at my parents' home when Dalilah was around four years old, Dalilah was playing in her room. I had followed my mom into her bedroom because we were talking about something, so we left Dalilah to play. After about a minute, we heard Dalilah running into the living room screaming and crying. We ran out to her and asked her what was wrong. She was crying hard tears, and she said that she thought we had left her at the house by herself. We assured her that we would never do that, and we asked her why she thought that we had left her. She said, "Because my mom left me at home by myself one time and told me not to open the door. I just sat there and cried until she got back." When I heard this, I was infuriated. I started to pick up the phone and drill in on Emily. However, my mom stopped me and said, "Calm down first before you talk to her because you know she's just going to lie and hang up if she did do this." I said ok, and that I figured this should be a face-to-face conversation.

When I dropped Dalilah off with Emily the next day, I said to her, "Emily, I need to ask you something. You're not leaving this child at home by herself when you go somewhere, are you?" She replied, "Boy, no! I would never do that! You know how that girl just be talking sometimes." I said, "Well, if you ever need to do something, you have either me or my parents that can watch her so just let us know. But she's too young to be left alone in a house by herself so that should never be an option." Emily said she would not do this, so I left it alone after that because if she had done that before, I did not think she would do it again. However, as Dalilah aged, she kept this fear of being left alone, even for a few minutes, so I truly believed that Emily had left this child at her house on at least one occasion at a very young age.

I also believed that Emily would drop Dalilah off with other people on weekends when she was supposed to have her in her care. There is nothing wrong with a break from your child because we all need that sometimes, even though in Emily's case, we were still keeping Dalilah about fifty percent of the time. However, it was irritating because Emily would act as if Dalilah was with her instead of just saying that she was dropping her off at a sitter. This was critical because, as a parent, I need to know where my child is at all times, and with Emily I could not always confirm Dalilah's whereabouts. She simply would not answer the phone when she did not have Dalilah, so it was easy to see when she was up to something.

During these early years as well as in later years, I did not tell anyone, other than the people that I told initially when I found out the truth, that Dalilah was not my biological child. This was a tough thing for me to deal with when interacting with people because of some of the things that they would say. I always felt uncomfortable when I was with Faithe or my parents and someone would say something such as, "That girl looks just like her grandmother," or "She looks like you, Floyd." All I could do was say, "Yeah, a little," and try to crack a smile. Deep down, I knew Dalilah had none of our blood in her. It was very uncomfortable to watch talk shows where they conducted paternity tests because I had been lied to just as some of those men in the shows were being lied to.

I loved Dalilah and knew that nothing mattered to her but my presence, but in my heart, I felt like I was somewhat living a lie. *I felt like I was lying to my own child.* I felt that, while I was trying to do the right thing as a man and a father, I was also lying to everyone that played a role in Dalilah's life, from her godfather and all of my family to my own friends. This was a heavy burden for me to carry, and you could not possibly be able to relate to this feeling unless you are a man that has been in this boat. I often wondered if I was doing the right thing by not telling anyone the truth. I would talk to Faithe about how I felt, and she believed that people should know the truth so they can see how we were good people for accepting Dalilah while also having to deal with the woman that put us in this situation: Emily. She also believed that Dalilah should know for health reasons as she gets older, and I agreed.

I would also talk to my mother about my feelings, and her perspective was slightly different, as she also believed Dalilah should know the truth one day but it is not something that we have to broadcast because families all over the world deal with all kinds of situations, and they deal with these scenarios internally without airing their business out to everyone else. My mom and Faithe both had valid points. However, what bothered me at the root was how I felt that Emily had left me hanging with this burden because she never spoke about the truth, or asked how I was dealing with it. She simply acted as if it never happened, and this was very weird.

Dalilah started to take dance classes, and when we were at the dance recitals, as well as last day of school ceremonies, when they called Dalilah's name for an award, I would cheer for Dalilah, and definitely hug her and tell her how proud I was of her when she came over to us after the ceremonies. However, when they called Dalilah's name at these ceremonies, Emily would also look at me and yell, "That's our girl!" I really could not respond when she said that – all that I could do was nod in her direction and try to smile because *I had not forgotten the past.* This woman was very weird to me at those times because it seemed as *she had completely blocked out the past.* I later learned that she also did this with other people that she had negative experiences with, and that this was her trademark way of dealing with the not-so-good things that she had done…

She simply acted as if they never happened.

As Dalilah went into grade school, things were still relatively smooth with Emily. She slowly started to keep Dalilah more, and this tended to happen when she was dating someone because I think she wanted to appear as if she was providing the sole care for Dalilah when she actually was not. Whenever she was not with someone, she would go back to the same old Emily - keeping Dalilah about half of the time. Emily tended to date men of African descent. I have my own thoughts on why she gravitated towards these men and them towards her, but she was a grown woman and free to date whomever she wanted so I did not pay much attention to her relationships as long as these men treated Dalilah well. I also did not attempt to find out more about these men because I honestly felt that they would not be able to deal with Emily and her ways for a long period, and in turn, they would not be around for too long. That is usually the way the ball ended up rolling with the exception of one man, who I will speak about later in the chapter.

I would always ask Dalilah how her mom's "friends" treated her, and she would always say they were good to her. I got away from asking Emily about certain things because you never knew when you were getting the truth from her, but Dalilah would tell what she could, and I knew that she would withhold some things from me out of a fear of her mother. Emily and I got along on most things, and we would discuss certain things regarding Dalilah and agree before moving forward, so we were able to co-parent effectively, or as good as this situation would allow. Faithe did not care too much for Emily once we found out that she lied about me being Dalilah's biological father, so their interactions were fairly limited - Faithe did not want Emily at our house so I would either meet her somewhere to pick up Dalilah, pick her up from Emily's house (which Faithe did not like me doing but she tolerated it), get her from school, or I would get her from my mother's house if Emily took her over there.

I talked to my mother more than my dad most of the time, so I reminded her that I viewed my relationship with Emily as strictly co-parenting and raising Dalilah, and that was it. I did not consider Emily to be "family" and never would, and I did not care for Emily to be at any of our family events unless she was dropping Dalilah off and leaving, nor did I care to be at any of her events. I understood my parents' perspective on the situation because they just wanted to be around Dalilah and knew that, in order to do that, they would have to give in to letting Emily come in sometimes. However, I would say that if you are a grandparent who may be in a similar situation, keep in mind that your child and his significant other may have a different perspective when it comes to your grandchild's other parent and their presence. Your son or daughter should respect your home, but as the grandparent, you should also realize that you have to respect your child's situation because he or she and the other parent should be the direct links to the child. When a triangle situation is created between two parents and the grandparents, things can get muddy at times because control of the child in question can sometimes seem to be stretched among all three parties. However, it must be communicated and accepted among all parties that, while grandparents are welcome to do for the child, control of that child ultimately lies with the parents. All parties must also respect that the grandparents can and will do what they want in their home if the child is allowed to spend time with them. If all three points of the triangle can work together, it can be a beautiful thing. However, certain situations such as the one with Dalilah would always be somewhat awkward, and I understand that.

Emily started to make some strides on the professional front as she matured. She met and befriended an accomplished woman who represented a local district in our area in the Georgia State legislature. When this woman went on to seek a higher office in the State in 2014, Emily ran to be her replacement, and she won the election.

Emily Thompson was now a politician. Oh Lord. Lol.

I guess she finally used that gift of gab for a positive purpose, huh? As I mentioned before, I had no emotional connection to Emily but it was good to see her win this position because I felt that it could somehow be used to benefit her and Dalilah. I never really wanted anything from Emily but to make sure Dalilah was always taken care of.

That was all that I ever desired of her. I also noticed that Emily cut off her hair around this time to a low Caesar cut, and eventually colored it blond, which was a good thing because she really did not know what to do with the hair that she used to have on her head, and you can tell that from the condition that Dalilah's hair would be in when she dropped her off sometimes. The short style fit her round head shape so it worked for her, and she has that style to this day.

When I first talked to Emily about her new position, she mentioned that she could use this public office and influence to benefit Dalilah, such as getting her into a charter school or just a better school in general. I did not have any problems with the elementary school that Dalilah was attending in Mableton, but I was always open to any school that would provide a good education for her. Emily told me that she inquired with a couple of charter schools but could not get Dalilah in, but I was not really clear on the reasons why. She had mentioned private school to me but, as usual, she had no plan on how that would work or who would pay for it, and I would not want to enter into an agreement with her on paying for private school because I believed that I would end up footing the entire bill as Emily would likely start slipping on paying her portion. Therefore, public school was the best option at that moment.

When it came to that public office that she held, Emily made sure that people knew who she was, no matter where she was lol. First, she would wear a pin with her name and the district she represented everywhere she went. If there was an opportunity for her to grab a microphone, she would definitely jump on it and introduce herself as well as the office she held. She even did this one time at an assembly at Dalilah's school. One speaker had finished talking, and there was a quick break before the next speaker so she hopped on the mic and did her spill. No one asked her to come up there. She just did it. That was Emily, though. Her confidence was a great attribute, but still lol.

As Emily got started with the public office, Dalilah ended up spending more time at my house, as well as my parents' home. We were fine with this because if she stayed with Emily, she would end up at town halls and other events that were not exactly suited for kids, and I know this because Emily took her to some of those things when she did not want to find a sitter, or we were busy. It may have been good for Dalilah to be exposed to different experiences on occasion but not all the time, as she still needed to be a "kid" while she was a kid. Dalilah would talk about some of the places that she went with her mother, and how some would be exciting while others were boring because she may have been the only child there.

As Dalilah was in grade school, she began to talk more about things that she was seeing and doing. I would ask her about how things were going at her mother's house, and she would say "ok." I know that Emily likely told Dalilah not to talk about certain stuff when she came to my house because sometimes Dalilah would hesitate when I asked her something. She had a fear of her mom, but it was a fear of retaliation, and not the "respect" fear that we generally regard as good when a child knows not to challenge his or her parents. This would keep her from opening up completely about things that may have been occurring at her mother's house. She later started to open up more as she got a little older once she realized that I would not say anything to her mother if she asked me not to. I noticed that Dalilah would open up to my mom more about some things that she was not comfortable telling me, and I know that this was because if she told me about something that might have been going on with her and her mom that I did not approve of, I would likely confront Emily about it, and if we got into it then Dalilah would not get to see me for a while. Dalilah wanted to avoid anything that would keep her from seeing me, and I think this is why she held a lot inside.

Dalilah did sometimes talk about her true feelings, and it often came out of the blue. One day, we were riding in my car and she told me, "I love my mom but I'd rather live with you, Daddy." I said, "I know you'd rather be with me, baby. You're a daddy's girl!" She replied, "Yeah. But I know I have to go home to my mom eventually. I guess I just tolerate her." I laughed a little, but I also knew that what Dalilah was saying held weight. Even in Dalilah's first few years of existence, it was obvious that she and Emily did not really share a bond like many other mothers and daughters do. Dalilah and I always had a strong bond, and some of that was due to daughters naturally loving their fathers, while the rest was that I just knew how to communicate with her, and I had spent so much time with her since she was born. Emily was not really one to open up about what was going on with her or her true feelings, so I believe that she really did not know how to communicate with Dalilah on an emotional level because she rarely tapped into her own emotions, and I do not believe that Dalilah really wanted to communicate with her mom, either. This would lead Emily to take Dalilah places and let her play to keep her occupied to decrease the time that she would actually have to communicate with Dalilah. I say this because Dalilah would tell me about how they would go places, and then when they got back home, Emily would get on her phone or go to sleep while Dalilah would have to go find something to do in her room, or watch TV.

Dalilah did talk about some things that her mom had said to her that I did not agree with. Faithe had bought Dalilah a salon chair and comb set for her dolls at our house. Dalilah loved this, and she would talk to her dolls while she styled their hair for hours. We noticed that Dalilah was pretty good at doing styles on these dolls. One day, Faithe was doing Dalilah's hair, and I was laying across the bed watching them. Dalilah said, "I wanna be a hairstylist like you when I grow up, Faithe." Faithe smiled and said, "Aww, that's nice, Dalilah. You sure can be one. I can teach you some things." Dalilah then lowered her head and said in a monotone voice, "But my mom said I can't be a hairstylist, and that I'll never be one so don't say that again." Faithe immediately looked at me, and I knew she was furious. I was mad as hell myself when I heard this, and I immediately said, "Dalilah, you can be whatever you want to be in this world. That is your choice, not your mom's. Do you hear me?" Dalilah said, "Yes, daddy."

I knew that Dalilah was still feeling some way about this because she knew she could not go home and tell her mom what I said, as Emily would probably get on her about it, and then Emily would say something to me that would likely cause us to start going back and forth, resulting in me not seeing Dalilah for a little while. Faithe and I talked about what Dalilah said that evening, and I tried to console Faithe because I knew that she already did not like Emily, and for this woman to put down her profession in front of a child was completely unacceptable to her. I told Faithe that I would speak with Emily about this. However, I do not recall if I ever had this conversation with Emily.

I want to briefly discuss two important points here that, as the reader, you should absorb from the last paragraph. First, never tell your child what they CANNOT be when they grow up. In my mind, I may want Dalilah to be a doctor, lawyer, or an actress when she grows up. However, if she walks around the house everyday ringing up items as if she is a cashier and tells me that she would love to be a cashier at a department store when she grows up, and she is extremely happy when she is doing this, then I am going to encourage my child to do whatever it is that will make her happy. It is HER life, not mine. I will show her how she can be a cashier and then run her own business, and she would then be able to show other cashiers how to do the same thing because

Dalilah loved telling people how to do things.

Now, I understand that we have to be reasonable with this and, as good parents, you will try to steer your child towards certain professions. However, if your child has a dream and he or she is extremely passionate about it, and it is something within reason, then please do not shit on their dream because if you steer your child in a direction that they never wanted to go as they grow into an adult, YOU will have to deal with their unhappiness and regrets later in life. I know these are harsh words, but when you crush a child by telling them what they cannot do with their life, you are essentially doing just that - shitting on their dream. I understand Emily's intent with her words, but she often does not know the magnitude of the things that she says sometimes as you will see again later in this chapter, and I am using her error to teach you a valuable lesson.

The second point is that while Dalilah was the one that repeated what she was told by Emily, I knew that these were Emily's words, and not Dalilah's. I know that there are relationships out there where one person or their significant other may not get along well with the co-parent of their child. However, when a child comes to your home and repeats something negative that their other parent said about you or your significant other, please keep in mind that your child is on most occasions speaking their parent's words, and not their own feelings. Faithe understood that Emily was the one that spoke negatively about her profession and not Dalilah, and she governed herself accordingly. However, I have seen situations through other people I know where a parent hears something negative from a child that was said by the other parent, and they take their frustration out on the child instead of the parent that made the negative statement. This is something that I would strongly encourage you NOT to do because the child is just the vessel - the captain is the one responsible for the orders. Remember this because if you repeatedly take out your frustrations with the other parent on your child, he or she will eventually stop confiding in you, and this could cause you to miss out on some critical information that your child needs to convey to you.

Dalilah had three different households that she called home with three different bedrooms that were hers - my house, Emily's house, and my parents' house. This is a blessing for a child to have so much to call her own, but Dalilah also had it tough because she had to adjust to each different household, and this can be tough for a young child. If you grew up in one household with one or both parents, you probably could never relate to this until you read this discussion. There were certain things that Dalilah could not say in my house, and I am sure there were certain things that she could not say in her mom's house, while she could probably talk about whatever she wanted at my parents' house. I understood that she constantly had to think about what she was saying and who she was saying it to wherever she was, and this can be a difficult thing for a child to deal with. However, children love their parents and they will do what they have to do to keep them in their life, so they tolerate it. If you have a child that is between your household and another household, please recognize this, and maybe even sit down with your child and talk about it. Let them know that they do not have to be afraid to talk about whatever they want with you because you understand that they may not have the same freedom in their other household. You may be amazed at what they will start to tell you after that.

Faithe has never been fond of Emily, and this was pretty much solidified in stone once we found out that Emily lied to me about Dalilah being my biological child. Any woman in Faithe's position in this same situation would likely feel the same way that she felt. One thing that I will mention is that while Faithe helped bathe and raise her child, and pretty much gave Dalilah better care than her own mother did, Emily never once directly told her, "Thank you." I believe that Emily may have felt as if that was my job, which I did show my appreciation for Faithe's attention to Dalilah. However, regardless of the verbal communications that transpired between two people in the past, for a woman to do so much for your child and you choose not to show appreciation for it is hard for me to understand. Some mothers may disagree with my statement but imagine how Faithe felt about what was done to me as she helped raise Dalilah.

Another reason that Faithe found it hard to associate with Emily is because Emily was given a child by God, and she did not seem to appreciate the blessing that she had, while Faithe and I had been working very hard to have a biological child of our own since 2012. For a woman to raise someone else's child while she is working hard on blessing her husband with a biological child is extremely tough, both physically and emotionally. I will digress from the story for a moment because it is important to me that I mention that Faithe has undergone two surgeries related to the creation of a child and has been giving her all to have one of her own. This is something that we are still working on as I write this book. Many people out there that have biological children cannot understand or may not even be aware that there are people in the world that have to actually "work" to have a child due to differences with their reproductive systems. People take this ability for granted, and you may have been one of those people until you read this paragraph. However, we do not take this for granted because we fall into that group of people who are "working" to have a child.

Some people are able to bring children into the world via In-Vitro Fertilization (IVF) or a surrogate mother that carries an embryo from another woman that is fertilized by a man. However, IVF procedures cost upwards of $15,000 to $25,000, while using a surrogate mother can cost even more due to the expenses that go towards the surrogate's care during the pregnancy. Therefore, these options are out of reach for many of us that do not have that kind of money sitting in the bank or the means to obtain financing for such an expense. This is something that Faithe and I are also battling, as I am far from rich at the moment that I am writing this book, so we are currently exploring other options that may lead to a successful pregnancy while we work on the financial part. Another fact that goes unnoticed by many people is that some of their favorite celebrities have used IVF or surrogate mothers to produce their children because they can afford it, and it preserves their physical bodies. In recent years, some famous actresses and others have brought awareness to the issue of infertility, and they have been bold enough to tell some of their stories. As we pray for our own biological child, I also want to bring awareness to this issue because it is another mountain that we are climbing while dealing with all of the other issues that I have written about thus far, as well as the ones that you will hear about as you continue to read.

Now I will get back to my story. While co-parenting with Emily was still awkward but somewhat ok, there were some things about our situation that made it hard to do things that may have benefited Dalilah if she was only in my household. This was not Dalilah's fault, but I felt bad about it at times. When Dalilah first started school, Emily was good (for a short time) about doing Dalilah's homework with her. As Dalilah went into the first and second grades, I would notice from Dalilah's homework folder that her mom often was not checking her homework. Dalilah went to the after-school program most days and they allowed the students to do their homework there, so Dalilah was able to get most of her homework done before she came home, and on days when I picked her up we would check it as soon as we got home and do any work that she still needed to do. Faithe actually worked with Dalilah on her homework more than I did, and my mom also worked with Dalilah on the days she picked her up from school, so I will give credit where credit is due.

During Dalilah's first three years of elementary school, including kindergarten, Emily and I never attended one parent-teacher conference together. I always attended when scheduled but Emily missed one or two that the teachers scheduled separately for her. I would also go to Dalilah's classes sometimes during each grade level, so her friends eventually knew when "Dalilah's daddy" was in the room. Emily would come to the school and bring snacks on occasion but sometimes there was something tied to it – some kind of opportunity that she wanted to take advantage of in relation to her career. She would also come around election time and show her face a little more since Dalilah's school was in her district, and the parents of the kids there were a critical voting block for her. My mother also visited the school often and knew the front office people well. They told my mom on multiple occasions that they were not fond of Emily doing minor "campaigning" at the school. However, from what I gathered from Dalilah's teachers, Emily would come to the school for different things, but they often did not discuss Dalilah's actual school work.

When Dalilah was in the second grade, she said that her mom often made her do her homework on her own, and that Emily did not check her folders often. I asked Emily about this from time to time, and she would tell me that she does check Dalilah's stuff. However, at this point, it was easy to see that this was not true most of the time because I could look in Dalilah's folders at the homework that was done on the days that Emily had her and clearly see that some of it was wrong, and these errors would have been caught if Emily was checking it. I guess Emily did not realize that as kids get older, it is easier to see what each parent is doing and what they are not doing. I also noticed that there were permission slips and other things in the folders that required a parent's signature, and much of the time these things would sit in Dalilah's folders until she came back to my house. This often resulting in either me, Faithe or my mom having to go up to the school to sign things and pay for field trips or t-shirts for Dalilah on the day of the actual events. On a couple of occasions, there were even unopened progress reports in the folders that Emily would have seen if she simply looked. I still have some of those report cards and assignments that went unchecked when Dalilah was not with me or my parents in my possession.

I wanted to put Dalilah into sports but this was hard because I could not guarantee that she would get to practice if her mom had her on a particular day, and I also could not work with her as often to get better at the sport that she may have been playing due to our arrangement. When Dalilah was in first grade, I told Emily that I wanted Dalilah to try softball because she needs to be exposed to a sport, and she could use the exercise. I explained that the team practices once or twice a week so I would take responsibility for getting her there and to the games, and Emily could take her on days that she felt like it. She was ok with this, so I signed Dalilah up for a seven and under team at a new park that was located right outside of my subdivision in Lithia Springs.

Dalilah was horrible at softball, and this was mainly because I did not have her with me every day to practice due to her mom having her on some days. My mom and I were present at Dalilah's first game, and Emily also came with two male friends of hers. One of the guys that accompanied Emily was an African guy that she would end up dating and is also the person that she is with as I am writing this book - just a nugget of information that I will expound on later. Emily introduced both men to my mom and I, and they were nice guys.

My mom had brought a cooler with her that had water and sports drinks for Dalilah and me. As the game went on, I noticed that Emily's conversations and cheering for Dalilah got louder. It is no surprise that Emily is always the loudest person wherever she goes, but this loudness was getting a little embarrassing. At this point, I knew that part of the reason for her behavior was because she was sipping small bottles of wine that she had brought and put in my mom's cooler. When the game was over, I just wanted to get out of there because it was hot, and I was also disappointed that Dalilah's coach only let her play one inning - the last inning.

When Dalilah's team practiced the next Tuesday, Faithe came with me to the practice because she had to miss the game that past Saturday due to work. Dalilah's coach had one of her assistants start the practice, and then she walked off the field and came over to Faithe and me, and asked if she could talk to us. We said sure, and the coach then led us over by the closed concession stand to a person whom she introduced as the director of the park. We had also observed a police car parked by the sidewalk that led to the softball fields, and as the director started to talk to us, we realized that an officer had exited the vehicle and was posted halfway up the sidewalk. It was at this moment that we realized that this meeting was organized by the director, and that the officer was there in case we got unruly.

The director began by telling us that she had received reports about two occurrences from the game on Saturday. First, it was reported by the other team that a woman (from their description of her, it was Emily) was at the fence behind home plate encouraging Dalilah to call the other team "losers" as they shook hands with Dalilah's team. Second, parents that were sitting around Emily and her friends in the stands said that they smelled alcohol coming from her direction as she moved around the stands and in front of them. Faithe was not even at the game, but the director seemed to be focusing her frustration at Faithe and I. This really angered Faithe and caught us both by surprise, and it seemed like the director was trying to hold us two accountable when Emily was the one that they had the issue with. The director also hinted that she was considering removing Dalilah from the team because she was trying to establish a great sports program at this new park, and she did not want any parents casting a negative shadow on the park that would be noticed by visiting parks that were already established.

We first apologized for Emily's behavior and assured them that we do not act like her. We then told them that Faithe and I are the ones responsible for Dalilah playing softball, so if they had a problem with Emily, they should take that up directly with her, and I gave them Emily's number. Dalilah's coach knew the kind of person that I was, and she knew that I had nothing to do with that behavior, but she seemed to be somewhat silent during this conversation. Then I noticed that she gradually started supporting the director when she suggested removing Dalilah from the team. I felt that she was doing this because Dalilah was one of the weaker players and she probably did not want her on the team anyway. Now, this coach was a nice lady for the most part, but I did peep this behavior from her and I felt that it was a little shady. The director then told us that Emily was banned from the park due to her bringing alcohol to the facility. I told them that they can call and let her know, but I will also communicate this to her as well. I called Emily that evening and told her what the program director had said. She took it much better than I thought she would, as she simply said, "Oh well, I guess you need to be at all of her practices and games going forward." She never came back to the field after that. Dalilah did finish the season and got her trophy at the banquet so she did get to enjoy that moment with her teammates. The other parents with the "superstar" athletes on the team were also super supportive of Dalilah; I really appreciated that, and I always will.

While I did not feel good about putting Dalilah into sports because I could not work with her often to learn how to play them, she did successfully attend a dance school for a few years in Douglasville that is run by a female friend of my late brother Brian. My mom, Faithe and I would take turns transporting Dalilah to practice, and Emily took her to a few practices too. Dalilah loved to dance, and when the spring and Christmas recitals came, she loved to be on the stage performing what she had learned with her age group. My parents and I attended every recital that Dalilah had. Emily came to most of the recitals but she missed one or two, and she also left early from a few of the recitals for miscellaneous reasons. In the last year that Dalilah danced, Emily was dating the African guy that I first met at the softball game, and he also came to a couple of the recitals. My first time really talking to him was at the second recital that he attended. Neither my family nor I knew his real name until I started to write this book, but he mainly went by his initials - R.J. He was a nice guy, about six feet tall with a thin frame. Faithe also thought that he was a nice guy and a decent person from her interaction with him. I am not sure which country in Africa he is from, but his accent was very heavy, so I understood maybe every third word that he spoke. However, it was enough to piece together what he was saying and he laughed often, so when he did that, I could stop trying to understand him and just laugh, too lol. I asked Dalilah about him from time to time, and she said he treated her fine. It seemed to work.

HERE COMES THE CURVES

Now, I am going to slightly backtrack in order to paint the full picture of the occurrences that would later lead to other events that you will soon read about. As Dalilah went into her elementary school years, Emily started to change when it came to her perspective on our co-parenting situation. In the years before this change started to occur, she would consult me on things that involved Dalilah that I should be aware of, and I appreciated that because that is what parents should do for one another. However, she eventually started to make decisions on things that involved Dalilah without consulting me, and some of these things were very disrespectful in my opinion but I will discuss a few of them and let you be the judge. I mentioned that Emily tended to act as if the custody case and the DNA test proving that Dalilah was not my biological child never happened, and she started to take this approach in some situations as we co-parented in the years to come, doing things that in her mind she seemed to believed that I had to accept as if I was legally obligated to be there for her and Dalilah.

One such instance took place back in 2015. I was working as a contract lease abstractor at a large firm in Buckhead, and I was at Phipps Plaza eating lunch one day when one of my good friends called me. We chatted for a couple of minutes, and then he said to me, "Hey man, did you see the cover of that book that Emily wrote?" My mother had mentioned to me that Emily was publishing a children's book on foster care, but it had nothing to do with me so I did not pay much attention to it. I said, "Nah, I haven't checked it out. Not sure if I'll ever read it." He then said, "I think you should go take a look at the cover when we get off of the phone." I said, "Cool, I'll do it now since I'm on my lunch break." We hung up with each other, and I then went online to look at the book. The cover had the book title, "It's Emily!" Then below that, it said, "By Emily Thompson and Dalilah Thompson." It took a couple of seconds before it hit me as to what was wrong with this: Dalilah's last name is Rounds, not Thompson. This woman actually changed Dalilah's last name on the cover of her book in an attempt to increase sales. Wow. She did this without saying a word to me, not caring about any embarrassment that I would encounter from her doing this because everyone that knew Dalilah and me knows that her last name is not Thompson.

I was mad as shit, and I immediately called Emily. She answered, and I said, "So, why am I looking at the cover of a book that you wrote with Dalilah's last name as Thompson?" She then asked,

"What's wrong with it?"

What's wrong with it? No, I cannot make this stuff up lol.

That was the question that I got. So, I responded, "You don't have any comprehension that you changing her name from Rounds to Thompson is very disrespectful to me and my family? I raise this child just like you do, and then you just erase my last name to benefit you?" I knew she was trying to think of something quick as she replied, "No, I wasn't trying to be disrespectful. I did it to give Dalilah a pen name to protect her since she is a child."

Now, this would make sense if that was Emily's actual intent for doing this, but I knew her well enough to know that this was not her intent. In fact, I knew exactly why she did it. Emily wanted to portray herself as a "single mother" that had been through foster care and was now raising her daughter completely ON HER OWN, when in reality she had never raised Dalilah on her own. This was a persona that she would continue to try to convey as Dalilah became older, and is still doing today, as I will elaborate on later in this chapter. I can prove this - if you know Emily on a personal or professional level and you are reading this book, then there is a strong chance that, if you are not a member of my family or a friend of my family, you probably did not know that neither my family nor I existed before this book. Am I right?

Let me get back to the story. I further explained to Emily why this was disrespectful to me, and that I believed that if she did not think this was disrespectful, she would have told me about the book because she could not hold water when it came to discussing exciting things that involved Dalilah. She apologized for how I felt and said she would see if her publisher would make the change. I am not sure if this was done, but I did a quick check when writing this portion of the chapter and I see that on a few popular book websites, and other not-so-popular websites, Dalilah's last name on the book and in the credits is still listed as "Thompson." It may not have been an easy fix for Emily, but I believe it could have been done if the effort was truly made to do it.

Emily displayed her transition into believing that she was the ultimate decision-maker regarding Dalilah on a number of occasions. While she would act as if she recognized me as a true parent of Dalilah, it was visible that she was now in a mindset where she was going to start doing what SHE wanted to do with the child because she stopped "asking" for my input on affairs involving Dalilah, and instead started "telling" me what she was going to do regarding Dalilah. This happened with no catalyst from me – I never did anything negatively to Emily, so this shift in mindset seem to have come out of nowhere.

I will discuss another occurrence relating to Emily's change because it illustrates an important point when it comes to co-parenting. I had picked Dalilah up from school one Friday early in 2018 because it was my weekend to keep her. The elementary teachers that she had never assigned homework on Fridays, so we went to the playground on our way home, and I let her play for about an hour. We went home, and I decided to fry some chicken since I like to do what I consider "fun" meals on Fridays, which is why I call them "Fun Fridays." Faithe and Dalilah were sitting at the dining room table chatting while I fried the chicken. Dalilah said, "That chicken sure smells good. However, my mom said I can't have any because we're not eating meat anymore." Faithe looked at me and I looked back at her. I know we were both thinking the same thing, so I said to Dalilah, "Your mom never mentioned this to me, Dalilah. However, this is my house, and unless she's buying food over here, which she isn't, you can eat what we eat over here. So, if you want meat then you can have it here. If you don't, then that's fine too." Dalilah replied, "Yes Daddy, I want some chicken." We gave her a plate with some sides and she tore it up lol.

We had a good weekend, and I dropped Dalilah off at school on Monday morning. As I was pulling up to a grocery store that evening to grab a few items for the house, I get a call from Emily. I answered, and as soon as I said hello, she went into a loud rant, "Floyd, how dare you make my child eat meat! We're vegans over here now and I can't believe you would disrespect me by making this child eat meat when we told her not to! Is this what we're doing now? You should never force a child to eat meat, especially when I told her not to!"

Now, there were two things on my mind while she was ranting. First, we never MADE Dalilah eat meat - she said that it smelled good and that she wanted some. However, I know that she told her mom that we made her eat it because she was scared that her mom was going to punish her if eating the meat was her choice. I was ok with Dalilah telling that lie because I knew why she told it, so I would take that one on the chin for my baby. Second, Emily never mentioned anything to me about her household switching to a vegan diet, and I want you to remember those keywords for discussion later: HER HOUSEHOLD. I let Emily finish until she got it all out because I was about to go in on her ass, and when she stopped, I did just that. I said, "Hold up, now. First of all, we never made Dalilah eat meat. She said it smelled good and that she wanted some. Second of all, you never told me anything about not feeding her meat. Dalilah has TWO parents, so you need to run this stuff by me before you make serious decisions regarding her, especially when it comes to her diet. We eat meat in my household so I'm not about to adjust our cuisine and spending based on what you are doing in your house. Now, we've had this discussion before a few times and we seem to keep having to have it - we are supposed to make decisions for Dalilah TOGETHER." Emily calmed down after that, and then said, "Well, I told your mom. I thought I told you." I replied, "No, you didn't. But that doesn't change the fact that you need to ASK me how I feel about that, don't TELL me that this is what we're doing now. There's a difference."

We went on to talk about it further, and I said that I will not force Dalilah to eat anything, but if she does not want meat, I will not give it to her. However, I am not denying her anything that she wants. Just so you know it turned out: all of this eventually went away after about two weeks or so, and Dalilah eventually ate whatever she wanted at my house after that time and I never heard a peep from her mother again about it. I think that this may have been an influence from her boyfriend R.J. but I cannot be sure, as I did not know him well enough to know what he ate - all I essentially knew about him was that he was African and that he treated Dalilah ok.

Now, let's get it straight – I am not against a vegan diet at all. I know that it is a healthy option, and I actually plan to one day give the diet a serious try once I can end my lifelong love story with steaks and juicy burgers. However, the lesson that I want to express to men and women who are co-parenting is:

Never tell the other parent what they WILL do in their home because of what you are doing in YOURS. If both of you are active in the child's life, you make major decisions regarding that child TOGETHER.

If both parents are active in the child's life and one of them forgets this, the co-parenting relationship will become strained and will remain that way until both parents are on one accord. The problem with my situation is that the other parent slowly started to act as if she was the ONLY parent, despite all of the other shit that happened between us in the past that you now know about. Yes, keep reading…

I have mentioned Emily's boyfriend R.J. a few times, and now I can elaborate a little more on his role in this story before I come to the significant event that changed our co-parenting relationship forever. As I mentioned earlier, I did not talk to R.J. much, and this was largely because I did not care to talk to Emily much except for when I had to. However, during the few times that I did encounter R.J., he was very friendly to me, and Dalilah always said that he treated her ok, so I have never had any issues with R.J. and I still do not. I cannot pinpoint exactly how long R.J. had been with Emily, but we did not see him with her regularly until 2017. During that year, she had referred to R.J. as her husband but I had never seen her with a ring on and there was no name change, so I cannot say if they were actually married or just "doing it for the cameras" as they say.

Emily never discussed what R.J. did for a living with me, but she talked to my mom about him and told her that they were working on setting him up politically for a run at the mayoral seat in one of the local towns that was near Emily's political district. However, Emily never really made an attempt to tell me anything about this man, especially since she would end up leaving Dalilah with him for days at a time. I did not know his full name, what he did for a living, or even what African country he was from. I know some of these things now but this knowledge did not come from Emily. R.J. and Emily used to spend some time at my parents' home when they dropped off and picked up Dalilah, so my folks got to know him much more than I did. After all that I had been through with Emily, I just could not sit around and pretend like we were a happy family, so I normally avoided my parents' house when I felt that Emily and R.J. would be there, or when I knew they were there. I was not sure how much R.J. knew about the backstory with Emily, Dalilah and I, but I am sure at that time it was not much, and he still may not know much about it as I write this book. However, regardless of what he thought he knew, he now has access to the full REAL story now if he wants to know it.

My parents talked to R.J. on many occasions, both in person and via video calling. I did not make a big deal about the relationship that my parents had with R.J. because there was no jealousy there, and my mom would also come back and feed me information about things that were going on in Emily's household because I did not care to really have small talk with Emily due to our history, which you as the reader should now have a decent understanding of. Now that I look back on it, I probably should have had a better handle on this association because it seemed like there was an element of my situation with Dalilah that I could not control due to there being three parties involved, but it had its advantages and disadvantages. My dad also had a pretty good relationship with R.J., and he even went to help R.J. one time when the tire on his car blew out close to the Alabama border, which is about forty-five minutes from where my parents live. Remember this relationship between my father and R.J. because it has some significance later in this chapter.

I spoke earlier about Emily's mindset seeming to change into her believing that she was the sole decision maker for Dalilah, and it seemed to become more prevalent during her relationship with R.J. As we had spats in recent years about Dalilah, Emily started to get away from the references of Dalilah being OUR child and started to move more towards Dalilah being HER child. I do not know if this shift was being caused by R.J.'s take on the situation due to what he had been told by Emily or if she had just gone back and read the legal documents that we signed early on giving her sole custody, or if she was just flipping the script on me mentally. Either way, this was a sign that things were moving in a different direction, and it was not the right one.

In the next phase of Emily's shift in behavior, I noticed that she gradually started to do what I considered "phasing my family out" of her and Dalilah's world. I believe that this was for two reasons. First, as Dalilah had grown, she was able to do more things on her own such as dress herself and bathe herself (we would let Dalilah bathe herself at my house but we would always make sure she cleaned herself thoroughly, while I do not believe that Emily always checked Dalilah after she bathed herself). Therefore, due to Dalilah's growing independence, Emily did not need me or my family as much as she did in the earlier years. I believe that the second reason for this shift is that, despite what she agreed on with me when Dalilah was a baby, Emily never planned to tell Dalilah the truth about her biological father unless Dalilah found out on her own one day. I think that as she settled into her relationship with R.J., she saw a way to possibly dodge ever having to explain anything to Dalilah. Therefore, in Emily's head, she could try to replace our family with her own involving R.J. and Dalilah. I do not believe that R.J. was behind this because I believe that he did not, and still does not, know the full history of Emily and me. However, he may have encouraged this somewhat by being ignorant to the complete facts of our story, which I do not blame him for.

The next thing that I noticed was that Emily started trying to get Dalilah from me on days that we had already designated as mine. At this point, which started in early 2018, she was already keeping Dalilah during the weekdays and I was getting her every other weekend, which I did not totally agree with because I learned from people close to Emily that R.J. was the person that was helping Dalilah with her homework most of the time since Emily would not be at home some evenings. This was another example of her dictating the days and expecting me to fall in line with that instead of asking me, which goes back to my earlier point that in situations where both parents of a child are active in that child's life, major decisions need to be AGREED upon and not DICTATED by one parent to another. It got to a point where I would ask Emily if she needed me to watch Dalilah on a weekend where she was designated to keep her if she had something to do or wanted a break. She would say, "No, I'll keep her because we're going to do some things together over the weekend." I would then learn the next week that Emily went out of town and left Dalilah with R.J. for the entire weekend, and sometimes longer than just a weekend when she could have just left her with me. Now, I cannot tell that parent what to do with her weekend because it is technically "her" weekend with Dalilah, but why leave her at home with her companion when she could have just left her with me? It would be different if R.J. wanted to watch Dalilah for a whole weekend, but from my conversations with my parents who would be in touch with R.J. sometimes during these periods, as well as things said by Dalilah, who was nearly eight years old at this time, I believe that R.J. did it out of respect for his relationship with Emily and would have not objected to Dalilah coming with me for the weekend. Some readers may not understand where I am coming from with this and why I felt the way that I felt, but I know many of you will.

Another occurrence happened on Easter Sunday in 2018. It was my weekend with Dalilah, and we had a good time hanging out on Friday and Saturday. On Sunday, my mom took Dalilah to church for the holiday. Emily called me around noon and asked if she could get Dalilah for the rest of the day. I told her, "Nah, this is my weekend so we're good. It's a nice day so we are going to enjoy it." Emily replied, "Well, that's MY daughter, and I want to get her for the holiday so I can spend time with MY daughter." I emphasize the word "MY" because that is how she used it. I said, "Well, she's actually OUR daughter, and I said it's my day. I only get her every other weekend so you can just pick her up from school tomorrow." Emily then said, "Well, I was planning to take her to an Easter egg hunt so she can have fun today." I thought about how much Dalilah loved egg hunts, so I said, "Well, I guess that's ok if you're doing something like that with her."

I called my mom, who was on the way home from church with Dalilah. I told her that Emily is going to get Dalilah and keep her for the rest of the day because she was taking her to an Easter egg hunt. My mom had the Bluetooth on in her car, so Dalilah heard this and immediately started crying. She did not want to go, and my mom tried to dispute me on this. However, I had had prior conversations with my mother about her questioning my decisions in front of Dalilah because the child would then think she could do the same, and I knew that Dalilah would be hurt, but I had to stand my ground and say, "No, she's going with Emily, and that's that." I still was not sure why Dalilah had gotten as upset as she did even after I said she was going to an Easter egg hunt because she loved those. I met Emily at QuikTrip, and Dalilah went with her for the rest of day.

I ended up getting Dalilah back that next afternoon because Emily had an event to attend that evening. As Dalilah and I drove off after picking her up from school, she said to me, "Daddy, I was very mad at you for making me go home with my mom yesterday but it's ok. I forgive you." Isn't this child the best? This makes me want to cry as I write this. I replied, "I'm so sorry, baby. You know I never want to make you mad at me for anything. I just thought that you would enjoy going to an Easter egg hunt. How was the hunt, by the way?" Dalilah said to me, and this shit still infuriates me to this day: "We didn't go to an Easter egg hunt, Daddy. I knew we weren't going to an egg hunt as soon as you told me, and I told Granny that. That's why I cried."

Now, you have already read about some of the horrible things that I have had to endure from Emily, but this had to be one of the things that she did that hurt me the most, and it hurt me to the core. This woman lied to me to get my child on Easter, and then sat at home and did not do a damn thing with her. And she did this knowing that Dalilah did not want to come home. This was tough before me because I felt as if I could not approach Emily with this due to her possibly taking it out on Dalilah for even telling me, and it seemed as if I was slowly losing my control of this co-parenting situation. I felt like Emily was starting to treat the situation as if she could do what she wanted when it came to Dalilah. But after all that I had done for her and Dalilah, why start acting like this?

Had she really forgotten about her past?

Dalilah was growing and was now more courageous in discussing her true feelings about her mother and the things that were going on in their household. She told me that Emily did not really have a reason for trying to keep her more, but it was more of Emily just not wanting Dalilah to come spend much time with us anymore. Dalilah did not completely understand why her mother was doing this, but it was starting to become apparent to me. I believe that Emily may have had some longtime emotions that she kept inside about how I viewed our co-parenting situation as just what it was to me: we were not friends or family - we were co-parenting and that was it. She also was not very fond of Faithe, and with her newfound "control" of our situation, she was able to do whatever it took to make things harder for Faithe and me emotionally. I think that these emotions and her current relationship with R.J. led her to conclude that she did not need me or my family anymore, and that it would be better for her image and future if it appeared as if she raised Dalilah completely on her own, and then completed the family with R.J.

I knew that Dalilah would not understand her mother's reasoning and actions, so I just told her I would work with her mother the best way that I could on seeing her more. Dalilah and I would talk about her feelings on the weekends and occasional weekdays as she came over, and we would go to the park near my home where she would ride her bike (which I taught her to ride since she said she never rode the bike that Emily had for her at her house - yes, I want my credit for this so I am throwing it in here). I could see Dalilah growing emotionally and mentally, and it was beautiful to see. However, I knew she had a lot on her heart, and I could tell because she would have occasional outbursts where she would cry extremely hard and say she just wanted to spend time with me. These outbursts would have me on the verge of crying myself because no man wants to see his daughter in this kind of emotional pain, especially at such a young age. However, I had to be tough for her in these moments because I was supposed to be her protector, but deep down I felt like I was failing at this, and I am crying now because, while I know that my child loved me with every ounce of her soul, she was slowly starting to see that it was becoming hard for me to protect her from the emotions that she was dealing with. I knew how she was feeling, but this was tough because we are dealing with a mother that would rather watch her child suffer emotionally while she looked after her own interests. This has been hard for me and others that I have talked about this situation with to understand, but that is "Emily." She will act like she is all about Dalilah in public, and she will not let anyone else hurt her child, but she is willing to hurt her own kid emotionally with her actions.

One day during that spring of 2018, the elementary school that Dalilah attended called me at 6:00 p.m. informing me that Dalilah had not been picked up. This was an issue because the after-school program shut down at 6:00 p.m. Emily knew this, and this was her day to pick Dalilah up, so I called her twice and she did not answer, of course. She then called back a few minutes later and said that something had happened to her tire, and that she and R.J. were on the way to pick up Dalilah. I said, "You know that it's not good for Dalilah to be the last child left at the school. You also know that you could have called me way before now to go get her until you got back over this way. Why didn't you just do that?" She had a slight attitude when she responded, "I'm on my way to get her now so don't worry about it!"

As she hung up, I started to think to myself, "Does Emily even care that Dalilah is the last child at the school?" I know that many single parents may have situations come up where you cannot make it to your child's school on time, and if you have no one else to pick your child up, then they just have to wait until you get there - yes, I get this. You would probably call the school as well to let them know that you are running late. However, Emily declined to let the school know that she would be there after 6:00 p.m., and Dalilah had a father, stepmother and grandparents that would have been willing to go pick her up with just a simple text or call asking us to do so. Instead, Emily chose to let her stay at school knowing that she would arrive well after the after-school program closed. I cannot come up with a positive explanation for this. Can you?

Things finally took a turn for the worst in April 2018. Emily called me up on a Monday and said that she wanted to sit down with me to discuss some things regarding Dalilah's future. This was weird because it seemed to come out of the blue, but since it was regarding Dalilah's welfare, I agreed. Faithe and I fell out right after that phone conversation for the rest of the evening because I agreed to meet Emily without consulting her about it. I later understood how Faithe felt and that it was wrong of me to not include her if she wanted to be involved, so I apologized and told her that I will let Emily know that she was coming, too. However, Emily texted me the next day and said she wanted to cancel, and that was that. I am not sure what she was planning on talking about, but I later got an idea as you will see in the next few paragraphs.

It was Wednesday, April 18th. Emily was to have Dalilah for the upcoming weekend based on our alternating schedule. I hit her up earlier in the day and told her that I did not have anything going on that weekend, and that I could get Dalilah if she needed me to but, if not, then I would just wait until the following weekend. She did not respond at that time, but sometimes she did not reply right away so this was not out of the ordinary. However, I was expecting an explanation at least by early afternoon because she would usually get back to me in a few hours at the latest. It was not until that evening when was leaving the gym that Emily finally hit me up.

I am going to separate this particular conversation in an effort to break it down so you can better understand it because it is critical to the rest of this chapter and the entire book.

Emily:

"Hi Floyd. Sorry, I'll be keeping Dalilah all weekend. And next Friday as well since it's her talent show. I know she would love for you to come."

Me:

"Ok. This weekend is fine since it's your weekend. However, next Friday is my day so I'll be keeping her. We need to just make sure we ask each other about these decisions as we've been doing."

Emily:

"Dalilah has worked very hard on this talent piece and I promised her that I would take her out after that. I'm sorry but this is NON-NEGOTIABLE."

(Yes, she told the man that she lied to about this child that still raised her for nearly eight years that this decision was NON-NEGOTIABLE. Meaning HE has no say so.)

Me:

"It is negotiable, and if you want to start making decisions and not respecting mine, we need to go ahead and have another conversation so we can decide how to move forward because I'm not going back to that old shit. Those days are long gone and they're not coming back."

Emily:

"Wow! Are you threatening me because I want to be with MY OWN child? You really have gone way too far. Tread lightly."

(There is that "MY" word again, and she even added "OWN" this time. On top of that, the woman that went 20 months before I had to take her to court and find out the truth about this child, and deal with all of her shit before and after that is telling me that "I" went too far? Really?)

Me:

"This isn't a threat - it's the TRUTH. Dalilah has a father too. I'm not sure what's gotten into you recently but don't ever tell me something is not negotiable when it comes to her. I'm done with this for the evening so you can call me tomorrow and we can discuss what we need to discuss about moving forward."

Emily:

"Yeah, you are right. You are DONE."

I will mention this here before I move on with the story because I feel it is important:

Believe it or not, aside from a simple "Hey" at a grocery store around four months after the above conversation occurred, as of the time this book is being published at the beginning of the summer of 2019, this was the last conversation that I had with Emily, and she has not attempted to put Dalilah in contact with me since then.

I was still sitting in the parking lot of the gym in Mableton while all of this took place on my phone, and I was in complete awe. There were many things wrong here, and I know that if you are a father who has been in a similar situation or you are a REAL mother, or any person with some sense in general, you can quickly see all the parts of this that were not good. First, as a parent, you never tell the other active co-parent that a decision regarding your child is "non-negotiable." Next, Emily referred to Dalilah as HER OWN child, which solidified how I was suspecting that she was now viewing my role in Dalilah's life. She then went on to tell me that I was "threatening" her by saying that we would have a conversation on how to move forward if this continued. If this woman views telling her daughter the TRUTH about her life as a threat, then she mentally is not in her right mind, and she really did intend on living a lie for the rest of her life. The icing on the cake was not even the "Yeah, you are done" part, but the "Tread lightly" statement. You can probably feel my pain at that moment I heard this, but she was really talking to me like I was some nigga off of the street, like I had not ever done anything for her. I had immediately made some decisions in my mind at that time that were very tough for me to do, but I knew they had to be made for the sanity and welfare of my home and my family. I cranked up my Hyundai Genesis and took it on to the house, in complete silence.

I walked into my home and went straight for the kitchen. Faithe was sitting on our sectional couch in the living room that is right in front of the stairs that led from the front door, so I had to walk past her as the kitchen was to the right, behind the couch. She said, "How was your workout?" I said, "It was good, but I'm not in a good place right now. That woman has crossed the line with me for the last time. I need a drink!" Faithe said, "You must be talking about Emily! What did she do now?" I unintentionally made her wait in suspense while I fixed my bourbon and Coke with a splash of lime, and I sat down on the couch and told her what happened. Faithe was in complete awe as I was, and said exactly what I had felt at the moment that conversation took place: "She had the audacity to say that to you after all that we've done for her? After all that your family has done for her? And she's out here acting like y'all don't even exist? That woman is disrespectful as hell. And she's disrespectful to someone that has never done anything to her - you've actually only done good things for her. Wow. I don't have any other words for this. I'm sorry that you've had to deal with her for so long." All I could say to this is, "Yeah, that's what she said. I'm not sure what's gotten into Emily, but she has burnt her bridge with me and ruined our relationship for good."

Faithe and I continued to discuss what had happened, and I told her that I have concluded that I need to back away from this entire situation with Emily because I could no longer deal with a person that has lost complete respect for everything that I had done for her. I was being treated as if I did not matter for unknown reasons, and it simply was not right. Emily had become TOXIC to my marriage, as well as my family because she was dangling Dalilah in front of us and then pulling her back whenever she felt like it, as she had often done when she did not get her way. This was not right, and I could not continue to allow Emily to do this to my family and me. The part of my decision that was going to hurt the most was that I would also have to back away from Dalilah, and that hurt me to the core. I had made the decision to cut Emily from my life completely, and I knew that this would include Dalilah until she was old enough to be able to interact with me on her own. However, this particular conversation on this particular night was the catalyst that sparked the creation of this book, so Emily changed the world that night and did not even realize it.

I wrote this book for other reasons as well, but it was also to deliver messages to Emily that she will likely hear indirectly as well as show other parents in similar scenarios on how to, and how not to approach certain situations. I know some readers may ask, "Why did you have to walk away from Dalilah, too?" I think that this may be hard for you to understand if you have not been a man in a situation similar to this, but after I had done all that I had done for Emily, even after being lied to years back, and then over and over again after that, and to then be treated like I was not shit when all I ever did was good for her, I had reached my breaking point.

Yes, I was a father to Dalilah, but I am a MAN first.

I could only tolerate so much disrespect, especially when it was not deserved. We did not always agree on things and that is the nature of human beings, but I would be surprised if Emily could tell you one truthful BAD thing that I did to her, while I have a whole repository of documents and images proving the GOOD things that I did for her, and you have already read about much of it. I am not a perfect man by any means, but I know without a doubt that I was a damn good co-parent to Emily and an amazing father to Dalilah, and no one can ever take that away from me. Not even Emily.

I called my mother the next morning and told her about the conversation. She was shocked and very pissed, as I knew she would be. I told my mother about my decisions on how I was moving forward with the situation. She was slightly hesitant to get all the way behind me because of her love for Dalilah, and that could be understood because we had dedicated so much to this child - my mom had a whole bedroom at her home just for Dalilah with customized pillows and all - but she eventually understood what I had to do and she supported me. She asked me about trying to get custody or some sort of legal visitation, and this is where I reminded her about the documents that I signed early on when I found out that Dalilah was not mine. I felt the need to protect myself but, in turn, I gave all rights regarding Dalilah to Emily. Do you remember earlier in the chapter when I said that would bite me in the ass? Well, the pit bull was locking his jaws into my ass at that moment lol. I could not foresee the future so I did what I did for me. However,

I would caution other men who are currently looking to protect their rights to their child to make sure that you do not sign a document relieving you of all rights to your offspring unless this is truly what you want. My mom asked, "Is there anything else that you can do to get rights to Dalilah?"

I told her:

"I don't think so unless Emily was a totally unfit mother and was on drugs, or endangering Dalilah to a point where I could prove it. And I have no proof of that. But you have to look at it from my perspective - the father in this situation. I was the one that was ultimately lied to about this child. I was the one that made the decision to still raise this child with a woman that I did not really even care for. And now this woman wants to make things difficult for me, after all that I did for her? I could call her and fuss with her every day for the next ten years about seeing this child, but why should I? Do I deserve that? Emily has forgotten about what really happened in the past, and if she does remember, she has sure lost respect for all that was done for her for the past eight years. Most importantly, Emily has forgotten that I never had to be here for her and Dalilah - THIS WOMAN SHOULD NOT MAKE ANYTHING HARD FOR ME WHEN IT COMES TO DALILAH."

When I agreed to raise Dalilah after Emily's lie had been exposed years back, I told her that if she ever made it hard for me to be in Dalilah's life, then I would no longer be in her life until it is on Dalilah's terms. Emily had started to make it tough for me to strengthen my relationship with Dalilah over the past few years for her own reasons, and her actions put strains in other areas of my life such as in my marriage as well as my parents having to deal with the stress of Emily dangling Dalilah.

If you do not get anything else from this book, please get this:

Emily had become TOXIC to my life. When something becomes toxic in your life, its toxicity will affect areas of your life much like a hazardous spill. Your life, relationships, and energy will continue to be toxic until you clean up the spill. I made the decision to rid myself of this toxicity for good.

It may come with some sacrifices, but to be completely happy, you must eliminate TOXICITY from your life.

My mom told me that morning after we talked about my decision that she was planning to go to Dalilah's school for Field Day. I had not seen Dalilah in a couple of weeks before that day and my mom had not either, so my mom said that Dalilah was happy to see her when she got there. She showed my mom off to her friends outside, as usual, saying, "This is my Granny. My Granny!" Then they would all laugh and play like kids play. My mom asked the teacher if she could take Dalilah for a walk. She agreed, and said that Dalilah could take my mom back to the classroom and show her a project that the class worked on together. When they got back to the room, my mom said Dalilah asked her to sit with her for a second. Dalilah then said, "Granny, don't tell anyone what I'm about to tell you, especially my mommy, ok?" My mom said, "Ok, I won't!"

Dalilah then said,

"My mommy told me why I won't be seeing you and Daddy that much anymore."

My mom asked, "And why is that?"

Dalilah answered,

"*Because my mommy said we aren't blood, and I won't see y'all much anymore. But out of R.J. and my Daddy, you know I love my Daddy the most.*"

Wow.

Really?

After all that I had done for Emily and this child, this woman robbed me of the right, the opportunity to sit with my child and have this conversation. Just dagger after dagger, and I still do not know what I ever did to this woman to deserve this kind of disrespect. A man raises your child after knowing that she is not his, and you do not even have enough respect to give him a chance to be there when you explain the truth to her? As the reader, don't you think that is a little fucked up? I am sure you do.

Emily had not said anything to me since that last conversation, and she still has not, but after knowing her for so long, it started to become clear what was going on. Once Emily gets mentally comfortable in a certain situation and believes she can finish the situation on her own, whether it is a financial arrangement with someone or a situation such as the one I had with her, she tends to let her pride overtake her mind, and this leads her to say horrible things that she really should think about before they leave her mouth. She will say these things to anyone, no matter how much they have done for her, as you have clearly seen here. However, instead of having the empathy (and common sense) to simply right her wrongs with people, there is just something in her that causes her to say whatever she needs to say to cut the cord, *and she simply walks away*. Has this theme started to sound familiar? In this case, Emily obviously felt that something was going to be said to Dalilah so she had to beat me to the punch. By this point, she had already done permanent damage to our co-parenting relationship by being extremely disrespectful with that last conversation, whether she intended to or not, but what is even more disrespectful is that she still made no attempt to repair the situation, acting as if I owe her, and not the other way around.

After Dalilah said that last statement to my mom, she said, "Let's go back outside so we can see what's going on, Granny." My mom took Dalilah back outside, and she commenced playing with her friends. I knew that Dalilah was mentally preparing herself to deal with not seeing me like she was used to by attempting to block it out, and while this was a horrible trait in her mother, I felt that Dalilah's acquisition of this trait from Emily would help her better deal with this absence of her "father." And until this book was written, and it may be some time after this book comes out because I know she will block this part of her life out as long as she can, Emily likely has no clue that Dalilah and my mom had that conversation, or that I am aware of what she said to Dalilah.

As my mother was leaving the school that day, she saw Emily coming in the front door. I did not ask much about what was said, but my mom said it basically involved Emily first acting as if nothing had happened, and then once my mother called her out on it, she said that it was something that was blown out of proportion, and that she would let things cool down and contact me about it later. My mom pretty much told Emily that she knew she had crossed the line and things would now be different, and that she knew that. However, my mom did not mention to Emily what Dalilah had just told because she did not want the child getting in trouble for simply saying what was on her mind and heart. There was no room for emotions and the TRUTH in Emily's home. We also knew that Emily probably did not think hard about what she said to me before she said it, and probably pushed things further than she planned to, so she reacted to that by saying what she said to Dalilah. That pride went to her head the night before and ended up changing Emily's and her daughter's life. As I just mentioned, Emily does not have the courage to correct her wrongs, so she just leaves it as is. *And walks away like it never happened.* Same theme, huh?

A few days after the visit to the school, my mom had a conversation with Emily's sister Cerita about what had happened. My mom also spoke to Emily's mother, who resides in Tennessee, about the situation because they talked on occasion. My mom said she received a text from Emily shortly after those conversations stating that if my mom contacted her mother again, Emily would have her lawyer contact my mom. We just laughed at this because it was funny and sad at the same time. It was funny because we knew Emily did not have a lawyer, and that was just her way of getting rid of people that she has gotten over on. However, it was sad because she was talking like this to a woman that helped her all the way from her pregnancy with Dalilah through the present day, when my mother never had to be there for her. This is what this woman named Emily considers "respect."

As I explained earlier, I had to eliminate Emily from my life because she had become toxic to it. Therefore, I was not going to contact her again. By doing this, I had to also step back from Dalilah. I would not speak to her on her birthday in May 2018, and that hurt me a lot. I could have called on her birthday, and even showed up on her last day of school, but I could not be cordial with her mom and act as if nothing happened like she would because those days were done for me. I believed that, while it would be hard for me to see Dalilah, it would be even harder for Dalilah to see me occasionally on these big days because she would not get to spend as much time with me as she wanted, and her mother would be there hovering to make sure I did not say something to Dalilah that she did not want her to hear, which would result in me likely saying something to her mother, and that would cause verbal conflict. I could maybe get Dalilah for a night or two, but eventually I would have to deal with Emily to keep her for as long as I deserved to, and I refused to allow a woman to dictate when I can and cannot see a child that I never had to do anything for. Dalilah would then have to go back home and not be sure of when she would see me again. It was not always like that with Emily, but she had changed, and I was not about to start playing the game.

I felt that Dalilah needed to get used to not seeing me often so she could adapt to the situation, and still be productive with her life mentally and emotionally until I could deal with her directly because I was no longer going through Emily. I know that if you are a woman who is a single parent with a child, you are probably saying to yourself as you read this that if you were in this situation, you view of the father trying to raise your child would be something like, "I was not honest with you for nearly two years of your life, and you found out that you are not my child's biological father, and you still want to be a part of her life? Shit, you can get her whenever you want for as long as you want. In fact, how much money do you need for the week? Wanna keep her for the summer? Ok, let me know how much summer camp is and I will put something on it. I appreciate you being here for my child when you did not have to. I am so lucky because there are SO many women out there that wish they had a man like you in their child's life." For some reason, Emily was the one woman out of probably a billion that just was not capable of appreciating what she had, and she eventually took it for granted.

Oh yeah - while I am mentioning summer camp, I paid for that for Dalilah as well, for multiple summers. Just one of the other things that I took responsibility for over the years I helped raise her.

I mentioned earlier that my dad's relationship with R.J. seemed to be a good one. Therefore, after not ever hearing from R.J. again after my last conversation with Emily, my dad was extremely disappointed with him because he could not see how a man that knew the kind of father I was and the kind of people that my parents were could just fade away into the shadows after a situation such as this unfolded. My dad believed that if R.J. was a real man, he would have questioned Emily as to why Dalilah was not going to see her father anymore, and if he did not get satisfactory answers from her, he should then reach out to my parents or me to find out why this was going on because he had contacted them directly before this happened.

I told my parents that I do not place any blame on R.J. because I truly believe that he did not know the truth about what was really going on, or he might have been told a little bit but definitely did not know everything about what his woman had done in the past when it came to our situation with Dalilah. Therefore, he was just being a man and going with what his woman had told him. We know that Emily has always been a master with the tongue because that is how we were manipulated into this situation back in 2009, and she has even talked her way into a political position. Therefore, there is no telling what this man had been told about our family and me.

Faithe believes that R.J. knows a little about the situation and may have just decided that, since I am not Dalilah's biological father, that maybe they should carry on and just be their own family. However, she agrees that R.J. likely does not know the full truth. I believe that R.J. does not know much of anything about what happened in the past, except for maybe Emily telling him that I am not Dalilah's biological father. I doubt that Emily has told anyone the full, REAL truth that I have revealed here in this book about the full history of Dalilah's coming into existence and the years after. However, I will not hate on any man and tell him what to do with his own relationship because that is breaking the G-code, but if R.J. ever wants to know more about the truth surrounding the daughter that he has spent a significant amount of his time helping to raise as this book makes its way around the world, *he knows exactly where he can go to find it, if he cares to.* I will just leave that right there for him to pick up if he so chooses.

Here is a quick note for you step-parents out there: if your significant other has a child with someone else and you slowly stop seeing that child as much or eventually not at all, or the child is starting to be kept more by your significant other and not seeing his or her other parent as often with no explanation from your partner, there is likely an issue going on between your partner and the other parent. You should explore this further because if it is affecting your significant other mentally or emotionally, it WILL eventually affect your household

.

The toughest part of this situation was knowing what Dalilah would have to go through over the next few years until I could interact with her directly. Emily's reaction to tough situations is to just walk away. However, I truly believe that she thinks that her eight-year-old child's mind is supposed to work like her thirty-one-year-old mind. I am sure that Dalilah cannot talk to her mom about not being able to see me and my family (as well as my extended family that was involved with her) because her mom simply wants her child to "forget" about her father, so she has to hold all of these emotions in, and that can be extremely tough and dangerous for a child. That is pretty deep, and if you are a mother, you are probably wondering how a mother can sit there and watch her child suffer emotionally like that.

My mom has spoken to a family member of Emily's that has been around Dalilah after my last conversation with Emily took place, and this person mentioned that they could observe that Dalilah was mentally distant at times due to the situation. I know that if someone that rarely sees Dalilah can notice this, then her own mother definitely does. If Emily really put Dalilah's emotions before her own pride like she will act as if she is doing when they are around other people, she would give Dalilah a phone and say, "Call your Dad. He doesn't really deal with me anymore, but YOU need to talk to him because he's an important part of your life." However, Emily's pride comes before her child's emotions, and she has chosen not to do this. Therefore, I continue to pray every day for Dalilah and her emotional health until I am able to interact directly with her again.

PRESENT DAY

So, I bet you are wondering what is going on with this situation as I write this book? Well, I can bring you to the present day. Neither my parents nor I had heard from Emily after my conversation with her in April 2018 and her text to my mom that May with the threat about the lawyer. I learned in August 2018 that Emily moved Dalilah to a different elementary school, and this knowledge came from an email generated by an online lunch and after-school payment program that was used at Dalilah's previous school and is also used at her new school. Therefore, once again, Emily did not give me the respect of telling me that she was doing this. If it was not for that email, I probably would not know what school that child was going to.

Emily also switched residences during this time, which I had no knowledge of. My mom mistakenly butt-dialed Emily's phone the day after Christmas in December of that same year, and Dalilah answered. She spoke to my mom briefly, and after a minute, Emily got on the phone. This led to Emily asking my mom if she wanted to keep Dalilah for a few hours that day, and my parents met them in Mableton. They brought Dalilah back to the house and let her play with her dolls, and some friends of the family that were already going over to my parents' home that day got a chance to see her as well. I spoke with Dalilah via video calling that say and she was so pretty. She had grown a little, and she was showing me that her top front teeth had grown back in. She said that she missed me and that she dreamed about all of us every night. This made me feel good, and I told her that I loved her and that I dreamed about her often as well. She was speaking very well and that was great to hear.

My mom told me later that day after dropping Dalilah back off that the child was understanding the situation, and that while she knew that my relationship with her mom was ruined, she also knew that I loved her very much, and that her mom was the reason why she was not seeing me. However, while this brief communication happened between Emily and my mother, Emily never spoke of the situation to my mom, and she has not said one word to me - the person that gave eight years of his life to her and Dalilah. I knew that she would take chances and deal with my mom instead of me because she knows that my parents will not exactly hold her accountable for her actions because they just want to see Dalilah, but I will. I also know Emily well enough to know that she is somewhat like a turtle - she wears a tough outer shell that is nearly impenetrable, but inside she is as soft as a marshmallow. She cannot handle the truth, so she walks away from it when it comes back to confront her, and she cannot face me after what I have done for her, so she will continue to avoid that until she has to. And when she does see me, she will not speak of anything in the past because she does not want to face it.

While Emily will not admit it, this situation, along with the many other negative things that she has done to others, has to weigh heavily on her conscience, and I hope one day she can rebuild who she is and release that box of crows from her soul. Even after all of the things that you have read about that are very true, I still will not say that I hate her because those are very powerful words. While I do hate what she did, and you probably do as well, I cannot carry hate on my heart because that would waste energy that God wants me to enjoy, and that would keep me from being happy. I also know that Emily will have to deal with the consequences of her actions one day, so she will have her time to answer for everything that she has done, especially in this situation. However, I will say that while Dalilah will always have a place in my life, and I know that I will have to see her mother from time to time because it is inevitable, I do not care to ever communicate with Emily any further, and she will not ever be welcomed into my life again under any circumstances.

All future dealings regarding Dalilah will be directly with Dalilah when she is able to contact and eventually see me on her own.

As for me, while I do miss seeing Dalilah, I am relatively happy at the moment because I know that I will be able to interact with her on her own in the coming years. At first, I was scared that Dalilah would forget about what I had done for her and eventually develop anger towards me and my absence that would be fueled by things that her mother might or might not say to her about the situation. However, with reassurance from Faithe and my family, along with my video conversation that I had with Dalilah in December 2018, I no longer have that fear, and I look forward to the day that I can walk and talk with Dalilah on my own. That may be a year out or a few years away, but I know it will happen, and Dalilah and I will embrace it. I know Emily will always have something to do with Dalilah's life, but I do not ever have to deal with her again regarding Dalilah and that is satisfaction in itself.

Faithe and I have moved to an exciting area in metro Atlanta, and we are enjoying our new environment. My parents are also living their best lives, traveling annually to different destinations such as Aruba, Jamaica, and Hawaii. My dog Lady is also doing well - she is currently twelve years old (in human years) and will be 13 in October 2019, Lord willing. Our BTRYA association started a Uniform Exchange at Dalilah's previous school, and it is thriving. It was put in place to help families save money on school clothes by being able to have access to new or gently worn school uniforms that are donated by other families at the school once their children grow out of them. The school can also use the uniforms to replace clothing that kids soil or stain during the school day.

I have not really broadcasted the situation with Dalilah to the world (well, until now), but I have started to tell those close to me the truth about what has transpired over the past ten years, all the way from Emily's lie at the beginning of her pregnancy up to my last conversation with her. When each person hears my story, they have the same reaction that you probably did as you read this chapter. They are simply shocked, and they often ask what is mentally wrong with Emily. They then always tell me that my family and I are angels for the life we gave to Dalilah, and that she will never forget what we have done for her, but her mother will one day have to answer for her actions, whether it happens on this Earth or not.

One thing that I will note that is interesting is that most of Emily's family, including those closest to her, have known the truth about Dalilah for years, and Emily likely is not aware of this until now. Some of them have known ever since I found out about it. They just do not approach Emily about it because they know her well enough to know how she will react - she will try to come up with something quick to say to push blame back on me and my family, and then she will either change the subject or start an argument with the person confronting her, and then disappear with Dalilah for a while. That "walk away" theme never goes away, as you see.

On my end, I am doing well. It is true what they say - once you release things that have weighed on you for some time, you feel much better. While I still have areas of my life in which I can improve, I can say that I did very well as a father, and when God brings Dalilah back to me, I can continue to be a good father to her while helping her to heal and seek the answers to the questions that she may have, as well as the answers to questions that we all have regarding our situation. I am doing well emotionally, but in the future, I know that Dalilah will help me patch up that area of my spirit that was damaged by her mother and Dalilah's absence from my life as a result of that damage.

From what I hear, Emily is still being Emily. I was informed during the composition of this book that she will soon be giving birth to another child. I wish her good luck with that because that child's support system definitely will not be the same as Dalilah's, and I hope she has matured maternally to give that child the care that it needs without repeating some of the mistakes that were made in Dalilah's early days. This particular human life will be solely on her and her husband, and while Dalilah will always be a part of my family and will be welcomed back in our lives when she is able, neither I nor my family will have anything to do with this second child because we no longer associate with its mother and father. I know that sounds harsh but it is what it is, and you probably do not blame me one bit for my position on this. However, children are innocent, precious creatures and they deserve the best, and I hope this next child can get that.

Emily is also still involved in her political career. She was first elected to her State legislature position in 2014, and was then re-elected in 2016 and 2018 so that gift of gab has served her well. You can catch her on TV from time to time hopping in front of the camera with a reporter at the latest event or tragedy, or on the radio discussing the next hot topic that may bring some attention to her political position.

However, you will not be catching her in public nor private talking about the things that I reveal in this book. This is because it would not be positive to her career, image or agenda, and I understand that.

But that is perfectly ok.

It is now my job to tell that story. For myself, for my family, and for Dalilah.

MESSAGE TO EMILY

Now, I will admit - I had roughly ten pages of straight heat, and I mean fire and brimstone, that were going to take up this section of the book because it is my chance to talk directly to you, Emily. However, at the advice of people close to me that have reviewed my book and after revisiting it myself, I believe that it is better to keep the integrity of this book intact and allow it to help others by not getting too personal. Therefore, I will keep it classy and brief so I can move on to Dalilah. However, there are some good things that all readers can get from these words.

This book may have never been written if you had been mature enough as an adult and co-parent to come to me and talk to me about your feelings instead of going silent on me and making the moves with Dalilah that you did without my knowledge. However, once you made your choices, God told me that I finally had what I needed to tell my story, and He told me to do it because it would be therapy for me to deal with the lies that I had to endure over the past ten years as a man while also helping so many other people. So, here we are. Your actions were, in a way, the catalyst for this book, so I will sarcastically say thanks to you for giving me what I needed to change the world.

You know everything that has happened since the day we met, and I know as well, so I can save my fingers some labor and not type all of that again. You also know the kind of person that you are, and you know the kind of person that I am. You knew that when you met me, and you know that now. There are just a few brief things that I want to say to you because you need to hear it. I know that you may never read any of these words because you want to forget that all of this happened, but they will be communicated to you in due time.

First, you must realize that while you try to forget about things in your life and act as if they did not happen, the people that are involved on the other end of your actions cannot and will not forget about what you do to them. I am not sure of everything that you endured as a child as you grew up, but it is clear to me and so many others that have been around you at some point in their lives that you have some things internally that need repairing because your failure to address your own demons has resulted in you inflicting your hurt on those that you have come across.

Those that are hurt will continue to hurt others.

Therefore, while you move through life bouncing from one situation to the next, the rest of us actually live in reality. You must remember that there are consequences to everything that you do, and one day you will have to deal with those consequences, whether you want to face them or not. I say this because, while I or any of the other people that you have hurt in the past may not be able to make you answer for what you have done, there is one person I know that will: *Dalilah.*

Dalilah has had to endure many things when it comes to you, and I know this because she has told me. Your child has never fully been your first priority, and while you may act like she is at times, understand that people have and can still see you in ways that you could never see yourself, and actions speak way much louder than words – I have even told you this myself during the trials and tribulations that we had while raising Dalilah. People can always see what is going on, no matter how hard you try to hide things or not address them. In the years that Dalilah has left to depend on you, I sincerely hope that your mind can change to put your child first in your life and actually care about her feelings because, while you may think that she has forgotten or will forget about us and what we have done for her, she will not forget and never will because she is simply not YOU.

You may not want to face it even though you know you will have to one day, but YOU are the one that will have to deal with the resentment that Dalilah is harboring due to your actions that have resulted in her alienation from an entire half of the family that she has always known, and this is because I know for a fact that she knows even better than me that YOU are the root cause of it. You have politics, bills, and life to deal with in life. As a child, Dalilah's life consists mainly of your family and MY family, and now half of that is not present in her life due to your actions. Imagine how that feels to a growing child, especially when they cannot talk to anyone about it. Imagine what that is going to do to her as she grows!

I could see in your eyes and actions that you had a jealousy for the love that Dalilah was getting from me and my family that you may have never had in your life, and maybe you want her to feel the pain that you felt as a child and a teenager so you simply walked away from us and forced her to do the same. That is a sad thing for a mother to do, and most mothers will agree with this, but maybe those demons inside you caused you to do this so I will try to give you a sliver of a pass and blame them, and I hope you rebuke them so you can do right by your child. I know you have a love for your child because she is your child, but Dalilah needs GENUINE love in her life. So, while you watch your child struggle with that missing piece of her life, prepare for the wrath that she will deliver to you when she is older, ready and able. I hope you can handle it and not walk away from her too. People can forgive but they never FORGET. This goes for Dalilah, me and everyone else in the world.

Remember that, despite what you may think, you will get back what you give out in life. If you constantly turn on good people that are only trying to help you because I know that you have done this many times, they will eventually eliminate you from their lives, and some will turn around and do the same awful things to you. If you burn every bridge that can help you get over a treacherous river, how will you ever get to the other side? You could try a hot air balloon, but if you cannot drop the sandbags filled with the burdens that you have to carry, you will sink to the ground every time. However, if you help others build a bridge to reach your goals as well as theirs, you ALL win, and the best part of this is that they will help you build another bridge to something greater. Try applying this in your life and see how it improves things.

The most important message that I want to deliver to you, Emily, as well as to everyone else that has read my story is:

You can walk away from many things in life,

but you cannot walk away from the TRUTH.

Good luck to you, Emily.

A LETTER TO DALILAH

My sweet Dalilah! I have been looking forward to writing this letter to you since I wrote the first word of the Preface. I hope that you are doing your best to live your life to the fullest as you can as a child. I miss you so much and I know you miss me too, and I know we think about each other every day.

It has been hard to wonder how you have been living, and how you have been treated every day. I know your mom would not let anyone else hurt you, but I know that she herself may hurt you emotionally in ways that no one else ever could, and while this may appear to be intentional at times, I feel that she honestly cannot help this because of who she is on the inside. You have had to live with her every day, and I know that can be tough much of the time, but continue to do your best, live your life and love her as you can. I know you carry her trait of being able to block things out, and I hope that has allowed you to continue to grow emotionally and still enjoy life as well as meet new friends.

I hope that you are still excelling in school. I remember that Friday where your mother refused to honor our agreement to let you come with me that day, and I ended up not seeing you or talking to you after that - you had a robot project due on that day that we were supposed to build together. I was told that your mother posted on her social media that she ended up taking you to the movies that Thursday night before it was due instead of honoring your schoolwork because I know you told her about the project, and your teacher told me that your project was never turned in, so I know it had to be tough to see everyone else turn in theirs. Despite not being able to see me for that last month of school, you still passed the second grade and I am very proud of you for that. However, I still want us to do that project when you come back to stay with me because I know you want to do it, too lol. It does not matter how old you are - we are going to complete that project!

The last night you were at my house, you asked me to read you a bedtime story. I told you that I would. However, that evening I had become upset at something that did not involve you, and when you came into the living room a couple of times to ask me when I was coming to your room, I told you to go lay down and go to sleep because I could not focus due to what I was dealing with. You were so upset at me, and the sounds of you crying yourself to sleep hurt my heart. On the way to drop you off at school the next morning, I apologized to you and told you that I never wanted to hurt you. You said, "It's ok, Daddy. I forgive you and I love you." That showed me how much of an amazing child that you were, and how much you loved me. If I would have known that would be the last night that I was going to spend with you for a long time, I would have come and read that story to you. It still hurts me to this day that I did not read it to you, and while I have been told by those close to me to let that go because you will still love me anyway, I cannot help but carry that on my heart, and I think that I will continue to carry that hurt until YOU one day tell me that it is ok to let it go. Forgive me - I have to now pause for a moment because I cannot see the screen because of my tears…

I know that you have gone through some things emotionally since the last time we saw each other, and I know this has had to be tough for you as a child because I am sure your mother forbids you to talk about it. Just know that you are not alone in this because I have had to go through some things too as I just mentioned in the last paragraph. Wow - you should know what a paragraph is by now! Lol! When I talked to you some months after your mom ruined my relationship with her, you said that you loved me and dreamed about me every day, and I told you that I did the same, but I know you may have wondered just a little why I never called again to try to see you. It may be hard for you to understand, but there were many things that I did for your mother and you all the way from before you were born through most of your life until she and I started having issues. When someone does as much as I did for another person when they never had to, and that other person eventually starts to treat you like you have not done anything for them, there is only so much disrespect that a man can take emotionally before he has to eliminate it from his life, and this is why I had to cut my communication with your mother. The hardest part of this was knowing that I would also be cutting my time with you, and I never wanted to do that. However, in order to be able to live a productive and happy life, I had to cut your mother from my life and sacrifice my time with you until you are able to come and let me be a father to you directly.

Your mother did not have to make it hard for me to be in your life, but she chose to. It was her choice. While she may tell you and others that "Floyd can call and come see Dalilah any time he wants," she will not speak to you or those people about the disrespect, dishonesty and ungratefulness that she had displayed towards me and our family, and that was what stopped the communication between us because I refused to deal with your mom if we were not going to be equal parents with equal roles after all that I have done for her. Therefore, this was her choice because she had the power to change it, and she will one day have to deal with the damage that has been done to you as a result. However, I know it may be tough for you to deal with this sometimes, and it is ok to cry when you have to because letting it out will help more than keeping it in. Please know that Daddy will always love you and be here for you when you are able to communicate with me directly. I am not going to tell you to disobey your mother because you have to live with her, and I know that is tough enough as it is, but when you can reach me on your own, please do.

I know you had to be a strong girl as we raised you because you had to deal with different households, and I hope that your adapting to the rules and events of each has helped you to adapt with the recent changes in your life as well as the ones to come. I want you to continue to live your life with the knowledge that all of us - me, Faithe, Granny and Papa, Eddie, Margo, "Tee-Tee" Sharee, Jeron, Meshai, Shamia, C.J., Geneva, Melvin, Jazzy, Angel, Lania, LaZandrea, Tre, Dwayne & Sabrina, Bussey, Charles, Shirlene, Kala, Wendy, Ieesha, Monica, Chace, Oni, Paulina, our Cali family, all of my friends from Atlanta, Chattanooga, and Phoenix, and all of the other family members and friends of the family that I failed to mention all still think about you, and we all will be here waiting for you when you can come to be in our lives on your own.

You are an amazing girl and you should live your life as such. I know your mother will take you places sometimes such as the pool or even amusement parks, and you will go on field trips with your school. I want you to enjoy those things and still be the child that you deserve to be. You and I know that sometimes your mom may drop the ball on things such as your schoolwork or filling out things that she may need to in order for you to do certain things at school. When this occurs, take it on yourself to make these things happen on your own when possible, as I am sure you are already doing, or stay on her until she does what she needs to do for you because when I was present in your life, I know these things were not being done consistently on that end, and I know that much probably has not changed due to her always focusing on her own stuff instead of yours unless R.J. is doing it. Doing these things will make you a stronger girl and woman, and you will have that element of independence that many other kids will not have.

The things that you have to deal with now will make you an amazing woman, and I cannot wait to be a part of your life as you grow into that woman because I will know that I played a part in it, and you will be wonderful and kind enough to acknowledge that. I also know when you are able to spend more time with us, you likely will not want to talk about the "blood" thing, or the existence of another biological father out there because you will just want to enjoy being with us. You may not even remember what your mom told you, or the conversation that you had with Granny back at Field Day. We will not make you talk about those things until you want to. However, when YOU are ready, and while I will always be your Daddy no matter what, we will help you find out who your biological father really is because I do not believe we currently have the truth on who that might be but you need to know who it is for your well-being, he needs to know about you if he does not already, and we need to know who he is as well.

I know that I will see you sooner than later due to how I have decided to proceed with life and tell OUR story, but I want to close this letter by saying that you should always know that I will be here for you, and while I have eliminated your mother from my life, you will always have an open door that you can and will eventually walk through. If you ever want to talk to me when we cannot be around each other, just look out of your window at the moon and the stars at night and talk to me. I will be looking out of my window at the night sky talking back to you. Talk to me about your day, about your feelings and your dreams, and I will do the same. And once we have talked about everything, say a prayer to God because He will help you continue to push on, and get some sleep because you must rest well in order to make sure the next day is a good one.

I loved you when I first set eyes on you, and I always will.

I'll see you soon, Dalilah!

Yours forever,

Daddy

7

M.A.N.H.O.O.D.

Well, that last chapter was a lot, huh! You probably need a cigarette and a glass of Bourbon on the rocks after reading all of that. If you are one of the people that have had the privilege to be blessed with my presence at some point in your life (lol), I know you are like, "Man, Floyd - I had no clue! You and your family went through all of that?" Well yes, we did. And we are stronger now because of it. It is often difficult to figure out why you are going through something while you are actually in the midst of it, but once you get to the other end, you can look back and see what it did for you and your life.

I did what I believed was right by Dalilah in the last chapter as I explained, and I eventually had to move on after realizing that I would never receive a real "thanks" from the person that brought me and my family into the situation from day one. That was a part of the portion of my life that I call MANHOOD because, as a man, I had to find an effective way to deal with it and keep living my life. Sometimes things will not seem fair, and we have to find a way to deal with these occurrences and move on without sacrificing our livelihood. This is manhood. Women also have to deal with similar transitions, so we will call that "womanhood." Yes - many, if not all, of the lessons in this chapter will apply to both sexes.

I decided to finish the book with this chapter because I had topics that I wanted to share with the world that did not quite fit into the previous chapters. This chapter is designed to provide nuggets of knowledge and observations that I have come across during my journey into and through manhood. My original vision was to feed the reader via quick excerpts resembling the Book of Proverbs from the Holy Bible, but nothing that I write here is by no means biblical lol. The topics to follow may seem random, and they somewhat are, but there is a method to the madness and they were indeed thought out. With my style of writing, no excerpt in this chapter will actually come across as "quick" so be ready to read because, as you should know very well by now, nothing that I write is truly brief. However, this chapter will not be as long as the past two were - I just believe that it will be a fun way to end the book. So, sit back and enjoy this last chapter of the book, and I hope that there is something in it that you or someone that you know can find useful and apply to some aspect of your lives.

Let us dive right into it. As grown men and women, we have many stressors that we bear from day to day in this thing that we call life. Some of us have children and spouses to maintain. Many of us also have jobs where spend one third of our lives at on a daily, weekly and monthly basis. If you're over eighteen years of age, you likely have monthly bills to add to this pile. If you let all these things soak into your skin without periodically getting into a virtual bathtub full of bubble bath or bath salts to relax you, your mental hygiene will stink. Why? Because everyone needs to escape from time to time. This brings me to my first nugget: you must find an OUTLET to relieve stress from time to time. These outlets can be in many forms. I will discuss some of mine to give you a few ideas.

One idea is to join an organization that is based on something that you are genuinely interested in. For as long as I could remember, I have always been fascinated with Freemasonry. I did not know much about it, but there was just something about the organization's emblem that really intrigued me. I watched just about every documentary on Netflix that was related to Freemasonry, and countless videos on YouTube covering the subject. One day, I decided to identify a lodge in my area and find out more about joining the order. I researched and came across the website for Square Work Lodge #596, which is a lodge chartered in Lithia Springs and governed under the Most Worshipful Prince Hall Grand Lodge of Georgia. I looked at the pictures of the members of the lodge and saw a person that I knew – I had played little league football with his cousin. I hit him up on Facebook and told him I was interested in becoming a Freemason. He invited me out to meet some of the brothers of the lodge.

A few months after I met the brothers of the lodge, I petitioned for membership, and soon after I was initiated to start the process of becoming a Freemason. On October 21st, 2014, I was raised to the Sublime Degree of a Master Mason at Square Work Lodge #596. As of the moment I write this paragraph, I have been exalted into the Order of Holy Royal Arch Masons, greeted into the Order of Royal and Select Masters, and most recently dubbed into the Magnanimous Order of the Knights Templar – all falling under the jurisdiction of the York Rite Masonic Bodies of Georgia, Prince Hall. Therefore, I am a member of all of the masonic houses on the York Rite branch of Freemasonry. I also later found out that my grandfather, his father, and grandfather were all Freemasons in West Point, Mississippi. I found this out from a distant cousin of mine, who is also a Freemason.

I know that people say all kinds of things about Freemasons, such as we worship the devil and other stuff based on no facts at all. I will clear this by stating that NO - we do not worship the devil, and no one is sacrificing any goats or anything like that lol. Freemasonry is Bible-based, and you cannot be initiated into the craft if you do not believe in God, or a higher power that represents the God that we Christians believe in. In fact, everything we do in the lodge is based on the Bible. Freemasonry was created by ancient master stonemasons who needed a way to recognize other master masons as they traveled from city to city. Their solution was to develop a system of signs and symbols that allowed them to recognize each other, share their elite skills with each other and earn better wages accordingly, as well as look out for fellow master masons.

The ancient operative master masons used certain tools to construct buildings, while the master masons of today use these same tools in a speculative manner to better ourselves morally. I have applied some of these tools to my life, and they have made me a better man. These tools, along with the support of my fellow Masonic brothers, also helped me to navigate through the tough situations that I discussed in the prior chapter. I love Freemasonry, and I will always be an active member of the order for as long as I am privileged to walk this Earth. Of course, we have rituals, passwords, and grips just as every other fraternity does because that is essentially what we are – a fraternity of men. We also pride ourselves on charity and helping the less fortunate, and you can find us doing that in my local geographic area as well as all over the world.

Another outlet you can explore is some form of exercise, such as working out or playing a sport. I joined an 8-man flag football league in the City of Atlanta back in 2014. It was called the Atlanta Sports Connection (ASC), which originated from a league known as MAFFA and has now transitioned into the A-Town League. It is a competitive league, and I really enjoyed it when I first came into it. However, I became disgruntled during my first season in the league because the captain that ran the team that I joined was also the quarterback, and he would not throw me the football that often. I felt like I was a capable wide receiver with good speed and hands (remember that I'm 6'4" and was in pretty good shape back then – I am no slouch now but you get my point), so with me being the talented mind that I am, the next season I started my own team in that same league because I was going to get some passes thrown to me lol!

I ran my team, known as PYTHON, with my co-captain for about four years before letting it dissolve and going on to play for a few other teams. I still play in this league that now contains nearly twenty teams with some of the most electric talent that you'll find anywhere in the country. I play for a team called the OUTSIDERS, as I mentioned earlier in the book, and I enjoy playing alongside those guys because they are great players, and even greater men. We also have a pretty cool offense that I like playing in. I have met some wonderful guys from this league that will definitely be lifelong friends, and the league is filled with people from all walks of life – from guys that work on garbage trucks to men that run multi-million dollar companies. However, on Sundays, when we step on the football field, we are all on the same level, and we leave all of our stresses and problems on the sidelines while enjoying the game that we love. We all have gotten something from each other that we can take with us when we leave the field. I also learned the value of hard work and staying in shape.

Another outlet is to join some social groups to meet people who have the same interests as you. There are websites that allow people to find groups for all kinds of interests and hobbies, from arts and crafts to singles' gatherings, chess clubs, bowling leagues and more. The options are endless. You can use an internet search engine to find those websites, and then discover groups and organizations that you may want to learn more about. You would be amazed at how you can relieve stress with an outlet that you really enjoy.

The last outlet that I will mention is to get a part-time job. You may not see "work" as an outlet, but there are many part-time jobs out there that people really enjoy, such as operating the scoreboard for basketball and kickball games, walking dogs or working at a pet store, physical training, and more. You also can put a little cash in your pocket at the same time. I found a cool part-time gig operating an iPad photo booth at different events. I was paid to take pictures and meet people, and this was easy money. I enjoyed this for nearly a year in my spare time and it was a fun outlet until I became fed up with the irritating ways that the owner of the company ran the business, which always made my job harder than it had to be due to him being too lazy to do what he should have been doing on his end to make sure his customers were satisfied. I had originally gone off on a tangent and wrote a long paragraph of how this outlet ended up going wrong due to the poor practices of the owner, but I deleted it in my final edit as it is not worth your time to read. What I will say is that I plan to dabble in the photo booth business on my own in the near future and do it the way that I believe it is supposed to be done because it is a great business, and it can be lucrative if done properly. Anyway, the moral of the story about this outlet is to get a part-time job if you really need something to do!

Now, on to the next topic. Many of us watch television from time to time, and as reality TV has become more popular, many viewers are now gaining a false sense of what their lives "should" be like instead of living the lives that they have been blessed with. Of course, I encourage all men and women to shoot for the stars and get that Rolls Royce, clothing line, or movie deal that you are dreaming of. However, also know that while some of the people you see on scripted television shows may be wealthy, the producers of the shows stage much of what you are seeing, and many of the fancy items that you see the people enjoying are rented. Therefore, in "reality", many of the people that you see in these shows are actually not rich at all. In fact, you may be worth more than some of them!

A person can make $150,000 per year from a reality show and live in an apartment while leasing a Range Rover. If you make $75,000 per year in your profession and own a $200,000 home, you are worth more than that person that grosses $150,000 annually. Why? This is because your net worth is based on the assets that you OWN, not the INCOME that you make. I am saying all of this to bring you to my main point: *work hard to achieve your goals and dreams, but also learn to appreciate the life that you have.* We often get so wrapped up in other people's lives that we forget that we have it better off than many other people around the world do. Appreciate what you have, because it could have easily been a blessing for someone else.

On the other side of this concept, also understand that if you find yourself having a bad day, *remember that there is always someone else in the world who is having a worse day than you are.* This sunk in for me as I watched a movie some years back in which there was a man standing on the ledge of a tall building, who was planning to jump to his death. There was a police negotiator sent up to a nearby window to talk the man out of jumping off the ledge. The negotiator and the man talked about the bad day that the man was having, and the entire movie consisted of the conversation between these two men.

As the two talked, the negotiator told the man that earlier in that same day he went to the doctor for a physical, and it was during this visit that he found out that he was sterile, and it was not possible for him to have children. This led him to realize that the two young children that his wife had birthed over the past five or six years that they were raising together were not his biological kids, and after bringing this to his wife, he then found out that the two kids actually belonged to his brother. His wife saw that the negotiator closely resembled his brother, and since she suspected that her husband could not help her produce a child, she secretly engaged with his brother to produce kids that the negotiator would think were his own seeds. Therefore, the negotiator was conveying to the man that, while the man was having a bad day, the negotiator was having a pretty fucked up day as well.

The man on the ledge eventually jumped to his death due to a back story that was shown in another scene right before he made the leap, so his day was pretty bad, too. However, I use this scenario to illustrate that, while your situation may seem bad, there is someone else somewhere in the world that would pray to be in your shoes. While my own situations from the previous two chapters were pretty bad, as I was going through those things, I would sometimes realize that there are people in the world who were going through things that were much worse, and that was one of the reasons that I wrote this book - to talk to these individuals and let them know that they are not alone. When you are having a difficult day, first pray to the Supreme Being that you believe in, and then remember this concept. It may help you better navigate what you are going through and get you to the brighter side of it.

The next topic that I want to jump to is mental health. When we were younger, which for me was the 1980's, 1990's and 2000's, mental health was not spoken about much in public aside from the people that were actively studying the subject. In school, we saw the kids that attended classes on the "special" hallway due to behavioral and learning disabilities that had been identified among them. However, most of us did not know much about exactly why they were there, or how they were selected for these particular classrooms. Many families also have members that are afflicted with mental issues, but they often do not talk about it unless it involves a person whose disability is visually apparent, and it must be addressed in order for them to maintain a decent quality of life.

The presence and growth of social media over the early part of the twenty-first century has allowed people to share their lives in a way that was not possible before. You can go to a social media website and see people doing live videos talking about every topic under the sun. The topic of mental health has also become more popular now, and this is partly because people from all over America, as well as the world, can share their stories with others. This has brought a higher mental health awareness to the world because people can now see that others are going through the exact same things when it comes to this topic, and ideas can be shared on how to diagnose mental illnesses as well as how to deal with them.

Some of us have people that are close to us that have been diagnosed as having a mental illness, or from your knowledge and relation to a person, you suspect that they may have a mental illness. You may even be this person that has a mental illness or suspect that you may have one. If you are in either of these scenarios, I ask that you seek professional help because it will benefit you as well as those that are close to you. When mental issues go untreated, they can have a negative impact on the lives of the people that possess them. They can affect and destroy romantic relationships, as well as impact the relationships between kids and parents. I am not a doctor by any means and will not pretend to be, but I mentioned in the last chapter that Dalilah's mother could possibly have some mental or emotional issues that she should address with a professional due to her awkward bond with her child that we noticed over the years, along with other things that my family and I, as well as other people, have noticed about her. Talking to a professional could cause a person to look closer at themselves and admit that they may possibly have issues that should be addressed.

Overcoming pride and admitting that there may be a mental or emotional issue present is the first step to treating it. I am not exempt from this - I have never been diagnosed with a mental illness and I do not believe that I have one, but I have been affected by my situation with Dalilah and Emily, which affects my emotions from time to time. While I have yet to do it, I would likely benefit from talking about my situation and my current feelings to a professional therapist, who could offer ways for me to view my situation as well as suggest ways to deal with it so I can continue to live a happy life no matter what happens in the future. However, I have found other productive ways to channel my thoughts and energy; this book serves as one method of therapy, along with the other outlets that I mentioned above. If you have a loved one that may have a mental illness, I know that it may be hard for you to approach them with your feelings on the subject. However, if it is affecting your relationship with them, the possible pain of confronting them about it now may be well worth the joy of a better relationship that could come later after helping them deal with their illness or issues.

This next section deals with a different topic. It was a last minute addition to the book but it should have been in the original composition because it is something that people often overlook. I am referring to the topic of social media.

Social media is a wonderful phenomenon. It has so many uses, and it has brought joy to many people around the world. It can be used for many wonderful things, such as spreading information on important topics, educational purposes, and allowing people to generate income in many different ways. Social media is also used for entertainment purposes, such as watching videos and keeping in touch with friends and family, which is likely its most popular use. On the other hand, social media has also been used in many negative ways by people who have bad intentions, or they just misuse it in a way that hurts others, whether intentionally or unintentionally.

The point that I want to make in this section is to *be very cautious of what you put on social media, and how you use it.*

I use social media in much the same way as many other people do. I may post a few times a week, and when I do, I may attach pictures from an event that I attended or make videos of fun things that I do such as barbequing or hanging out with family and friends. I also share posts that have to do with sports, education, or just positivity in general. However, I do not post content that I believe the world does not need to see or hear, such as issues that may be personal to my family and myself. I also do not speak negatively about others. However, I often see people doing what I consider as "misusing" social media. Sometimes I observe people creating posts in which they speak negatively about a family member or friend, or they disclose things that the world simply does not need to know about. Unless you are trying to let the world know that you are single and ready to mingle, it does not need to know that you caught Johnny or Linda cheating on you, and that you broke up with him or her yesterday. Unless you are trying to prevent others from harm or sickness, the world does not need to know about your yeast infection or pus coming from your elbow. Unless you are trying to become a reality star, or bring sexual attention to yourself, the world does not need to know that you had the best sex of your life last night. I think you see where I am going here: *you do not need to put all of your business on social media.*

Some people live on social media because they can be someone electronically that they cannot be in real life. You can look at the social media profiles of celebrities and see who I refer to as "cyber thugs" making negative comments about whatever the celebrities are doing. However, if these same cyber thugs were to confront the celebrity in real life, nine times out of ten they will not say the same things in person that they said online. Some people just create totally different personas from who they actually are in the flesh. I cannot say that this is a negative thing because you can choose to represent online yourself however you choose. However, if you are doing it to purposely mislead people or "catfish" someone that you are interested in romantically, then this is a negative thing, and you should think about how you are portraying yourself so that you do not waste your time or the time of someone else. This can be dangerous because some people have gone on to kill others that portrayed themselves as one person online and then disappointed the person by being someone else when they met in person.

To close this topic, I will ask this question: *If you put all of your business online, what do you have to offer the world in real life?* There are some people that spend so much time putting everything that they do on social media that I can bump into them at a store and tell them everything that they did the previous day, or that day. No one outside of your family and close friends should know that much about you because if someone wanted to cause harm to you, they will know exactly how to get access to you. It is great to celebrate positive things in your life, and it is totally acceptable to post about these things on social media. However, be careful not to post all of your problems on social media because, while you may just want attention or sympathy, *not everyone actually wants to see you happy, and your misery serves as entertainment for some people that are your social media "friends."* It is sad, but true. Now, I will say that if you are battling a serious issue such as depression or are contemplating suicide, and social media is the only way that you can think of to get help, then please reach out however you need to in order to get the help that you need. If going to social media for help with a serious issue will save the life of husband or wife, father or mother, son or daughter, then please use it because staying alive is more precious than pride on any day.

To reiterate my main point: *social media can be a wonderful tool. Use it wisely.*

The next topic deals with what many of us call "haters" in the twenty-first century. Yes, I told you I would be jumping around in this chapter and I meant it. Now back to the haters. You can go onto the social media profile of a person and view a post that shows them doing something great for someone else. They may have donated a kidney to someone or bought a house for a homeless man. You will see comments of other people praising this person for their benevolent action, as the person is truly deserving of this praise. However, there will ALWAYS be one or more people, also known as haters, who will say, "He knows he doesn't have the money to be doing that. Why is he helping that person? He probably has bills that he ain't even paid yet. He probably doesn't even have a job and is helping someone else. The nerve of this dude!" The cyber thugs that I spoke about in the last topic are a perfect example of this.

Haters are fueled by that invisible force that exudes negativity, and this can arise for a number of reasons. Many people that hate on others usually have problems that they are battling in their own life, and their way of dealing with them is fostered by a false belief that making another person feel bad like they do will help the person that is hating feel better. Often, when haters do this, they do not realize that others can see exactly what they are doing, and they will not realize this until someone calls them out for hating. This will either wake the hater up and make them change, or it will cause them to go on to hate on another person because their hating on this particular person has been exposed and will be challenged. So, they move on, and they hate. And hate.

In many cases, people simply hate because they cannot help it. I believe this is a natural trait of many, if not all human beings. I have even been guilty of it myself. We have all had friends that have done beautiful things, such as buy homes and have babies. You may already possess these same things yourself, and your version may even be better in some cases. While we are genuinely happy for these people, a small cell in our bodies naturally says to us, "My friend has a nice, new house. I want a new house, too. Let me find something wrong with their house so I can focus back on my house. Oh, there it is - my master bedroom is bigger than theirs. That is all I need. I can now focus back on my own house and continue to fully support my friend now." You may not admit it, but you have had these kinds of feelings before. It is ok - I believe that this is the one form of hate that is completely natural so do not feel like you are the only one that has felt that way. For my friends reading this, you all know that I love you lol. I just like addressing the elephants in the room that people do not discuss.

Human beings have a natural propensity to desire things possessed by someone else that they themselves do not have. This will cause them to subconsciously "hate" on those who have what they do not. This is illustrated by the common example of the single person versus the taken person. When a man is single and goes out in public by himself, or with other men, he may get some attention from women, especially if he is an attractive guy. However, when a man goes out and he is accompanied by a woman, other women will naturally pay more attention to this man than they would if he was by himself or with other men. Why? *It is because they are wondering what he possesses internally or externally that allowed him to get the woman that is with him.* These women may not even be physically attracted to this man, but they will want to know more about him because he has a woman with him, and they will also pay more attention to the woman that is with him than they would if she was alone. If these women do not have their own man, they may have that one cell in their brain that wants to "hate" on this woman simply because she is with this man.

People also naturally hate on others because they simply want to get a reaction to satisfy their curiosity. For example, Tanya may be friends with Kesha, and she knows that Kesha strongly dislikes Rachel. Rachel may do something that brings attention to herself, such as post pictures or videos of a celebration that she recently had on social media.

Tanya is well aware of Kesha's dislike for Rachel, but something inside of her will still force her to say to Kesha, "Oh yeah, Rachel celebrated her 5th anniversary with her husband this past weekend. Here's the video and pictures that she posted." Tanya knows that this is not something that Kesha cares to hear about or see. However, she will still say it because deep down she wants to see Kesha's reaction. Tanya could try to hold it in, but she will not be mentally satisfied until she says this to Kesha. This is a subconscious form of "hate" that many of us have been guilty of at some point in our lives. Our minds work in amazing ways.

I want to get back to the main point that I want to convey about people who intentionally hate on others: *the best way to deal with haters is to simply let them hate.* You can easily do this by understanding that they are likely not as happy as you are if they choose to hate on you, so if people are continuously hating on you, and you truly believe that you are doing everything that you know to be good and true, then you are likely doing something very right. Keep it up and make those haters mad until they can see the light!

Another topic that I want to touch on builds a little on the last point and is a deep concept in my eyes: *people will subconsciously take advantage of others.*

What does this mean? It means that people will continuously take advantage of others simply because they have been allowed to do it for so long, and it may not even be intentional in some cases. For example, in the last chapter I discussed some situations where Emily started to challenge me on some issues as Dalilah got older, such as asking to get her back for no particular reason when I was spending time with her, and telling me that I am not going to get Dalilah on a day when she clearly knew that it was my time to get her due to Emily having sole custody of her. Emily might not have awakened on those mornings with the intentions of taking advantage of me, but she started to naturally do this because she had been allowed to do it for so long, and my parents had also allowed her to do this to them as well. In Emily's mind, it became almost a game for her to challenge me just to see how I would react. Eventually, I had to let her know that it was not a game to me because she was playing with people's lives when she did this, and it led to me stepping back from the situation. Other people that have spoken to me about her as I composed this book also said that she exhibited the same behavior with them.

This happens so often to many people. One parent takes advantage of the other parent; boyfriends take advantage of girlfriends, and vice versa. Parents take advantage of their grown children, and men and women take advantage of their older parents. Everyone is not guilty of this, but some people just have a natural tendency to take advantage of other people - it is just the world that we live in. They cannot function if they do not do this. However, our world is balanced out by those of us that do not enjoy taking advantage of other people. It is the devil's advocate - good versus evil. I am not saying that people that take advantage of others are evil, but in most cases, it is not a good thing.

If someone continues to naturally take advantage of you, your life will not be as good as it could be if that person was not taking advantage of you. You can try telling the person how you feel about what they are doing to you, and they may stop. However, if they have a natural disposition to take advantage of you because it has become a habit, they will eventually resume it. I know that this can be tough because sometimes it involves parents, significant others, and even your own children, but if someone often takes advantage of you and you believe that they will continue to, *you should eliminate them from your environment.* Cut off contact with them. This is the only sure way to stop the behavior that they are exhibiting towards you. Your absence from their life may cause them to change their actions if they truly care about you. However, if it does not, they are no longer your problem.

Next, I want to talk about something extremely important: *taking care of our bodies.* It is commonly known that women are usually very proactive about going to their doctors for regular check-ups, and they often go for doctor visits as soon as they realize that something may not be right with their bodies. Men, on the other hand, are very reactive, and we wait until the pain from our ailments literally forces us to go to the doctor. We may feel a pain in our foot but will not go to the doctor until gangrene sets in and our foot is nearly hanging off lol. As a man, I have to speak to the men that are reading this book: we have to get better about maintaining our health. Get annual physicals and go to the doctor as soon as you feel that something might not be right with your body because there could be something wrong with you. I recently attended the funeral of a friend that I met while playing flag football. He passed away at the age of forty from colon cancer, and he was diagnosed nearly two years before he died. I do not know the details of his diagnoses, and they may have caught it at an early stage and it still spread, but many forms of cancer can be controlled for a significant amount of time if they are caught early. Prostate cancer is also one of the top killers of black men, so it is recommended by medical professionals that all men start getting tested for this cancer at the age of forty.

Whether you are a man or a woman, you know that your family needs you. Therefore, govern yourself accordingly and make strides to preserve your health. In addition to getting regular check-ups, try incorporating a healthier diet and a regular exercise routine. Some people can go cold turkey with unhealthy foods or start a rigorous workout routine and maintain it for a long time. However, it may work better for some of us to take baby steps and change our routine gradually. For example, anyone that really knows me knows that I love beef, especially a juicy burger or a nice, tender steak. However, I am aware that beef is considered as not being as good for the human body as other meats, such as chicken, turkey, and fish. I used to eat beef nearly every other day or at least every three days. Since I am making an effort to eat healthier, I have now attempted to cut my beef intake to just weekends. I can admit that, when I do this, I feel a little lighter on my feet. I do cheat on this from time to time, but that is neither here nor there lol. I am also trying to limit my sugar intake by substituting sodas and juices for water when possible. This gradual approach to living a healthier lifestyle has worked better for me than suddenly cutting beef and drinks containing sugar from my diet completely. Play around with the methods that work best for you, but at the end of the day, make an effort to work hard to achieve the ultimate goal of becoming a healthier individual. Do this not only for your family and friends, but for YOURSELF.

The last topic that I want to end this book with is the concept and action of *chasing your dreams*. So often, we hear celebrities and motivational speakers say, "Follow your dreams and do what it is that you're meant to do! If you want to be your own boss, be your own boss!" Man, if it were only that easy lol. I know you can definitely relate to that last sentence. When we hear someone say words such as these, many of us often ask ourselves, "Well, how do I find out what I am meant to do? And how do I just start doing that for the rest of my life?" Those are indeed very good questions. Some of us know what our true talent is, and some of us do not. Therefore, there are two parts to this dilemma - those that know what they are meant to do but are uncertain about how to bring it to fruition as a way of sustaining themselves financially, and those that are unsure of what they really want to do.

I first realized that I was a talented writer while I was in high school. I wrote poetry back then and into college, but I eventually stopped because I felt that I would never make money writing, and my energy could be better spent doing something fun, or something that would generate income. After my brother passed away at the end of 2008, I decided that I should follow my dreams while I still had a chance, so I created a business where I wrote academic papers for college students and graduate students, as well as drafted resumes for job seekers. I advertised my new business mainly on Craigslist, and I made decent money doing this part-time. However, even though the money was good, I was burned out after a few years due to the research that academic papers required, so I cut that from my service offerings and I only committed to writing content for websites that were run by small businesses, or for digital marketing specialists that would take my content and put it on their clients' websites.

I still do assignments in my spare time for a few clients, and I have spoken of doing this for a living here and there over the years, but I have never fully dedicated myself to making this a full-time business. I had also told many people that I would never write a book because I never felt that I had enough to write about, or anything of significance that people would want to read about. Then in 2018, my situation with Emily came to an end as I discussed in the previous chapter. Guess what happened then? God told me that now is the time to write a book, and that my dream of being a successful writer will be realized. And here we are! The point that I want you to get from this is that, like some of you, I knew what my purpose was, but I was not ready to accept it and do what I needed to do to make it a reality. Then life happened, and suddenly, I was ready.

You have to be ready to accept your purpose. When you truly accept it, you will naturally be pushed to make it a reality.

For nearly a year, I poured my heart and soul into this book, and I literally could not help it. I used online cloud storage to store my book chapters, so whenever I had a moment to write, I pulled out my smartphone, tablet or laptop and I wrote. Whether I was on the toilet at work, at a stoplight, in line to check out at the grocery store, or on my porch - if I could write, I was writing. It was magical! It was fun. These words all came with ease. I laughed aloud as I wrote the earlier chapters in this book about growing into adulthood, and I cried real tears as I wrote the chapters about my brother Brian and Dalilah. This is because I was passionate about my purpose, and you may possess that passion for your true purpose as well, but you have to be ready to accept it. Once you do, you will then start to take the necessary steps to bring it to fruition.

Once you are ready to turn your passion into a career, start researching the ways in which other people have turned your passion into businesses that are sustaining them financially. You can go online to find web pages and videos where people talk about how they started their businesses, and what it took for them to become successful. Once you have a blueprint, set goals for yourself and stick to your plan. If you work hard and believe without a doubt that you will achieve your dream, you will mentally have no choice but to attain it because your mind will not let you give up on it.

The other group of us may not be sure of what we want to do, or what our talents are. There are a few ways to tackle this dilemma. One suggestion that I have is to write down five activities or services that you do well, and enjoy so much that you would do them for free. Once you have five options, rank those options from the one you enjoy the most to the one that is the least enjoyable of the five. Once you have identified that option that you enjoy the most, start researching how people are earning an income doing just that. You can also do this for the other four options until you find one that people are doing for money that would suit you well. When you have chosen the option that you want to pursue, create a step-by-step plan based on your research to create a business in which you can make money. Set goals with deadlines to hold yourself accountable and put your plan into action!

For those of you who are open to a new career but are unsure of what you want to do, go online and search for a new career - it is that simple. You can pull up a search engine and use search phrases such as "career options", "occupations," or "finding a new career" - you can see where I am going with this. The Bureau of Labor Statistics also publishes the Occupational Outlook Handbook (OOH) that literally lists just about every career imaginable that people are working in throughout the United States. This is a great resource to get you started and can be accessed online completely free. The OOH not only lists every career in the U.S. that people have paid taxes on, but it also identifies the hottest careers, and you can search or sort careers based on average annual salaries, type of labor involved, and much more. You should get something in return for those federal taxes that you pay each year, huh? Also, if your situation allows it, be willing to relocate for a job that you believe you will enjoy. Traveling and living in a new environment can be life changing, as I experienced this when I traveled to Phoenix, Arizona to live and work from 2006 to 2008

.

Your dream is within your grasp. You have to first see it, and then find the path to it.

Well, we have finally made it to the end of the book. It was a journey, won't you say? I hope you enjoyed my story, and I really hope that you got something from this book that you can apply to your life and carry with you as you continue to live. I put all that I had into this book, and I hope you felt that as you read it. I wanted to give something to every reader that they could take with them - every man, woman, mother, father, son, daughter, husband, and wife. Of course, this book will generate some income for my family and me, but that was never my purpose for writing it. I wrote this book to show those who have gone through situations similar to the ones that I have encountered over the course of my life that there are other people in the world that can relate to you because they have been where you have been, although no two human beings' journeys are the same.

I wrote this book to help those who have lost siblings and other loved ones, and to show them ways in which they can deal with those losses. I wrote this book to show people how life lessons can come from unexpected life forms, such as an animal. I wrote this book to show men who have been misled about the paternity of their child or children that there are other men who have gone through the same thing and know how they feel, and how to move forward with life after going through such a situation. I wrote this book to deliver messages to actual people. I wrote this book to change the world. I wrote this book as therapy for myself. I wrote this book for YOU.

Share my story with as many people as you can and encourage them to get this book. As my ultimate goal is to help people, if you know of someone who can benefit from some of the things that I talk about in this book but they are unable to purchase a copy for whatever reason, let them borrow your copy, or simply give it to them. Giving someone peace of mind where they never had it is more important to me than money on any day.

Thank you for reading and continue to live your BEST LIFE.

ABOUT THE AUTHOR

Floyd Rounds Jr. is a new author that resides in Smyrna, Georgia. He is a corporate real estate professional that has always been passionate about writing, and he has high hopes that this debut book about significant events in his life will help him achieve his dream of being a full-time writer. Floyd has a beautiful wife and has raised an amazing child that was referenced throughout this book. He loves to bowl, play flag football, barbeque, spend time with family and friends, hang out with his dog Lady, and just enjoy life.

You can catch up with Floyd online at www.floydsstory.com or on social media:

Facebook: @floydsstory
Instagram: @floydroundswriter
Twitter: @ftrounds
Snapchat: infinniti2015

Made in the USA
Columbia, SC
24 June 2019